Kettl, D...

HN
90
C6
K47
1987

The regulation of
American federalism

Kettl, Donald F/The regulation of Americ
HN90 .C6 K47 1987 C.1 STACKS 1987

DATE DUE

+HN90 .C6 K47 1987

COLLEGE FOR HUMAN SERVICES
LIBRARY
345 HUDSON STREET
NEW YORK, N.Y. 10014

THE REGULATION
OF AMERICAN
FEDERALISM

THE REGULATION OF AMERICAN FEDERALISM

WITH A NEW EPILOGUE

DONALD F. KETTL

THE JOHNS HOPKINS UNIVERSITY PRESS
BALTIMORE AND LONDON

Copyright © 1983 by Louisiana State University Press
Epilogue copyright © 1987 by The Johns Hopkins University Press
All rights reserved
Printed in the United States of America

Originally published 1983 by Louisiana State University Press
Johns Hopkins Paperbacks edition published 1987 by
The Johns Hopkins University Press
701 West 40th Street
Baltimore, Maryland 21211
The Johns Hopkins Press Ltd., London

LIBRARY OF CONGRESS CATALOGING-IN-PUBLICATION DATA

Kettl, Donald F.
  The regulation of American federalism.

  Bibliography: p.
  Includes index.
  1. Federal aid to community development—United States. 2. Block grants—United States. 3. United States—Social policy. 4. Intergovernmental fiscal relations—United States. I. Title.
HN90.C6K47 1987   353.0081'8'09746   86-46272
ISBN 0-8018-3508-9

For my wife, Susan

CONTENTS

FOREWORD / xiii
PREFACE / xv

Chapter 1   The Regulation of Governments / 1
Chapter 2   Who Decides? / 24
Chapter 3   What Procedures? / 42
Chapter 4   Who Benefits? / 58
Chapter 5   Getting the Facts / 76
Chapter 6   Framing the Agenda / 99
Chapter 7   Uncertain Brides / 128
Chapter 8   Loosening the Regulatory Strings / 154
Epilogue   Riding the Trojan Horse / 174

APPENDIX: CROSSCUTTING REGULATIONS / 181
BIBLIOGRAPHY / 187
INDEX / 195

FIGURES AND TABLES

Figure
1   Federal Outlays for Community Development / 20
2   Federal Payment to State and Local Governments / 26

Table
1   Regulation of Grant Programs / 36
2   Crosscutting Regulations / 43
3   Major Crosscutting Rules / 44
4   Discrimination Complaints in General Revenue Sharing / 55
5   General Revenue Sharing Cases Investigated / 56
6   Federal Civilian Employment: Percent Change by Decade / 87
7   Interest Groups Active in CD Rule Making / 108

FOREWORD

WITH THIS BOOK, the Miller Center of Public Affairs at the University of Virginia continues a sponsored series of analytic works on the American presidency. These works represent the scholarship of those whose research and writing have been encouraged by the center and who have participated as visiting scholars in the center's Program on the Presidency. Through this program, the center undertakes to contribute to the building of a new science of the presidency for our time. The focus is on the study of the organs and philosophies of central power and leadership in the American constitutional system; the underlying concern is how to reconcile the need for effective central leadership with the constitutional imperatives of limited government and divided but shared power—particularly under the twentieth-century conditions. Three main areas of inquiry are embraced in the center's presidency program. One is concerned with the nature and purposes of the presidency as an instrumentality of governance and of leadership in its larger institutional, political, cultural, and historical setting. A second area of inquiry concentrates on particular problems in which the presidency is deeply involved or which carry far-reaching implications for the conduct and organization of the office. A third area of inquiry concentrates on the study of individual presidencies to learn what lessons may be drawn from the past.

Donald F. Kettl holds the Ph.D., the M. Phil., and the M.A. from Yale University and the B.A. summa cum laude. In 1979, he earned the William Anderson award of the American Political Science Asso-

FOREWORD

ciation for the best dissertation in American intergovernmental relations. In 1980, he published the book *Managing Community Development in the New Federalism*. The research for his latest volume was completed during an appointment at the Miller Center.

Don Kettl has been a leading member of the Woodrow Wilson Department of Government and Foreign Affairs, serving as director of its graduate program in public administration and public affairs and graduate adviser in the department. Before coming to the University of Virginia, he was program coordinator of the graduate program in public affairs and administration at Columbia University. Thus, he has already contributed significantly to the life of two of the leading departments of government in the United States through his scholarship and his administration.

The Regulation of American Federalism represents a new and original approach to American federalism and a searching analysis of changing patterns of intergovernmental relations.

KENNETH W. THOMPSON, Director,
Miller Center of Public Affairs

JAMES STERLING YOUNG, Director of
the Program on the Presidency

PREFACE

MOST STUDIES of federal regulation have concentrated on rules that apply to the private sector. But just as the federal government has through regulation increased its influence over private institutions, it has vastly extended its control over the states and cities through a large—but largely unnoticed—system of public sector regulation. Federal regulations have grown to define not only who should benefit from government programs but how states and cities must run those programs: what accounting standards they must follow, what environmental effects they must measure, who can be hired under the programs, and how much they must be paid. These regulations have made the nation's states and cities into uncertain brides in the partnership of American federalism. The marriage has drifted between two extremes: on one hand, generous federal grants accompanied by increasingly burdensome rules; and on the other hand, fewer rules but less money. The causes and effects of these rules have escaped careful review by scholars or prolonged attention by policy makers. This book will explore the steady, creeping growth of these public sector regulations and the federal government's use of irresistible intergovernmental grants as a vehicle for carrying these regulations into all of the nation's state houses and city halls.

The principal focus of this investigation will be a case study of federal regulation of the Community Development Block Grant Program from 1974 through 1980. Originally passed in 1974 to consolidate six previous federal grant programs into a simpler, more flexible program to help rebuild urban areas, the program gradually became encrusted with rules. By 1981, Congress attempted to simplify the program once again; the program ironically had become part of the problem it was designed to solve. The first two chapters of the book explore the burdens and historical roots of these regulations, and Chapters 3 and 4 explain the different kinds of regulations the Community Development program has developed. Chapter 5 investigates the crucial role that good information plays in managing government regulations and programs. Chapter 6 seeks to answer the crucial question of who sets the regulatory agenda. Chapter 7 examines the attempts that have been made to reform these regulations. The conclusion suggests several alternatives for breaking the regulatory cycle.

This study relies predominantly on primary sources. The *Federal Register* and the *Code of Federal Regulations* contain the formal rules affecting the program, and extensive public comments contained in the U.S. Department of Housing and Urban Development's docket files provided enormously useful public comments on regulatory proposals. Congressional hearings highlighted important administrative questions as well as strong congressional concern about the Department of Housing and Urban Development's management of the program. Extensive interviews with about twenty-five key officials provided clues to questions left unanswered in the written record. Officials interviewed included policy makers and civil servants within HUD charged with rule making; officials in the White House and the Office of Management and Budget; staff members of the key congressional committees; and spokesmen for the most active interest groups. Their contributions proved invaluable; in return for their help, all officials interviewed except those in policy making positions were promised anonymity.

Secondary sources proved extraordinarily helpful as well. Few federal programs have been as thoroughly studied (especially by nervous interest groups) as community development, and these studies yielded a wealth of background information as well as confirmation of several arguments.

Because this study focuses on the regulation of community development, it does not try to draw authoritative conclusions about federal regulation in other policy areas. Two things, however, make the book's findings suggestive for the general problems of federal regulation of the public sector. First, many of the regulations that plagued community development were crosscutting rules that applied across-the-board to all federal grant programs. What was true for community development thus was likely true in other areas as well. Second, students of other areas have reached very similar conclusions. Wherever relevant, those conclusions are noted in this book. This study of regulation in community development, therefore, has broad implications for how the federal government deals with the nation's states and cities.

No author can complete a project like this without gratitude to the many hands that helped it along. I have special appreciation for the many government officials who freely shared their time, willingly guided me through their records, and most importantly, gave generously of their most important resource, their many years of rich experience.

Several of my colleagues commented extensively on earlier drafts of this book, and their perceptive words saved me from many errors. I am indebted to James W. Fesler, Matthew Holden, Frederick C. Mosher, Peter Petkas, Heywood Sanders, Deil Wright, James S. Young, and an anonymous reader for their criticisms and suggestions. They may not agree with the book's conclusions, but they have my lasting thanks for their challenging comments.

Carol Kotsher, Mary Ann Curtin, and Barbara Keller energetically searched through mountains of material in helping me research this book. Cynthia Miller, Anne Hobbs, Shirley Kingsbury, and Nancy Lawson somehow managed to translate my arrows and mountains of scotch tape into an intelligible manuscript. Beverly Jarrett, Marie J. Blanchard, and the staff at LSU Press have my thanks for their enthusiasm for this project.

Partial support for this project came from the Summer Grants Committee of the University of Virginia. I am grateful to the committee for providing time to puzzle over these problems.

Finally, I have a special debt of gratitude to the White Burkett Miller Center of Public Affairs at the University of Virginia. I give grateful thanks to the Miller Center, to its director, Kenneth W.

Thompson, and the project director for the Program on the Presidency, James S. Young, for support—financial, intellectual, and moral—of this project. The field research, clerical support, and time for reflection that the Center provided most certainly improved the final product.

Portions of Chapter 7 originally appeared in the *Publius Annual Review of American Federalism: 1981* (Washington, D.C.: University Press of America, 1983). I wish to thank the director of the Center for the Study of Federalism, Daniel J. Elazar, for permission to reprint those portions here.

THE REGULATION
OF AMERICAN
FEDERALISM

CHAPTER 1

THE REGULATION OF GOVERNMENTS

WHEN MOST PEOPLE think of federal regulation, they think of rules on factory safety or airline fares. Pressed a bit more, some people might also remember federal rules that affect individual citizens, such as the Internal Revenue Service's rules on how to count and report personal income. Regulation in common parlance means governmental control of the private sector, control of both business and individuals. A large volume of federal regulations, however, is of a different sort: federal rules that influence the operation of state and local governments. Federal regulations affect whom state and local officials hire, how much those workers get paid, how the officials keep their financial records, and whom federally funded programs benefit. Many of these rules are relatively invisible to the public, but cumulatively their impact is enormous.

Federal regulation of state and local governments is but part of a complex system of federal rules. There are, in fact, at least five varieties of federal regulation.[1]

Traditional private sector regulation. The classical argument for regulating businesses is that market mechanisms sometimes break down, with costly consequences for consumers. Congress created the

---

1. I am endebted to Frederick C. Mosher for suggesting this typology.

earliest regulatory agencies to defend the marketplace against monopolies and the high prices coupled with inadequate service they sometimes produced. The Interstate Commerce Commission, for example, controlled for decades the entry of truckers into the market, the prices they could charge, what they could haul, and how many hours per day a driver could work. The rules resulted, as Merle Fainsod and Lincoln Gordon pointed out in 1941, from "a series of empirical adjustments to felt abuses."[2] And although private interests have regularly complained about federal intrusion on their sovereignty, they have also found convenient protection in federal rules. Rules sometimes inhibit competition, and reduced competition enhances the position of successful industries.[3] In the 1960s, the federal government extended its regulation of the cost and availability of private goods to their quality and safety. Some rules ordered decreased exposure of factory workers to carcinogens while other rules sought safer toys.[4] As a group, all of these regulations were "command and control": the federal government would publish a rule that ordered the private sector to take specified actions.

Private sector regulation by inducement. Not all federal regulation occurs through direct order. Many rules apply to the private sector, including both profit and nonprofit organizations, as conditions for subsidies and contracts. Some of the rules are general standards, like rules requiring contractors to "buy American" or to ship their goods on American-flag carriers. Other rules require universities to count the hours faculty members spend on federally sponsored research projects and to account for the grants in prescribed ways. Some of the rules, on the other hand, are terms specific to individual deals. Loan guarantees to the Chrysler Corporation set standards of operation and reporting that opened its operation to federal inspec-

2. Merle Fainsod and Lincoln Gordon, *Government and the American Economy* (New York, 1941), 226.
3. See, for example, Marver H. Bernstein, *Regulating Business by Independent Commission* (Princeton, 1955), 17–18; and Louis H. Kohlmeier, Jr., *The Regulators: Watchdog Agencies and the Public Interest* (New York, 1969), 17–18.
4. William Lilley III and James C. Miller III, "The New 'Social Regulation,'" *The Public Interest*, XLVII (Spring, 1977), 49–61.

tion. Federal subsidies and contracts establish a *quid pro quo*, federal rules in return for federal aid. As the federal government has relied more on such subsidies and contracts, this style of regulation has become increasingly important.[5]

Internal federal regulation. The federal government regulates itself more than it regulates any corporation. Executive orders and Office of Management and Budget circulars prescribe operating procedures for all federal agencies while each agency develops its own memoranda to guide its workers. Every program has its own manual, every office its own procedures, every department its official forms, and every official a fat file of "departmental issuances" to interpret the rest. As part of a campaign to eliminate "unnecessary" internal federal rules, just one office—Community Planning and Development in the Department of Housing and Urban Development—in one year—1981—eliminated 114 handbooks that provided guidance on the department's policies.

Regulation of individuals. Private citizens find themselves the object of other federal rules. Every taxpayer slogs through IRS forms and booklets; individuals receiving federal entitlements like social security must abide by restrictions like limits on outside income. Every citizen finds himself affected directly by federal rules.

Public sector regulation. Especially since the 1960s, the federal government has set numerous conditions for its aid to state and local governments. Like private sector regulation by inducement, public sector regulations come as a *quid pro quo* for federal support. The federal government cannot constitutionally order state and local governments to examine the environmental impact of projects they propose or to keep their financial records in specified ways. The federal government can, however, set those standards as conditions for fed-

---

5. According to best estimates, more than half of all federal expenditures for goods and services are contracted out. See Frederick C. Mosher, "The Changing Responsibilities and Tactics of the Federal Government," *Public Administration Review*, XL (1980), 542.

eral grants. And even though acceptance of that support is voluntary, the nation's states and cities have become financially dependent on their Washington uncle.

The rules come in many forms. Congress empowered the Environmental Protection Agency to prescribe the treatment that local governments must give their drinking water and the inspections that some states must conduct on automobile emission controls. Regional health planning organizations mandated by federal rules prescribe the facilities and rates that hospitals can charge, with other regulations governing the operation of federally funded, but state run, Medicaid programs. Federal mine safety regulations set standards for the operation of state and local gravel pits. In all of these areas, the federal government has spun out elaborate requirements about who can make decisions, who must be consulted, and even how records of performance must be filed. Rules stipulate who must benefit from federally aided programs and how state and local governments must administer those benefits. These regulations have created a wide channel of federal influence over the most intimate details of state and local operations. They have also made state and local governments front-line administrators for numerous national programs.

The importance of these programs is enormous. In financial terms, federal grants are big business. They totaled $95.1 billion in 1981, 14.5 percent of all federal spending. The 539 grant programs funded that year provided an amazing array of services: mass transportation, mental health centers, control of automobile junkyards, forestry research, housing rehabilitation, and many more.[6] The programs have been the principal vehicles for presidential strategies since the New Deal. And especially since the Johnson administration, they proved to be the largest controllable part of an increasingly uncontrollable federal budget. The aid proved an increasingly vulnerable target for budget cutters, but by that time the programs had developed strong and vocal constituencies. For state and local governments, the programs provided an important source of income. For every dollar state and local governments raised on their own in 1981, they received

---

6. U.S. Advisory Commission on Intergovernmental Relations, *Significant Features of Fiscal Federalism, 1980–81* (Washington, D.C., 1981), 58.

thirty cents in federal aid.[7] Mayors, governors, and county supervisors depended on the aid to fund programs for which they otherwise would have to find local revenue—or eliminate altogether. Grants, furthermore, provided support to local interest groups ranging from working mothers to neighborhood organizations. They depended upon federal grants to fund day care centers, health services, and job training programs, to build new houses, roads, and airports. And just as the programs developed a national constituency concerned about the strategy of federal aid, they acquired as well a collection of local constituencies that benefited from the programs.

The more important the programs became, the more irresistible they became as targets for federal regulation. Federal rules dictate how grant recipients must keep their financial records. In job training programs, the regulations put an upper limit on salaries; in construction programs, a lower limit. Congress originally passed the Elementary and Secondary Education Act in 1965 to provide grants with few strings to the states. But although the program had begun as a lean 32-page law, it had grown through amendments by 1978 to 3,237 pages, with a ten-page table of contents.[8] The growing popularity of formulas that automatically distributed federal grants, furthermore, brought these regulations into nearly all of the nation's state houses, county office buildings, and city halls.

These regulations have developed in two varieties: crosscutting rules that apply across-the-board to many, if not all, federal grant programs; and program-based rules that apply to individual grant programs. As grants have grown into more functional areas and have gone to more governments, they have become attractive vehicles for transmitting a broad range of crosscutting rules. Some rules govern administrative and fiscal policy. The earliest of these rules came from the Davis-Bacon Act, passed in 1931 to prevent contractors from paying their workers substandard wages. Davis-Bacon requires that state and local governments (among others) who spend federal funds must pay construction workers according to wage rates determined by the

7. *Ibid.*
8. See Carol Weissert, "The Politics-Administration Dichotomy Revisited: An Intergovernmental Perspective," paper presented at the 1981 Annual Meeting of the Midwest Political Science Association, Cincinnati, Ohio, April 17, 1981.

federal government. Congress added other requirements in 1934. The Fish and Wildlife Coordination Act set standards for wildlife conservation in federally funded water projects, and the Copeland Act sought to prevent kickbacks in federally financed construction. In 1940, the Hatch Act prohibited not only federal employees but also state and local employees paid by federal grants from engaging in political activities. Federal agencies naturally insisted that state and local officials keep careful financial records of how they spend the money, and over the years these rules have grown into conditions that apply across-the-board.

Other rules govern social and economic policy. Federal grants became an important mechanism for forcing state and local governments to comply with the 1964 Civil Rights Act. The National Environmental Policy Act of 1969 requires all grant recipients to consider the environmental effects of any projects they plan; other rules require facilities built with federal money to be accessible to the handicapped. Still other rules have emerged to govern wetlands, clean air, historical properties, and lead-based paint.

No one really knows how many of these crosscutting requirements there are. One count by the U.S. Office of Management and Budget in 1980 uncovered fifty-nine rules that apply to state and local governments (although OMB officials found two more rules after the report's publication).[9] There were relatively few crosscutting rules before 1960, but the number grew quickly during the 1960s and even more dramatically during the 1970s. Nearly 60 percent of all of the rules, in fact, were issued during the 1970s. (For a complete list of the fifty-nine requirements, see Appendix 1.)

In addition to the general regulations that apply across-the-board to all federal assistance, state and local governments also face different rules for each grant program. Although the rules vary widely, they fall into three categories. Some rules define extensive procedures that state and local governments must follow as a condition for funding. Every program has its own application form. Many programs, furthermore, require state and local governments to alert their citizens about planned projects. For example, 155 federal grant programs require

---

9. U.S. Office of Management and Budget, *Managing Federal Assistance in the 1980's* (Washington, D.C., 1980).

some form of citizen participation—boards, committees, or public hearings—before recipients can spend the money.[10] Most programs, furthermore, require grant recipients to measure and report periodically on their performance.

Some rules define who should receive the benefits of federally funded programs. The federal government's job training program in the 1970s, the Comprehensive Employment and Training Act (better known as CETA) defined who was eligible for job training, what kind of training they should receive, who could provide the training, and how much job trainees could be paid. Programs from social service grants to housing subsidies set income limits for beneficiaries. The standards vary widely, but every federal grant program sets conditions about who should benefit from grants.

Finally, some rules attempt to eliminate the despised trio of "fraud, waste, and abuse" from federal programs. Few federal programs have ever received the caustic attacks and hostile press attention that CETA received during the 1970s. Charges abounded that mayors were using the money as patronage to hire relatives, that some workers received exorbitant wages, and that there was little training and even less employment occurring. The Department of Labor responded with new rules on who could be hired, how much they could be paid, and what kind of training they should receive in an attempt to eliminate the problem.

THE BURDENS OF PUBLIC SECTOR REGULATION

Most of these crosscutting and program-based rules individually make much sense. No one would want rigged construction bids, discrimination against the handicapped in hiring, or destruction of a city's last park. The federal government would not want to abet local fraud by subsidizing it with a grant. No one knows, however, what all of the rules are and no one is in charge of finding out.[11] Before the Office of Management and Budget's survey, in fact, no one knew how many crosscutting regulations there were, to which programs they applied,

---

10. U.S. Advisory Commission on Intergovernmental Relations, *Citizen Participation in the American Federal System* (Washington, D.C., 1979), 113.
11. U.S. Office of Management and Budget, *Managing Federal Assistance*, 20.

or who was responsible for them. But no matter what sense the rules make, they bring substantial burdens to the state and local governments that struggle to comply with them and the federal administrators who seek to administer them. In a classic understatement, the Office of Management and Budget concluded that "cumulatively the conditions may be extraordinarily burdensome on federal agencies and recipients."[12] The costs, both financial and administrative, are usually borne by state and local governments that discover—often belatedly—that the regulations impose hidden carrying charges for the grants.[13] The regulations have in particular created four burdens for state and local governments. They have imposed high financial costs for compliance and have led to the creation of new state and local agencies to keep the records needed to prove compliance. They have subjected state and local officials to uncertainties and delays in planning their projects. They have created adversarial proceedings among governments. And they have created pressures toward token compliance: meeting the terms of the rules without conforming with their goals.

FINANCIAL COSTS

Some of the rules required large investments and those costs became political causes in themselves. The rhetoric of regulation's costs sometimes far outclassed the accuracy of the estimates. But since no one truly knew how much compliance with the rules did cost, the rhetoric took on a political importance of its own. Mayor Edward Koch of New York City, for example, estimated that complying with forty-seven major federal and state mandates from 1980 through 1984 would cost $711 million in capital expenditures, $6.25 billion in money from the city's current expense budget, and $1.66 billion in lost revenue.[14] One seemingly innocuous phrase in a 1973 law created particular problems for New York City and other cities around the country. Section 504 of the Rehabilitation Act of 1973 pro-

12. Ibid.
13. U.S. Comptroller General, *The Federal Government Should But Doesn't Know the Cost of Administering Its Assistance Programs* (Washington, D.C., February 14, 1978), Report GGD-77-87.
14. Edward I. Koch, "The Mandate Millstone," *The Public Interest*, LXI (Fall, 1980), 42.

vides that no otherwise able handicapped person "shall ... be excluded from participation in ... any program or activity receiving federal assistance." This phrase, adopted by Congress without hearings or debate, led to new rules requiring rest rooms, elevators, and public transportation to be accessible to the handicapped. The rules on transportation proved especially controversial—and costly. Mayor Koch faced the prospect of making the entire New York City subway system accessible to citizens in wheelchairs, while the U.S. Department of Transportation estimated that wheelchair lifts for existing buses and the development of a new generation of buses with low steps and wide front doors would cost $100 million. For educational institutions, the law meant an estimated $400 million in capital investments plus $2 billion annually for special educational services for the handicapped.[15] The Reagan administration withdrew the requirements that mass transit systems be accessible as one of its first regulatory relief actions, but not before earlier rules had led to a new and enormously more costly generation of buses.

Two Urban Institute scholars, Thomas Muller and Michael Fix, tried to measure the cumulative cost of such regulations on seven local governments. They investigated six rules that local officials found especially expensive or intrusive: Clean Water Act amendments, the Unemployment Insurance Compensation Act, bilingual education requirements (under the 1974 Bilingual Education Act and the 1964 Civil Rights Act), the Education of All Handicapped Children Act, accessibility requirements for local transportation systems, and the Davis-Bacon rules that set minimum wage standards. Muller and Fix found that the regulations led to increased operating costs of $51.9 million, or $19 for each resident in the seven communities. Capital costs increased $113.5 million, or $6 per capita (when amortized over twenty years at 8 percent). The $25 per capita in total costs roughly equaled the amount the seven local governments received annually in the federal government's general revenue sharing program.[16] What the federal government gave with one hand it took away with the other.

15. Timothy B. Clark, "Access for the Handicapped—A Test of Carter's War on Inflation," *National Journal*, X (October 21, 1978), 1672–75.
16. The jurisdictions are: Alexandria, Virginia; Burlington, Vermont; Cincinnati,

Beyond the financial costs, each regulation creates substantial administrative burdens. Someone must do the paper work that demonstrates compliance to federal officials. With the need to prove compliance have come files, new officials, and sometimes whole new agencies devoted to servicing the regulations. Many cities by 1980, for example, had established separate departments of community development whose principal function it was to administer federal grant programs.

All of these regulations, of course, exist for some good reason. All are aimed at curing important problems and many are effective in doing so. Many of these regulations, however, also impose high costs without prior consideration of what they would accomplish. The regulations requiring access to federally funded projects are the most infamous example, but many other regulations have been established without any consideration about the costs they would impose or the results they would produce. Put together, as Muller and Fix suggest, the financial costs imposed by public sector regulations are staggering.

UNCERTAINTY AND DELAY

Public sector regulations often breed uncertainty and delay. Simply discovering which rules apply to which programs is often a huge chore. Some crosscutting regulations are included only by reference in a program's rules. A regulation may state, for example, that an applicant for federal community development assistance shall comply with the requirements of federal environmental review and cash management procedures, a short reference that sends state and local officials into a different volume that details the full requirements of those rules. Furthermore, many regulations that apply across-the-board are often not included even by reference in a program's legislation. It often takes many months, consequently, to uncover all rules that apply to a grant program. Eighteen months after the passage of the Community Development program in 1974, for example, the Department of Housing and Urban Development (HUD) was still

---

Ohio; Dallas, Texas; Fairfax County, Virginia; Newark, New Jersey; and Seattle, Washington. See Thomas Muller and Michael Fix, "Federal Solicitude, Local Costs: The Impact of Federal Regulation on Municipal Finances," *Regulation*, IV (July/August, 1980), 29–36.

discovering crosscutting requirements that had to be added to the program's rules. Local governments, meanwhile, found that HUD's area offices could not supply them with copies of the rules that applied to the program.

Obtaining copies of the regulations of course does not end the uncertainty. There are inevitably questions of interpretation, and often different federal agencies interpret the same law differently. State and local officials naturally are expected to comply simultaneously with each interpretation. The access for the handicapped legislation required twenty-nine federal agencies to write regulations. The regulations appeared at different times and many of the rules were inconsistent or conflicting, particularly about the deadlines for compliance. "To date," the Office of Management and Budget reported in 1980, seven years after the passage of the act, "interagency coordination has not been very effective."[17] The lack of coordination, in turn, breeds uncertainty among state and local governments about what the federal government requires them to do when.

Other regulations impose long and costly delays on state and local governments. Roy Eckrose, director of public works in Janesville, Wisconsin, a city of 50,000, complained that federal rules cost the city five years and $760,000 more than originally planned. In 1973, the city applied for a $2 million Urban Mass Transit Administration grant to buy nineteen new buses, build shelters at nine bus stops, and improve a city garage. UMTA first required a plan on how the city's transportation system could be improved, a plan that took two years to write, even though the city was planning no changes in the system. Then UMTA invalidated a local public hearing because the city advertised the popular local name for the location instead of its street address. The city held a second hearing and no one attended. The city heard nothing from UMTA for sixteen months, and finally got approval for its new buses a month after the bus company stopped making the buses the city ordered. The delay forced the city to purchase a new "advanced design" bus that, among other things, would comply with the access for the handicapped regulations. It

17. U.S. Office of Management and Budget, *Improving Government Regulations: Current Status and Future Directions* (Washington, D.C., 1980), 9.

also cost the city "$760,000 more than we would have paid in 1973, and $380,000 more than we would have paid last year for the standard design bus. I attribute that difference to regulations," Eckrose complained.[18]

ADVERSARIAL PROCEEDINGS

The regulations often create adversarial relations among the federal, state, and local governments. Grants are designed as cooperative arrangements, with the state or local government receiving federal money for something it wants to do and the federal government granting aid for those projects it wants to fund. Public sector regulations have, however, created conditions that amount to legal orders. The environmental impact of a project must be assessed; a specified number of public hearings must be held and the hearings must be advertised in a certain way. With the regulations come as well the federal right to inspect state and local operations for compliance, and if the inspectors are not satisfied, orders for corrective steps follow. "The thing that bothers me more than anything else," Janesville city manager Philip L. Deaton said, "is when someone from the federal or state government comes down here to talk with us about regulation and the first thing they do is pull out a document and point to the section that says they have the authority to tell us what to do. In a legal proceeding, the theory is that you are innocent until someone proves you guilty. In a regulatory proceeding, you are made to feel guilty until you can prove your own innocence."[19]

Public sector regulation is a process of the regulated demonstrating compliance to the regulator. Proceedings often begin with an inspection or a complaint that raises the suspicion of noncompliance with a rule. The federal agency responds by informing the state or local government of the complaint, by citing the regulation in question, and by asking for evidence to the contrary. The presumption is that compliance must be demonstrated, rather than assumed except with evidence to the contrary. The result is an adversarial relationship between the federal government and the state and local govern-

18. Paul Danaceau, *Regulation: The View from Janesville, Wisconsin and a Regulator's Perspective* (Washington, D.C., 1980), 12-13.
19. Ibid., 11.

ments, a relationship marked by charges, threats of suspension of funding, official demands for information, and inspections. The fact that federal agencies rarely carry through with their threats does little to reduce the quasi-judicial spirit of regulatory investigations.

TOKEN COMPLIANCE

Federal pressures for compliance lead state and local governments to concern themselves with the details rather than the spirit of the rules. Ramps into public buildings might make access for the handicapped easier, but some are so steep that they pose a hazard to anyone on wheels. In the CETA program, the program's rules and the uncertainty of future funding led many local governments to spend a substantial share of the money on the salaries of government officials instead of on training programs.[20] Pressure is often heavy for token compliance, compliance with federal regulations as written but not conformance with their intent.

The regulated naturally explore the boundaries of the regulations. They often seek to maximize their own goals while minimizing the chances of federal intervention. The Community Development program in its first years, for example, required communities to design projects principally benefiting low- and moderate-income persons, and HUD's regulations required communities to identify the location of each project by census tract. Many communities responded by identifying some projects as "city-wide," a strategy that allowed them to place the projects where they chose while satisfying federal rules. The cleverest of the regulated can usually find ways to do what they want to do while complying, at least on paper, with what the federal government wants done.

On the other hand, some rules do not pursue the goals for which they were written. After his investigation of regulation in Janesville, Wisconsin, Paul Danaceau concluded that the regulated "often see little connection or relationship between the activities regulation has imposed on them and the social goals regulation is supposed to achieve."[21] Providing ramps for the handicapped does not necessarily

20. Richard P. Nathan and associates, *Public Service Employment: A Field Evaluation* (Washington, D.C., 1981), 7–35.
21. Danaceau, *Regulation*, 31.

improve their access. Compliance with federal regulations does not guarantee the fulfillment of federal goals.

The central problem is this: how can the federal government pursue its goals without intruding excessively or needlessly into state and local affairs? The federal government, especially through the 1960s and 1970s, relied increasingly on public sector regulation to define and seek its goals. These regulations, however, not only carried heavy financial and administrative costs but also often did not achieve the planned results. We will explore the creeping regulation of the Community Development Block Grant Program, passed by Congress in 1974 to streamline federal aid for urban development, for clues about the sources of and alternatives to this steady growth of corrosive federal power.

THE PROMISE OF DISCRETION

By 1970 federal grants for urban development had become a complicated hodgepodge. The largest of the federal programs was urban renewal, a program that traced its origins to the Housing Act of 1949 and America's postwar concern with eliminating slums. With the Housing Act of 1954, federal attention shifted from urban redevelopment—the clearance of land for future development—to urban renewal—"a comprehensive process of maintaining urban vitality," according to one of its early proponents.[22] Rebuilding the nation's cities would take more than just eliminating slums, the urban renewers contended. Revitalized communities would require better housing, improved police and fire protection, adequate health service, well-equipped recreational areas, good transportation, and most importantly, a plan to coordinate all of the new services.

It quickly became evident that no one federal program could solve so many problems, and Congress enacted a host of new programs to attack them one by one. The Office of Equal Opportunity launched its war on poverty; the Department of Commerce established economic development districts; the Department of Labor administered

22. Miles L. Colean, quoted by Mark I. Gelfand, *A Nation of Cities: The Federal Government and Urban America* (New York, 1975), 171.

comprehensive manpower training programs; the Department of Health, Education, and Welfare funded health planning agencies. Perhaps the most ambitious program of them all was the Model Cities Program, enacted in 1966 and administered by the year-old Department of Housing and Urban Development. Urban renewal, in the eyes of many of its critics, had transformed the physical structure of central cities while doing little for the people who lived there. Urban renewal, in fact, was often translated as "Negro removal."[23] Model Cities was the federal answer to these critics. The program would combine social and construction projects and concentrate them in "model neighborhoods" within "demonstration cities." The program was to be proof of the power of coordinating federal programs with local problems.[24]

By the late 1960s, however, these programs—and many other similar programs—encountered heavy and sustained criticism. One program designed to build new towns on federally owned land in central cities failed, Martha Derthick argued, because of "the limited ability of the federal government to influence the actions of local governments and from its tendency to conceive goals in ideal terms."[25] Another study of several economic development projects in Oakland lamented in an elaborate subtitle, "How Great Expectations in Washington Are Dashed in Oakland; Or, Why It's Amazing that Federal Programs Work at All."[26]

Most criticism of these programs centered on their overly ambitious goals and their hopelessly complex administrative structure. Critics complained that there were too many grant categories, a problem that made finding the right program for the right problem a burdensome chore. Critics also complained that the federal government exercised too much control and that that in turn created too much uncertainty for state and local governments. Urban renewal regula-

---

23. For a critique of the urban renewal program, see Martin Anderson, *The Federal Bulldozer* (Cambridge, Mass., 1964); and James Q. Wilson (ed.), *Urban Renewal: The Record and the Controversy* (Cambridge, Mass., 1966).
24. See James L. Sundquist with David W. Davis, *Making Federalism Work: A Study of Program Coordination at the Community Level* (Washington, D.C., 1969).
25. Martha Derthick, *New Towns In-Town* (Washington, D.C., 1972), 83.
26. Jeffrey L. Pressman and Aaron Wildavsky, *Implementation* (Berkeley, 1973).

tions were measured in thickness by the foot, and the average application review took 4⅓ years.[27] The complexity of the grant process thus tended to favor those governments best equipped to probe the rules and produce elaborate applications, the critics charged. Excessive federal control, they concluded, had made the grant system harder to administer at the same time it weakened the very state and local governments it sought to aid.[28]

In his 1971 State of the Union Address, Richard M. Nixon proposed a "New Federalism" to rid the intergovernmental system of these problems. He pledged to establish a new generation of federal grant programs that would transfer power from Washington to the nation's states and cities. The long application reviews, the uncertainties that surrounded them, and the proliferation of grant categories, Nixon concluded, had hamstrung state and local officials. His new programs, he said, would "provide the States and localities with more money and less interference."[29]

The complicated intergovernmental grant system, furthermore, had posed an impediment to Nixon's attempts to control domestic policy and the federal budget. The many Great Society programs had brought new administrators into control of large amounts of money. Assigning state and local governments the primary responsibility for planning and administering the programs would outflank administrators Nixon could not hope to control and gain him leverage over the size of federal grant expenditures. The "New Federalism" was thus an attempt both to sort out intergovernmental responsibilities and to shift power within the executive branch.

Earlier federal grants to state and local governments had principally been categorical grants that distributed money for specific and, usually, narrowly defined projects. There were federal categorical grants for highway construction, health centers, urban renewal, and Model Cities. Categorical grants in turn came in four basic varieties.

27. National Commission on Urban Problems, *Building the American City* (Washington, D.C., 1968), 165.
28. See Michael D. Reagan, *The New Federalism* (New York, 1972), 86–88; and U.S. Comptroller General, *Fundamental Changes Are Needed in Federal Assistance to State and Local Governments* (Washington, D.C., August 19, 1975), Report GGD-75-75.
29. U.S. Office of the Federal Register, *Weekly Compilation of Presidential Documents*, VII (January 25, 1971), 93.

Some grants, like aid to families with dependent children, distributed aid to state and local governments according to a formula set by law or administrative regulation. For other grants, including urban renewal and Model Cities, state and local governments had to submit applications to the federal agency administering the program. The application process was often highly competitive, and project grants generally required the recipient to contribute from 10 to 50 percent of the cost of the project. A third variety was a mixed grant where a formula determined how much aid a state received while potential recipients submitted applications for a share of the money. These grants funded projects as different as civil defense emergency operating centers and general aviation airports. Finally, some programs like Medicaid automatically reimbursed state and local governments for a specified share of their expenditures.[30]

Nixon's New Federalism included plans for a "general revenue sharing" program and six "block grants." General revenue sharing would guarantee grants to all state and general-purpose local governments with few restrictions on how they used the money. Block grants would combine existing categorical grants in a functional area and would give state and local governments much greater flexibility in spending the money. Congress previously had established two block grants: the Partnership for Health Act (1966) and the Law Enforcement Assistance Act (1968). Nixon proposed new block grants for manpower training, urban development, education, transportation, rural development, and law enforcement. Formulas within the programs would automatically entitle state and local governments to the money, and there would be very limited federal review of state and local plans. The keystone of Nixon's rhetoric was maximum local discretion and minimal federal control.

Congress approved general revenue sharing in 1972 but balked at yielding federal control over the other programs to state and local governments. A compromise manpower block grant, the Comprehensive Employment and Training Act (CETA) finally emerged in 1973. CETA combined seventeen existing categorical grant programs

---

30. For a discussion of these grants, see U.S. Advisory Commission on Intergovernmental Relations, *Categorical Grants: Their Role and Design* (Washington, D.C., 1978).

into a single program and guaranteed by formula the grant each state and local government would receive. However, it also required local preparation—and federal approval—of a comprehensive plan to chart and meet the area's manpower needs. The program was not as free from federal control as the one Nixon proposed, but neither was it as restrictive as the collection of programs it replaced.

Congressional opposition to further decentralization blocked all of the other block grant proposals except urban community development. Finally, in the midst of preparations in 1974 for the expected impeachment trial, Congress passed the Community Development Block Grant Program (CD). CD followed CETA's middle path between the Nixon proposal and the six categorical programs for water and sewer facilities, open space, neighborhood facilities, and public facilities loans. It contained a formula (counting population and the overcrowding of a community's housing stock and double counting the extent of poverty) that automatically entitled cities with a population of more than 50,000 and counties with a population of more than 200,000 to an annual grant. Communities had to submit applications for the funds, but federal review was limited in time to seventy-five days and in substance to insuring that applicants had not violated any basic requirements. Applications, in fact, were automatically approved if HUD had not rejected them during the seventy-five-day period.

CD provided funds for three general goals: the elimination of slums and blight, attacks on the problems of low- and moderate-income families, and projects to solve urgent community development needs. Local governments could use the funds for a wide array of projects, including housing rehabilitation, downtown improvement, parks, clearance of substandard buildings, and many other local development projects.

The distribution formula, however, soon provoked controversy. A provision in the program's legislation guaranteed that no community would receive less money for CD's first three years than they had received in the programs it replaced. For many older cities in the Northeast and Midwest, the gradual introduction of the formula thereafter would mean a substantial loss of money. Congress eliminated that problem in 1977 by enacting a second formula (based on: the age of a community's housing, counted 2.5 times; poverty, counted 1.5 times; and the community's lag in population growth, counted once) and allowing communities to choose whichever formula gave them the higher amount. The dual formula thus eliminated a major concern that would have seriously weakened political support for the program.

The federal block grant for community development proved a boon to local governments. The formula provided predictable grants and the dual formulas protected older and newer communities alike from a decrease in funds. Federal support for community development grew from $1.85 billion in fiscal year 1973, the last full year of the categorical programs, to $2.55 billion in fiscal 1975, the first year of CD—a 15 percent increase above inflation. Federal spending for CD, after allowing for inflation, remained relatively constant until the overall decline in federal grants during the late 1970s. (See Figure 1.) The program, furthermore, spread federal aid to more communities. The number of communities with a population of more than 25,000 that received funds increased by two-thirds, from 794 to 1,313.[31]

Local governments were enthusiastic about not only the predictable flow of funds but also the program's administrative flexibility. HUD's first regulations were little more than a restatement of the legislation's broad guidelines. They filled only 25 pages in the *Federal Register*, the federal government's daily regulatory journal, compared with about 2,600 pages of regulations in HUD's handbooks for the categorical programs. Compared with average applications of 1,400 pages per year required for the categorical programs, CD applications averaged between 40 and 50 pages the first year. Compared with the categorical programs in which HUD's Washington office reviewed most of the applications, the agency's forty area offices had primary responsibility for reviewing and approving CD applications. The streamlined application review procedure in the first year resulted in an average review time of forty-nine days, and HUD approved all but three applications.[32] The communities' own performance reports were to be the federal government's primary measure of progress.

---

31. U.S. Department of Housing and Urban Development, *Community Development Block Grant Program: First Annual Report* (Washington, D.C., 1975), 5, 24.
32. *Ibid.*, 3.

FIGURE 1: FEDERAL OUTLAYS FOR COMMUNITY DEVELOPMENT

(AMOUNT in billions of constant 1972 dollars; FISCAL YEAR 1971–1981 est.; curves labeled "Community Development Block Grant" and "Categorical Grant Programs")

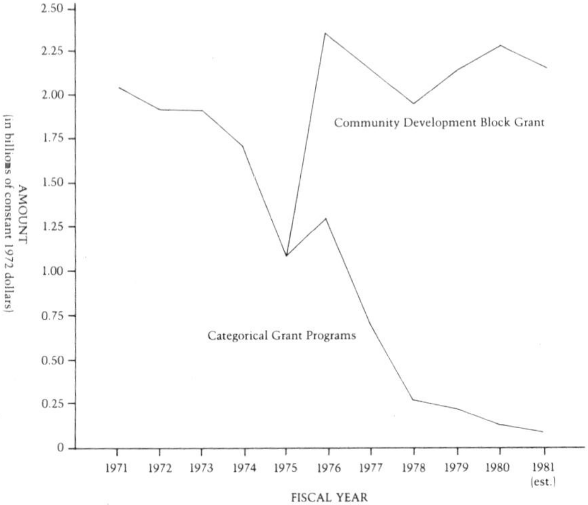

SOURCE: Derived from U.S. Office of Management and Budget, *Budget of the United States, Appendix*, various years; and *Economic Indicators*, prepared for the Joint Economic Committee by the Council of Economic Advisers.

NOTE: Grants for the 1976 transition quarter (the changeover of fiscal new year from July 1 to October 1) are included in fiscal 1976.

The promise of discretion, however, proved difficult to keep. When charges surfaced that some communities were using their CD money to benefit the rich instead of the poor, HUD began taking a much closer look at CD applications and insisted that communities document how much each project would benefit the poor. More stringent rules emerged to govern the crosscutting regulations as well—how environmental reviews should be conducted, how affirmative-action hiring plans should be drawn. Communities found themselves under increasing regulation; as one rough measure, the number of pages of CD regulations in the *Code of Federal Regulations*, the federal government's annual compendium of rules, grew from 56 pages in 1975 to 202 pages in 1979.

In the first months of the Reagan administration, an internal HUD memorandum complained about the costs these rules imposed: "Local discretion and flexibility are the cornerstones of the CDBG program. Over the past few years, HUD has imposed additional administrative requirements which have tended to reduce the freedom of localities to decide which activities to fund and have increased administrative costs."[33] Local officials themselves complained that more extensive regulations required more staff members to complete more complex applications, that they asked for data that often were unavailable, and that they raised conflicts with local plans.[34] In revising the program in 1981, Congress reverted to minimal requirements. Instead of preparing applications that were becoming increasingly long and complicated, local officials had only to choose their goals and select projects to meet those goals; publish their plans and allow citizens an opportunity to comment; and certify that they had met all other program requirements and crosscutting regulations.

The 1981 revisions of the CD program sounded, in fact, very similar to the program that Richard Nixon had proposed ten years earlier —including the argument that existing programs had become bogged down in federal regulation and had shifted the intergovernmental balance toward the federal government. CD itself had become the regulatory problem which it had been designed to solve.

THE CHALLENGE TO STATE AND LOCAL AUTONOMY

Public sector regulations have, especially since the 1960s, become an important part of the federal government's regulatory framework. As the size and scope of federal grants have grown, they have become increasingly attractive instruments for enforcing these regulations. Extensive rules have been added as conditions for aid: crosscutting rules that transmit requirements from equal opportunity to environmental protection and program-based rules that specify who decides and who benefits. The complaints lodged against these rules seem much like the second verse of the familiar song criticizing private sector rules. Indeed, the basic problems are the same. Regulations

---

33. U.S. Department of Housing and Urban Development, Community Planning and Development Notice 81-5, May 15, 1981.
34. Statement of HUD Secretary Samuel R. Pierce, Jr., U.S. House of Representatives, Committee on Banking, Finance and Urban Affairs, Subcommittee on Housing and Community Development, *Housing and Community Development Amendments of 1981*, hearings, 97th Cong., 1st sess., 1981, p. 2253.

that individually seem to make sense impose large costs on states and communities, just as they do on individual businessmen. Nearly all rules exist for some good reason (or at least it seemed that way when they were drafted). Whether to make cars safer or to prevent local abuse of federal programs, federal regulations are a barometer of the national interest. And as Herbert Kaufman has argued, "One person's 'red tape' may be another's treasured procedural safeguard."[35] There is a basic impetus in the federal government's policy making toward identifying problems and writing rules against them, whether those problems be dangers to the public health and safety, assaults on equality and freedom, failure of private markets and services, or misuse of federal money and authority. At the same time, such regulatory attack is always at least partially inadequate. It sometimes imposes costs that exceed benefits, produces regulations that conflict, and creates burdens that defeat the regulations' original intent. Such federal policy making is thus at its core a balancing act. The trick is to find just the right balance between the attempt to insure the national interest and the burdens those attempts create.

Even more fundamentally, regulation is a dynamic process of making adjustments and readjustments in the relationships of individuals and groups.[36] Regulation can provide an opportunity for asserting administrative power and can provide more pressure points to which political influence can be applied. It can furthermore be a way of shifting decisions from one level of government to another, for substituting the outcome of a national political process for decisions that otherwise might have been made at the state or local level. Regulation, finally, can serve a wide range of unexpected purposes. Interest groups can press for regulations that guarantee them a predictable share of federal money while state and local officials can use federal rules as a shield against the demands of their citizens. Regulation is thus a dynamic process with the potential for substantially altering the distribution of money and power, a political process in the largest

---

35. Herbert Kaufman, *Red Tape: Its Origins, Uses, and Abuses* (Washington, D.C., 1977), 4.
36. For example, see Merle Fainsod, "Some Reflections on the Nature of the Regulatory Process," *Public Policy*, I (1940), 299–323.

sense of that term: "choices between competing social and economic values and competing alternatives for government action," according to Lloyd N. Cutler and David R. Johnson.[37]

American federalism is precisely that kind of process: a choice between competing state and local interests, between interests represented at the national and subnational levels, between uniformity and diversity. Attempts to deal with these questions have drawn intergovernmental relations, and especially intergovernmental grant programs, into an increasingly complex federal regulatory web. In the chapters that follow, we will explore that web by examining the case of the Community Development program, a program originally promoted to eliminate regulatory strings but which itself became encrusted with rules. We will also explore a broader issue: why is the promise of state and local discretion so difficult to keep?

---

37. Lloyd N. Cutler and David R. Johnson, "Regulation and the Political Process," *Yale Law Journal*, LXXXIV (1975), 1399.

CHAPTER 2
WHO DECIDES?

THE FEDERAL GOVERNMENT has never reconciled its ambivalent policies toward grants for state and local governments. Since the first federal land grants in the eighteenth century, the federal government has provided intergovernmental aid for two reasons, to give financial assistance to often hard-pressed state and local governments and to induce these governments to administer programs with national goals. These two goals, however, have always been incompatible. Every recipient of aid wants as much discretion as possible in using it, and every donor wants to maintain at least some control over the money given. Federal aid has always been couched in the promise of minimal federal supervision of state and local decisions, but the lesson of two hundred years of federal aid—and particularly of the years since the New Deal—is that the federal government cannot simply transfer money to state and local governments and expect them to follow federal goals. This is not necessarily because state and local governments are more venal than the federal government (although we will explore this question later). Rather, state and local governments simply have different motives than the federal government. Faced with the same decisions, they usually decide differently.

This presents a problem for federal officials administering these programs. Whose decisions prevail when federal, state, and local officials differ over what to do with intergovernmental aid? Concentrating the money on federal goals means defining by law or regulation who should benefit, distributing money to those recipients who need it most and are most likely to spend it well, and supervising those projects funded to make sure the intended beneficiaries actually benefit. The federal government cannot set its goals without creating administrative problems for the governments receiving the programs. Each step creates its own rules, its own paperwork burdens, and its own avenue for federal interference in state and local decisions. There has thus always been a fundamental trade off in federal aid: concentrating benefits on federally defined targets versus providing state and local governments with administrative discretion. It is a trade off with which neither the donor nor the recipients have ever been comfortable. It is also a trade off that has created a complex administrative system governing intergovernmental aid.

Federal grants to state and local governments have grown through two massive spurts in spending. From the depths of the Depression came the presidency of Franklin D. Roosevelt, who pledged to a desperate nation that he would lead them out of their troubles. Much of Roosevelt's strategy relied on new federal grants to state and local governments, both to ease their own financial crises and to use their agencies to run the new programs. The scale of Roosevelt's efforts was not matched for another thirty years, until Lyndon B. Johnson's war on poverty. Johnson promised an attack on the societal problems that kept the nation's underprivileged citizens from a larger share of the country's wealth. As with Roosevelt's New Deal, Johnson's Great Society campaign was fought primarily with federal grants using state and local governments on the front lines. Both eras were marked by unusual social conditions and strong presidential leadership, and both campaigns brought a large growth in federal assistance to state and local governments, as Figure 2 shows. Each era, furthermore, took the federal government more deeply into the nation's state capitols and city halls. Governors and mayors came to rely more on federal assistance. The federal government meanwhile identified more problems as national ones and sought to insure that these national goals were met. Thus with this broadening of national concern came the problem of devising administrative

FIGURE 2: FEDERAL PAYMENTS TO STATE AND LOCAL GOVERNMENTS

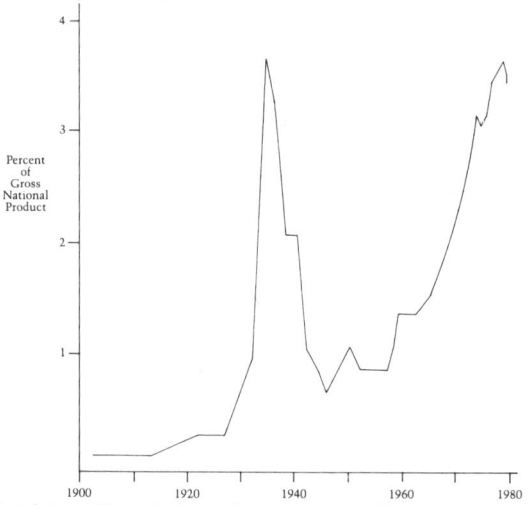

SOURCE: U.S. Advisory Commission on Intergovernmental Relations, *A Crisis of Confidence and Competence* (Washington, D.C.: U.S. Government Printing Office, 1980), 61.

strategies to insure that state and local governments met the federal government's expectations.

Federal attempts to control intergovernmental grant programs have evolved through three stages. In the first stage, control by category, the federal government exercised only loose control over state and local administration. From the New Deal to the Great Society, federal influence centered on the creation of new programs that drew state and local governments into new activities like income support for the elderly, public housing for the poor, highways for rural areas, and public works for growing cities. The federal goal principally was to induce state and local governments into new activities.

In the second stage, control by application, the federal government exercised control principally by selecting which state and local projects would receive aid. Many earlier grant programs required applications through which the federal government selected grant recipients, but during the Great Society the application process became a far more important mechanism for controlling the flow of federal money. Federal aid was distributed in more categories while federal administrators had greater authority to choose the local plans that best seemed to meet the programs' goals.

In the third stage, control by regulation, the federal government relied on increasingly specific rules governing the programs. Complaints about the increasing complexity and restrictiveness of the Great Society programs led to a new generation of federal grant programs in the 1970s that guaranteed state and local governments their grants in advance of application, determined grant amounts by formula, and allowed recipients broad freedom in choosing which projects to fund. Without extensive application reviews, federal administrators often found that their only effective control over the programs came through rules conditioning how the money could be used.

These stages of control were each marked by different social conditions, different presidential strategies, and different policy goals. The strategies, however, developed along a consistent path: distribution of federal aid to more state and local governments, more goals becoming defined as national, and stricter federal supervision of state and local progress toward national goals. It was a path that led to regulation.

THE NEW DEAL: CONTROL BY CATEGORY

March 1933 saw the confluence of three strong tides. State and local governments had reached their financial limits while the desperation of the unemployed worsened. Into these problems stepped Franklin D. Roosevelt, a president of supreme pragmatism and self-confidence and a president with a mandate to raise America out of its troubles. Roosevelt's kinetic activity during the first one hundred days of his administration set a standard by which presidents since have been judged. He created a spate of new agencies designed to cut through the government's lethargy and, perhaps even more, to restore hope that the nation would recover. He also altered forever the relations among the country's national, state, and local governments.

Roosevelt's programs were based on a novel sense of the national government's purpose. Serious problems that affected the country, even if they were economic as opposed to military or diplomatic, were *national* problems that deserved a *national* solution. Economic disaster nullified the relatively compartmentalized responsibilities that had characterized American federalism before the New Deal.[1] During the 1930s, the federal government moved into a dozen new functions, from social security and conservation of natural resources to housing and law enforcement.[2] The grants provided a device to unify the federal, state, and local attack on pressing problems. It was government by indirection, and cooperative administration by inducement.

Mark I. Gelfand has argued convincingly that Roosevelt did not intend to alter permanently the federal government's role or to usurp the role of the states.[3] Events, however, rendered the president's intentions moot. State governments found themselves hamstrung by fiscal and political constraints, while the national government was financially stronger and politically more eager. Federal borrowing capacity was far greater than that of state and local governments, and the programs proved easier to pass in Washington than in the forty-eight state legislatures.

The sudden growth of federal grant programs, however, worried state and local officials. "Both municipal and state officials fear that the grants-in-aid system will be used as a vehicle to force a Federal pattern upon them," Raymond S. Short reported in 1940.[4] As an example, he pointed to a 1938 congressional debate where the Senate tried unsuccessfully to force the states to adopt uniform drivers' license regulations as a condition for federal highway aid. Such regulations, however, existed more as a feared specter than as an established mechanism. Most grant programs during the 1930s operated relatively simply by formula, with the federal government reimbursing state governments for a specified share of their expenses. The federal government would occasionally, in cases like old age pensions or

1. See George C. S. Benson, *The New Centralization: A Study of Intergovernmental Relations in the United States* (New York, 1941); and Harry N. Scheiber, "The Condition of American Federalism: An Historian's View," in Frank Smallwood (ed.), *The New Federalism* (Hanover, N.H., 1967), 19–55. Their views conflict with the theory of "cooperative federalism" advanced by Morton Grodzins in *The American System: A New View of Government in the United States*, ed. Daniel J. Elazar (Chicago, 1966).
2. Benson, *The New Centralization*, 45.
3. Gelfand, *A Nation of Cities*.
4. Raymond S. Short, "Muncipalities and the Federal Government," *Annals of the American Academy of Political and Social Science*, CCVII (January, 1940), 47.

child welfare programs, pay the states in advance of their expenditures. But the most common case was national reimbursement of a portion of state costs.

Federal control was initially straightforward and used four basic tools. Federal agencies administering the grants insisted on approving project plans before agreeing to reimburse state agencies for their expenses. Federal agencies also wrote regulations to insure that each state as well as the ultimate recipients of federal aid received uniform treatment. Field inspections, financial audits, and program reports helped federal officials supervise the integrity of state programs. Finally, federal officials had what V. O. Key called the "shotgun behind the door," the right to withdraw funds for inadequate performance, a gun always loaded but rarely fired.[5]

The predominantly post-funding controls of the earliest grant programs—periodic status reports and financial audits—were gradually supplemented with stronger pre-funding reviews. As mechanisms to prevent abuse of the programs, post-funding controls were often much like spilled milk, for crying would not get the milk back into the bottle or undo the abuse. Pre-funding reviews, particularly advance approval of project plans, lessened the risk that local activities would vary from the federal design. For some projects like public works that did not recur, furthermore, advance approval was the only effective means of controlling what the state and local governments did with federal money. Most federal agencies awarding grants consequently grew to rely more on advance review of state and local plans, an approach that Key contended was "far superior to the post-audit as a means of insuring that the policy of Congress will be carried out as laid down in the federal act."[6]

The federal government also developed more sweeping conditions for its aid. Some grant programs required the states to create specified administrative structures to be eligible for aid. The Social Security Act of 1935, for example, mandated that the states establish a single agency to administer grants for dependent children. States had to establish merit systems for their employees and to insure that federal funds did not go for patronage. Federal officials were suspicious of the

5. V. O. Key, *The Administration of Federal Grants to States* (Chicago, 1937), 373.
6. *Ibid.*, 80.

integrity of state and local officials, and they created ever-bigger sticks to go with the carrots of federal aid. The grant programs provided a useful mechanism with which to promote reform.

For Roosevelt, the grants were administratively useful. By delegating management of the programs ultimately to state and local officials, Roosevelt avoided the administrative burdens of creating large new federal agencies or of trying to set policy for the complex variety of local conditions from Washington. The grants were politically useful because they reaffirmed the central role of the states in administering domestic policy. They also provided a way of expanding the federal government's role at a time when the Supreme Court was hostile to the New Deal.

The grant programs of the New Deal confirmed important changes that had begun to occur in American federalism. They gave an activist president a wide frontier across which to enlarge the federal government's activity. At the same time, the programs preserved the principle if not the fact that most areas of domestic policy were reserved for the states. Federal control was subtle; application reviews were not harsh and supervision of states' activities was not tight. Far more important was the development of new relationships. The grants drew the states into new partnerships with the federal government across a large number of functional areas. From conservation programs to highways, state governments accepted federal money and agreed to be bound by federal conditions. By expanding the categories of the federal-state partnership, the New Deal created the groundwork for further expansion of federal influence.

THE GREAT SOCIETY: CONTROL BY APPLICATION

When the nation returned its attention to domestic problems after World War II, the public discovered a new generation of problems. Existing roads were inadequate for increasing numbers and higher speeds of automobiles. Returning veterans led the rush to suburban houses, and in the process the nation rediscovered slums as well. New federal grant programs emerged to attack these problems. The federal government in 1956 began a 40,000-mile system of interstate highways, built by the states but largely funded by federal grants. The urban renewal program, meanwhile, provided grants to local governments for clearing substandard buildings. These new programs took the federal government further into the nation's state capitols and city halls. Cities found themselves bypassing state governments to deal directly with federal officials.

New grant programs for the states and the emergence of a broad federal-local partnership set the stage for Lyndon B. Johnson's Great Society. By any measure, federal grant programs grew explosively during the 1960s. Federal aid to state and local governments more than tripled from 1960 to 1970, from $7 billion to $24 billion.[7] Even more important than the growth of money was the proliferation of categories in which the money was awarded. The number of programs grew more than seven times between 1964 and 1967, from 51 to 379.[8] The explosion of categories marked a watershed in American federalism akin to the New Deal. What characterized the Great Society was a new, expansive definition of which problems were national ones. Johnson turned national attention to problems of structural inequality: inequality that grew from societal weaknesses and that no amount of economic growth could cure. Poor health care and inadequate housing seemed to affect some groups, notably minority groups, far more than others. Discrimination and poverty had left too many Americans too far away from the benefits of American life. If the thrust of the New Deal were economic recovery, the theme of the Great Society was social equality. If some people could not find jobs because they had no skills, the federal government would create a program to train them. If some neighborhoods suffered from a lack of services, Model Cities would aid them. If mothers needed to work to support their families, day care centers would look after their children. All of these federal grant programs shared a central theme: inequality in the United States was a national problem; the federal government would attack it with intergovernmental aid.

The growth of federal grant programs came predominantly through the establishment of new narrow-purpose, competitively

7. U.S. Advisory Commission on Intergovernmental Relations, *Significant Features*, 58.
8. Kenneth N. Vines, "The Federal Setting of State Politics," in Herbert Jacob and Kenneth N. Vines (eds.), *Politics in the American States: A Comparative Analysis* (Boston, 1976), 21.

awarded grants. Earlier categorical programs had been almost entirely formula based, with grants distributed to reimburse costs according to statutory criteria. In the 1960s, project categorical grants grew into an important new strategy. Like the formula categorical grants, they provided aid in narrow categories. But unlike the earlier grants, state and local governments had to submit extensive applications that explained what they planned to do with the money. There often was not enough money to fund all applications, and so the federal officials reviewing the applications gained increased authority. They could choose which projects seemed most deserving, which state and local governments were most likely to meet federal objectives, and which groups would benefit from federal money. The federal government could become more discriminating in deciding which projects to fund, and the application process thus became a crucial form of control.

The project grants greatly increased the federal government's control of intergovernmental aid programs. In addition to choosing which projects would be funded, the application review also gave the federal government greater opportunities for setting conditions for its assistance in advance of funding. The war on poverty's requirement of "maximum feasible participation" by the poor was only one of a wide range of new rules attached to the program. The federal government used the programs as vehicles for transmitting equal opportunity rules to state and local governments. And if the state and local governments could not or would not direct their programs to the poor, the federal government stood ready to impose even stronger conditions—and if necessary to bypass the governments and deal directly with the poor themselves.

Federal application review became the key mechanism for insuring that state and local governments were using federal money for federal goals, and as those goals broadened the reviews became more important. It also created applications that were voluminous and reviews that were lengthy. Local governments had to develop detailed plans for the land they proposed to clear, how they planned to relocate the citizens and businesses displaced by the project, what new development was planned, and how the whole package would be financed, all before the federal government would approve the application. Federal reviews often meant detailed federal consultation with local officials as well as technical assistance to help local governments draft plans to meet federal standards. The national mark on projects funded with federal project categorical grants was unmistakable. Complaints about excessive federal control and too much red tape led Richard M. Nixon to propose a "new federalism" to transform intergovernmental relations.

THE NEW FEDERALISM: CONTROL BY REGULATION

Despite the apparent simplicity of the New Federalism programs proposed by Nixon and passed, in greatly altered form, by the Congress, the programs proved administratively difficult and politically volatile. As Chapter 1 described, the programs vested state and local governments with substantial new responsibilities for planning and managing programs for which the federal government had previously been primarily responsible. Many members of Congress had serious reservations about the discretion the programs allowed state and local governments. Many interest groups feared that the programs would benefit the locally powerful instead of the needy. Would local politics corrupt national policy goals? Did local governments have adequate management expertise to implement the programs? The new programs promised only minimal federal supervision of local projects, and many suspicious observers in Washington doubted that the trust embodied in state and, especially, local governments was well placed.

It did not take long for such fears to receive support. An armada of monitoring groups set forth to examine local performance, and these monitors found trouble wherever they looked. There were reports that cities were choosing many projects that benefited the rich instead of the poor and that, in any case, they were spreading the money too broadly to have any real effect. Charges of corrupt hiring practices plagued CETA projects. Regardless of the strength of the charges, two problems dominated the debate. First, cities dealt with the money differently than had the federal government in earlier programs. Local officials responded to the need to develop a broad constituency for the programs by scattering the money around local neighborhoods. Second, local administrative capacity varied widely, and some cities had a very difficult time in controlling and executing their projects. In some localities this meant that little happened; in others, it meant sloppy administration that led to abuse or outright fraud.[9]

Federal officials in Washington consequently tightened their review of state and local performance. The Department of Housing and Urban Development began taking a much closer look at CD applications and insisted that cities document the extent to which each project would benefit the poor. In the CETA program's 1978 renewal, Congress put limits on how long CETA participants could work and how much they could be paid. In addition to supervising local applications more closely to insure that local governments fulfilled their federally defined obligations to the poor, the federal government also began to conduct far more stringent monitoring.

All of these actions created a complicated mix of federal controls: extensive regulations detailing what had to be done; application reviews to determine whether the cities were meeting the regulations; and monitoring procedures to examine whether the cities had complied with the regulations. Programs that had promised more freedom from federal control had, ironically, produced new and complex federal regulations designed to prevent abuse of the money.

No program, of course, can function without rules. A regulation-free agency would be open to capricious actions by administrators, and even if every administrator tried faithfully to execute the law, there could be no assurance without written rules that officials in Atlanta and Boston would interpret the law in the same way. Even officials across a Washington corridor from each other could easily come up with different approaches to managing the same program. The new breed of grant programs during the 1970s, however, brought many new rules affecting many more state and local governments. Agency regulations specified who could receive federal money, how

9. See Donald F. Kettl, *Managing Community Development in the New Federalism* (New York, 1980). From the U.S. Comptroller General, see *Weak Internal Controls Make the Department of Labor and Selected CETA Grantees Vulnerable to Fraud, Waste, and Abuse* (Washington, D.C., March 27, 1981), Report AFMD-81-46; and *The Community Development Block Grant Program Can Be More Effective in Revitalizing the Nation's Cities* (Washington, D.C., April 30, 1981), Report CED-81-76.

they could spend it, and whom it should benefit. CD regulations specified that senior-citizen centers, street lights, and playgrounds were eligible for funding; stadiums, cultural centers, and bus stations were not.[10] Fire stations were eligible (because they protected neighborhood property) while police stations were not (because they primarily protected people). As the programs evolved, they became encumbered with increasingly detailed rules, some to prevent the recurrence of abuse and some to answer questions of interpretation that arose in the administrative process.

Although programs often acquire more rules as they age, rules for some of the new programs expanded at a far greater rate than others. Regulations grew most rapidly for the new formula grants, especially those awarded to local governments. Table 1 shows the amount awarded in the eight largest grant programs for fiscal year 1981. Although they were only a few of the approximately five hundred grant programs, grants in these programs totaled $37.4 billion, 68 percent of all federal grants to support state and local governments. (Grants to state and local governments in fiscal 1981 totaled $94.8 billion. Of this money, however, $39.9 billion went to grants for eventual payment to individuals—income transfer programs like Medicaid, housing subsidies, and unemployment assistance—and hence were not grants to support state and local governments. These eight programs accounted for more than two-thirds of the $54.9 billion that remained.)

Two themes emerge from Table 1. One is that regulation, as measured roughly by the number of pages in the *Code of Federal Regulations*, the federal government's annual compendium of its rules, grew substantially. (The *Code* provides a better indicator than the more commonly used source, the number of pages in the daily *Federal Register*. Compared to changing type sizes and formats in the *Federal Register*, the *Code* has stayed in the same format over the period measured in Table 1. It also lists all rules in effect and hence is a better measure of the total volume of rules.) In just six years, from 1975 to 1980, regulatory growth ranged from 50 percent in the Elementary and Secondary Education Act programs to 400 percent in

---

10. 39 *Federal Register*, November 13, 1974, pp. 40142–43, Sections 570.200–201.

TABLE 1: REGULATION OF GRANT PROGRAMS

Program	FY 1981 Outlays (in millions)	Regulation: Percent Change 1975–1980[1]	Type of Grant	Recipient: Type of Government
Mass Transit (UMTA)	$3,771	+400	C/F+P[2]	Local[4]
Manpower Training (CETA)	5,926	+334	B/F	Local[4]
Community Development (CD)	4,042	+298	B/F	Local[4]
General Revenue Sharing	5,137	+200	R/F	State+Local
Sewage Treatment	3,881	+106	C/P[3]	State+Local
Social Services (Title XX)	2,646	+ 83	B/F	State
Highways (Trust Funds)	8,641	+ 60	C/F	State
Education (ESEA)	3,345	+ 50	C/F	State[5]

TYPE OF GRANT: CODE
  C = categorical   F = formula
  B = block   P = project
  R = revenue sharing

NOTES
  1. Pages in the *Code of Federal Regulations*.
  2. Operating assistance is largely distributed by formula; facilities and equipment are funded through project grants.
  3. There are some project grants subject to distribution by formula.
  4. Predominantly local governments, although state governments receive a share of the money.
  5. Predominantly state governments, with money passed through to local education agencies.

SOURCE: U.S. Office of Management and Budget, *Budget of the United States Government, 1983*, "Special Analysis H: Federal Aid to State and Local Governments" (Washington, D.C.: U.S. Government Printing Office, 1980), 29–36; U.S. Office of the Federal Register, *Code of Federal Regulations*, various years; and U.S. Advisory Commission on Intergovernmental Relations, *A Catalog of Federal Grant-in-Aid Programs to State and Local Governments: Grants Funded FY 1978* (Washington, D.C.: U.S. Government Printing Office, 1979).

urban mass transit programs. No matter how rough the measure may be, it is indisputable that federal regulation in these programs grew substantially. The second implication is that the growth of regulation was especially large for the new, formula-based programs for local governments. In four programs—mass transit aid, CD, CETA, and general revenue sharing—regulation at least tripled over the six-year period.

The reasons for the regulation of these programs are complex. Some of the rules flow from federal attempts to rid the programs of local fraud, waste, and abuse. No program is free of such problems, but the new block grants attracted more than the usual amount of criticism. Federal officials followed the natural administrative reaction to such charges: write rules to insure they do not recur. Some of the rules grew as well from the lack of state and local administrative expertise. Programs like CETA were major new government enterprises and no level of government was administratively prepared to deal with the programs' demands. CD, on the other hand, brought major new responsibilities for planning and coordinating complex projects to city hall. In both cases, the lack of administrative expertise led to initial problems, and this led to regulations that attempted to resolve local difficulties.

Perhaps the most imporant reason for the greater regulation of these programs, however, was the formula-based entitlement itself. Many of the new formula grants of the 1960s and 1970s had been created to end the unseemly competition for funds created by the project categorical programs. The formula grants accounted for two-thirds of all federal grants in the mid-1960s, David B. Walker of the U.S. Advisory Commission on Intergovernmental Relations estimates, and three-quarters of the money by the mid-1970s.[11] Four factors increased the popularity of the formulas.

Rise of the intergovernmental lobby. Hand in hand with the growth of formula grants was the rise of the "intergovernmental lobby," a term coined by Samuel H. Beer to describe the organizations in Washington representing the nation's governors, mayors, city managers, county supervisors, and state legislators in Washington.[12] As the federal government relied more on state and local governments to administer its programs, those governments came to rely more on federal grants. Although these groups were among the oldest of Washington-based lobbies, they gained more influence on policy during the late 1960s. State and local governments changed from passive recipients of what the federal government offered to active participants in designing new federal grant programs.

The formula grants were particularly attractive to these groups.

---

11. Letter to the author from David R. Beam of the commission staff, August 8, 1980.
12. Samuel H. Beer, "The Adoption of General Revenue Sharing: A Case Study in Public Sector Politics," *Public Policy*, XXIV (1976), 129.

They guaranteed their members an entitlement to aid instead of forcing them to compete among themselves. Furthermore, by guaranteeing all—or nearly all—members an entitlement the formulas enhanced the internal unity of the lobbying organizations. A lobby that could bring home the bacon for a broad cross section instead of a small clique of its members naturally strengthened its position. Members of the intergovernmental lobby thus strongly supported the new formula grant programs.

Decline of party unity in Congress. The intergovernmental lobby's growing strength meshed with growing congressional enthusiasm for formula programs. As party leaders in Congress became less able to deliver votes, each program increasingly had to stand for itself. This decline in party discipline, R. Douglas Arnold suggests, made formula-based grants more attractive because they provided a mechanism for building coalitions for each program.[13] The formulas provided a measure in advance of the program's value to every member's district and an easy way to adjust the program's benefits to help assemble a winning coalition. In its crudest form, a formula could guarantee that many if not all members could take a share of the money back to their districts. The entitlement formulas thus became the glue that held coalitions for the grant programs together. But getting programs enacted required spreading the glue thinly. The formulas drew many more governments into the grant game.

Attempts to outflank the federal bureaucracy. Few presidents have approached Washington with more suspicion toward the federal administrative establishment than Richard Nixon. Many of the Great Society's programs were staffed by career officials with strong commitments to the programs they had helped to build. One White House aide referred often to "the White House surrounded"—surrounded by bureaucratic interests opposed to the president's goal of trimming and decentralizing federal domestic policy.[14] In the new programs,

---

13. R. Douglas Arnold, *Congress and the Bureaucracy: A Theory of Influence* (New Haven, 1979), 210–14.
14. Richard P. Nathan, *The Plot That Failed: Nixon and the Administrative Presidency* (New York, 1975), 82. See also Richard L. Cole and David A. Caputo, "Presiden-

federal officials lost the most important leverage over the programs: control over who gets how much money. Formulas dictated which governments were eligible for the money and how much they would receive. The formulas also created a presumption of funding. In previous programs, the burden of proof was on state and local governments to demonstrate why they should receive the money. In the New Federalism programs, the burden was on federal officials to demonstrate why a government should not receive money to which it otherwise was entitled.

Attempts to outflank the president. Many members of Congress had their own suspicions about Nixon. Foremost among them were that the White House would penalize some members' districts by withholding grants or that the White House would impound money for programs it opposed. Casting the distribution formula in law provided some reassurance for members of Congress. Reducing administrative discretion left fewer avenues for presidential intervention and thus protected some of the members' favorite programs—and the grants for their constituents.

DISTRIBUTIVE POLITICS AND REGULATORY ADMINISTRATION

Formula grants developed widespread support for disparate reasons. They also created grant programs much different from the New Deal programs of the 1930s or the Great Society programs of the 1960s. Earlier programs centered on the *politics of purpose.* Congressional attention revolved around the objectives that the programs would seek—reconstruction of urban housing, improvement of rural health care, jobs for the unemployed. Decisions about who would receive how much money were left to the federal agencies that administered the programs. The formula grants of the 1970s, by contrast, centered on the *politics of distribution,* the logrolling between rural and urban states, large and small governments, states and cities, that determined the allocation of federal aid. Federal legislation dictated who

---

tial Control of the Senior Civil Service: Assessing the Strategies of the Nixon Years," *American Political Science Review,* LXXIII (1979), 399–413.

would receive how much money while state and local governments acquired more freedom to choose the projects they would fund. This is not to suggest that congressional debates over general revenue sharing, CETA, or CD were free from questions over the money's use or that the legislation was silent on administrative directives. The distributive questions, however, were the ultimate questions, and the administrative issues were ultimately left to federal, state, and local administrators to haggle over. That haggling eventually led to regulations that spelled out just what actions the federal government would permit. When they lost the sanction of distributing funds selectively, federal administrators fell back upon rules that conditioned how the money could be spent.

Distributive politics in Congress thus led to regulatory administration of the grant programs. While all federal grant programs have demonstrated a tendency to become encrusted with regulations as they grow older, the tendency has been particularly strong (as Table 1 shows) in formula-based grant programs. The broad license granted to state and local governments in the formula grant programs—and particularly the block grant programs—has produced predictable administrative problems and federal regulations to correct them.

The 1970s thus brought a wide range of new regulations to the administration of federal grant programs. If there had been any doubt about whether the federal, state, or local government was the major partner in the union, the new programs stifled it. The federal government, through regulation, defined in growing detail which problems were national problems. It supplied money to attack them, and it wrote increasingly stringent rules to govern how the money was used. This movement to regulatory federalism only marked the next step on a path to greater federal control set by the New Deal, but it broadened that path by applying more rules to more state and local governments about more detailed national goals than ever before. For example, of the 38,776 state and general-purpose local governments in the United States in 1979, 37,704—97 percent—received general revenue sharing grants.[15] All of them had to comply with the program's rules.

15. U.S. Advisory Commission on Intergovernmental Relations, *A Crisis of Confidence and Competence* (Washington, D.C., 1980), 84.

The regulations were of two types. As we shall see in Chapter 3, some applied in crosscutting fashion to all grant programs and posed particular problems for some of them. Other rules, as we shall see in Chapter 4, applied to particular programs. Together they grew into an imposing feature of American federalism.

CHAPTER 3
WHAT PROCEDURES?

THE FEDERAL GOVERNMENT never gives money without strings attached. At the very minimum, state and local governments have had to have their financial records audited and to allow federal inspectors to survey their projects. These strings, not surprisingly, grew stronger as the size of federal grants increased through the New Deal. Even in the 1930s, the federal government showed a penchant for establishing crosscutting conditions for all of its programs, conditions that set wage standards for construction workers, forbade kickbacks, and sought to preserve fish and wildlife. Congress's goals came to include procedural as well as substantive goals. In part, the federal government simply identified some procedures as national goals in themselves. There was no better way to transmit such broadly ranging objectives to state and local governments than by attaching them as universal conditions to irresistible federal grants. In part, these regulations also grew because the federal government was suspicious of the administrative capacity and personal integrity of state and local officials. Through both routes, *how* state and local governments ran the programs came to be just as important as the projects the programs were established to fund.

In the years since the New Deal, Congress and the executive branch have added increasingly thick layers of procedural require-

TABLE 2: CROSSCUTTING REGULATIONS

Date Established	Social/Economic N	%	Administrative/Fiscal N	%	Total N	%
Prior to 1960	4	11	2	9	6	10
1960s	9	25	9	39	18	31
1970s	23	64	12	52	35	59
TOTAL	36	100	23	100	59	100

SOURCE: U.S. Office of Management and Budget, *Managing Federal Assistance in the 1980s, Working Papers* (Washington, D.C.: U.S. Government Printing Office, 1980), Vol. I, p. A-2-11.

ments. By 1960, there were only six crosscutting regulations, but the steady growth of the rules became a torrent in the 1960s and 1970s. As Table 2 shows, 90 percent of the fifty-nine crosscutting rules the Office of Management and Budget counted emerged from 1960 to 1980, and 59 percent were issued during the 1970s alone. The federal government published new rules to require coordination of grant applications, to standardize record keeping, and to account for the time university faculty members spent on federally funded research projects. Administrative and fiscal rules specified how grant recipients were to keep their books, how they had to be audited, and how public meetings had to be conducted. Social and economic rules required state and local governments to pursue affirmative action, to purify their air and water, to protect endangered species, to provide the handicapped with access to public facilities, and to protect historically significant structures. Just the major activities (see Table 3) kept state and local administrators busy.

The growth of crosscutting rules, especially the socioeconomic rules, was but part of a new "social regulation."[1] Old-style rules in the private sector had since the late nineteenth century controlled the market: entry, rates, and the obligation of firms to serve the public. With the 1960s, however, came a new style of regulation that sought to control the public's health, safety, and social condition. Social regulation set the conditions in which workers manufactured products as well as the safety and reliability of the goods they pro-

1. Lilley and Miller, "The New 'Social Regulation.'"

TABLE 3: MAJOR CROSSCUTTING RULES

Socioeconomic Rules	Administrative/Fiscal Rules
Civil Rights Act (1964) Historic Preservation (1966) Access for the Handicapped (1968, 1973) Environmental Assessment (1969) Clean Air Act (1970) Clean Water Act (1972) Endangered Species Act (1973) Flood Insurance (1973) Age Discrimination Act (1975)	Cost Accounting (various years) Freedom of Information Act (1965) Relocation Assistance (1970) A-95 Application Coordination and Review (1973) Privacy Act (1974)

SOURCE: Derived from U.S. Office of Management and Budget, *Managing Federal Assistance in the 1980's, Working Papers, Vol. I* (Washington, D.C., 1980), A-2-11.

duced. The Occupational Safety and Health Administration, for example, issued rules to govern the safety of the workplace while the Consumer Product Safety Commission probed the dangers the products might cause in normal use.

With the growth of a new social regulation came the establishment of new regulatory agencies. Of the twenty federal agencies involved in old-style economic regulation, nineteen had been founded before 1960. Six of the thirteen health and safety agencies were founded after 1960, including the National Highway Traffic Safety Administration, the Environmental Protection Agency, and the Consumer Product Safety Commission. All but one of the eight social equality agencies were established after 1960, including the Civil Rights Division of the Department of Justice and the Federal Elections Commission.[2] Many of these new agencies generated rules with which state and local governments had to deal. All of them were part of the trend of increasing federal involvement in social and economic policy. Federal mandates on state and local government for two decades grew geometrically.[3] The reasons for the rapid growth of these rules and the agencies that issued them are complex, but among the most important are three factors.

2. U.S. Advisory Commission on Intergovernmental Relations, *A Crisis of Confidence*, 78–79.
3. For one study of federal mandates on local government, see Catherine Lovell and Charles Tobin, "The Mandate Issue," *Public Administration Review*, XLI (May/June, 1981), 318–31.

First, the federal government defined more problems as national problems. Some of the new rules attacked problems that simply had not previously been seen as problems requiring a federal regulatory response. Preserving historic structures in towns across the nation had not been a problem that seemed to demand extensive regulations. Nor had newly asserted citizens' rights to privacy and access to governmental records and meetings. Other regulations dealt with problems that previously had been under state and local jurisdiction. The federal government moved into environmental protection and civil rights in part because of perceived state and local failure to maintain acceptable standards and in part because a new national constituency for these regulations demanded national attention. For a variety of reasons, then, more problems became national problems and those problems bred federal regulations.

Second, many of the same pressures that created a new national awareness of some problems led to demands for equal treatment. Particularly in civil rights but also in areas ranging from access for the handicapped to protection for wetlands, advocates for a stronger federal role argued that the only defensible policy was a national policy enforced uniformly by the federal government. Environmental activists wanted to eliminate any economic advantages some states might acquire by issuing less strict standards. Other organized forces contended that the equal protection clause of the Fourteenth Amendment to the U.S. Constitution required uniform federal standards for civil rights. Pressures for equality led to federal rules that would apply equally across the country.

Finally, such salient issues provided a convenient way for members of Congress to engage in what David R. Mayhew calls "position-taking."[4] By adding affirmative action or environmental review regulations as conditions for federal aid, members of Congress could go on record as favoring these positions without having to devise an administrative strategy for insuring those conditions were met. A short, innocuous-sounding phrase slipped into the Rehabilitation Act of 1973, without substantial discussion or analysis, and required that projects funded with federal money had to be accessible to the handi-

---

4. David R. Mayhew, *Congress: The Electoral Connection* (New Haven, 1974).

capped. It seemed reasonable that federally funded projects should be available to all, and the provision provided an easy way for members of Congress to go on record in favor of equality of access for the handicapped (and to please the large and vocal lobby for the handicapped in Washington). Only after federal rules interpreting that provision emerged—rules that took the provision literally and required everything from subways to city halls to be accessible to citizens in wheelchairs—were the full implications of the phrase evident.

Congressional lawmaking has in many cases moved from the drafting of specific legislation to the endorsement of broad principles, from what Theodore J. Lowi calls the denotation to the connotation of public policy.[5] Law, especially law dealing with the new social policy issues affecting the public and private sectors, has become more vague: broad injunctions to serve the poor, to provide workers with a safe workplace, to promote equal opportunity, without instructions on how they are to be accomplished. The laws inevitably include language that authorizes the cabinet secretary or agency head to issue regulations to implement the policy, and it is only in issuing the regulations that the full language of the law is written. The result has been a series of problems: for Congress to oversee the programs and requirements it created, for federal bureaus to manage the programs, and for state and local governments to cope with the burdens the programs brought. Even in programs designed to return substantial responsibility to state and local governments, state and local officials found federal procedural regulations a distorting force.

We will examine in detail two of the crosscutting regulations that applied to the CD program. From their passage in 1974, rules for equal opportunity and environmental protection proved especially difficult for federal officials to supervise and for local officials to follow.

EQUAL OPPORTUNITY

Federal civil rights legislation dates from the ineffectual Civil Rights Act of 1866. For the next century, federal policy evolved in piecemeal

---

5. Theodore J. Lowi, *The End of Liberalism: The Second Republic of the United States* (New York, 1979), 105.

fashion with little real impact. Not until the Civil Rights Act of 1964 did the federal government authoritatively ban discrimination by race, sex, and religion in all parts of national life. By 1975 federal civil rights policy grew into a complex collection of laws and presidential executive orders. No employer, union, educational institution, or government could discriminate in its activities. Each had to keep records demonstrating its compliance and was subject to court-ordered changes if a case of discrimination was made against it. For recipients of federal aid, the ultimate sanction for noncompliance with federal civil rights policy was the denial of assistance.

Each local chief executive applying for the community's entitlement had to sign a form certifying that the government would comply in particular with four laws and two executive orders.[6] HUD officials in Washington instructed field officials in the area offices to accept local certifications except where there was convincing evidence to the contrary. This process established a presumption of compliance and federal officials, burdened with the chores of administering the program and supervising the other crosscutting requirements, initially did little more than check to make sure the certification was signed.

In the first year of the program, however, several studies charged that local governments had violated the equal opportunity rules. The Michigan Advisory Committee to the U.S. Commission on Civil Rights conducted a case study of one city's application—Livonia, Michigan—and concluded that the city "demonstrates no affirmative action" to overcome the effects of past discrimination. Furthermore, the committee charged, "the Livonia plan locks the city into its already 'all white' and 'middle income' housing characteristics."[7] In another Michigan city, Sault Ste. Marie, the committee found a "pat-

---

6. They are: Title VI of the Civil Rights Act of 1964, which prohibits discrimination; Title VIII of the Civil Rights Act of 1968, which mandates fair housing; Section 109 of the Housing and Community Development Act of 1974, which prohibits discrimination in the provision of program benefits; Section 3 of the Housing and Community Development Act of 1968, which compels affirmative action in employment for the residents of project areas; Executive Order 11063, which stipulates equal opportunity in housing built with federal funds; and Executive Order 11246, which prohibits discrimination in employment funded with federal money.

7. Michigan Advisory Committee to the U.S. Commission on Civil Rights, *Civil Rights and the Housing and Community Development Act of 1974, Vol. I, Livonia* (Washington, D.C., 1975), 26.

tern of discrimination that has failed to provide adequate and appropriate housing and community development programs" for a community of Chippewa Indians.[8] The committee placed the blame with HUD. Its policy of checking only for signed certifications instead of conducting a thorough review of local compliance, the committee charged, "jeopardizes those provisions of the law requiring affirmative action." The committee argued that HUD "should conduct a more vigorous front end review of applications," and, if necessary, deny funding to communities that do not comply.[9]

By the second year of the program, HUD faced thirty-one complaints on the equal opportunity regulations and HUD's own application reviews showed that a majority of applications had at least one equal opportunity deficiency.[10] The complaints were based in a set of interrelated problems. This was the first time many communities faced these requirements, and many CD recipients simply did not know how to comply. For other communities, the equal opportunity requirements were more paperwork that had to be processed to get their money, and some did not take it seriously. Some of the cases were enmeshed in the technical difficulties of devising affirmative strategies for righting past discrimination and, undoubtedly, some of the charges pointed to genuine discrimination. HUD, however, had no way to differentiate one cause from another and its acceptance of local certifications provided the agency with no defense against the charges.

HUD responded in May, 1976, with a memo to its field officials that directed them not to accept local certifications unless recipients could demonstrate "meaningful action" toward meeting equal opportunity requirements. If a community did not meet this requirement, HUD froze its grant until it did. In Middletown, Connecticut, for example, HUD gave the city sixty days to contract with fair-housing groups to assist minorities, undertake a survey of housing conditions, and begin a fair-housing campaign. In Euclid, Ohio, HUD insisted the

8. Michigan Advisory Committee to the U.S. Commission on Civil Rights, *Civil Rights and the Housing and Community Development Act of 1974, Vol. III, The Chippewa People of Sault Ste. Marie* (Washington, D.C., 1976), iii.
9. Michigan Advisory Committee, *Livonia*, 26–27.
10. U.S. Department of Housing and Urban Development, *Community Development Block Grant Program: Second Annual Report* (Washington, D.C., 1976), 140–41.

city pass antidiscrimination ordinances, set up an affirmative action plan, and contract with a local fair-housing group to handle discrimination complaints. HUD showed itself ready to use the ultimate sanction—revocation of funds—to force local governments into compliance with the equal opportunity regulations.[11]

HUD's stronger supervision of local governments ran directly against the New Federalism philosophy: minimal federal control and maximal local discretion. That philosophy weakened when in the first months of the program complaints arose that CD recipients were violating the law. HUD's control moved to a trial by paper: stronger monitoring of local performance and more aggressive review of local applications. CD recipients could demonstrate their compliance with the equal opportunity regulations by writing adequate fair-housing plans, providing satisfactory mechanisms for collecting and judging the complaints of their citizens, and keeping copies of all reports in a file HUD officials could examine. It was control that operated less through review of performance than monitoring of paperwork.

ENVIRONMENTAL REVIEW

Earth Day in 1970 marked the summit of a new environmental consciousness in the United States. It was, ironically, the recognition of scarcity within a decade of enormous growth in both the public and private sectors. A growing consensus saw natural resources as limited and pressured Congress to prevent the use of federal funds for projects that would further dirty the air or pave over more open space. Congress passed the National Environmental Policy Act in 1969 and ordered all federal agencies to review whether any proposed action would have a "significant impact on the human environment."[12] The act included any activity funded with federal money, whether directly administered or operated indirectly through a grant program. If an agency determines that any action will have a "significant impact" on the environment, the agency must develop a formal

---

11. U.S. Department of Housing and Urban Development, *Community Development Block Grant Program: Third Annual Report* (Washington, D.C., 1978), 351–52.
12. 42 U.S.C. 4321 *et seq.*

statement of all effects, positive and negative, and must examine any alternatives to the proposal. An adverse environmental impact statement would not in itself automatically cancel a project, but because all statements must be made public, it would provide opponents with ammunition. Citizens, furthermore, could file suit against an agency to challenge a decision not to prepare a statement or to contest the adequacy of any report prepared.

The National Environmental Policy Act in turn bred fifteen more laws and executive orders during the 1970s to protect the environment. New regulations sought to clean up the air and water and to protect endangered species and wetlands. Other rules aimed to preserve the shoreline, scenic rivers, and historical treasures.[13] The long gamut of environmental policy rules provided environmentalists with important ammunition with which to fight projects they opposed. Perhaps the most famous case was that of the snail darter versus the Tellico Dam, where fears that the dam would destroy the darter's habitat led to a lengthy delay in the dam's construction. Although Congress eventually allowed federal officials to complete the dam, the struggle firmly established the place of environmental reviews in national policy making (and, fortunately for the darter, environmentalists later found several of his cousins downstream).

The CD program brought a major change to national environmental policy. Before CD, the federal agency whose funds paid for a project was in charge of conducting the review. Thus, if HUD awarded a grant to a city for a neighborhood development project, it was HUD's responsibility to determine if the project would have a "significant impact" on the environment and, if it would, to prepare the full impact statement. The CD legislation, however, delegated to local governments for the first time the responsibility for the review. Congress' delegation was both an experiment in decentralization and a strategy for efficiency. If local governments were to have primary administrative reponsibility for administering the program, federal officials reasoned, that responsibility ought to include the environmental reviews as well. Furthermore, if HUD had itself undertaken the chore to review the multitude of local projects, the program would

13. See Appendix, rules 10 through 24.

have been immediately halted by a tide of paperwork. HUD passed the chore to local governments and required them to certify (as they did with the equal opportunity rules) that they had complied with all of the applicable environmental review requirements.

Local officials found the requirements extraordinarily troublesome. HUD's regulations mandated an environmental assessment for every project regardless of type or scale. Thus, before local governments could spend their money, they had to determine for each of perhaps one hundred projects whether it would have a "significant impact." Most local projects were extremely small and few projects had an impact on the environment whatsoever, let alone a "significant" impact. But even for projects like health screening centers or housing rehabilitation, local governments had to assess their impact on the environment. "This," the General Accounting Office complained, "is a waste of time and money." Furthermore, GAO concluded, "some communities are not effectively carrying out their responsibilities."[14] HUD's own surveys in late 1975 and early 1976 found that 75 percent of all local governments surveyed did not complete one or more of the steps HUD regulations prescribed. Eight percent of the assessments were prepared even before the recipients decided how or where the money would be spent. The problems were not so much the result of deception by local governments as ignorance of the regulations compounded by inexperience. Nearly all local governments in one HUD survey thought they were complying with the requirements; another survey found that more than one-fourth of the recipients had no one on the staff with any experience in environmental matters.[15]

Local governments found HUD of little help in the first few years of the program. In keeping with the New Federalism philosophy, HUD was reluctant to give advice or assistance on how to conduct a

14. U.S. Comptroller General, *Environmental Reviews Done by Communities: Are They Needed? Are They Adequate?* (Washington, D.C., September 1, 1977), Report CED-77-123, pp. i, 21. For a similar argument, see U.S. House of Representatives, Committee on Banking, Finance and Urban Affairs, Subcommittee on Housing and Community Development, *Community Development Block Grant Program*, committee print, 95th Cong., 1st sess., 1977, p. 57.

15. The review was conducted by HUD's Office of Inspector General, which surveyed 259 projects of 49 grantees in 24 states. See U.S. Department of Housing and Urban Development, *CD Second Annual Report*, 137.

review, and HUD's regulations on the review inadequately spelled out what was required. Criticism by the Council on Environmental Quality, the General Accounting Office, and HUD's own inspector general prompted HUD's CD staff to draft more detailed instructions on how to conduct the reviews.[16] The environmental review regulations grew by a quarter,[17] and HUD's field staff began conducting more thorough monitoring visits to make sure communities understood and were complying with the law. Most importantly, HUD backed away from the nearly total delegation of authority to local governments for the environmental reviews. The agency no longer began by assuming local reviews were adequate and correct. HUD asserted a right to examine the reviews and, if the agency felt it warranted, to challenge local findings. After the early problems arose, HUD moved to insure that the agency, not local governments, would ultimately pass on the quality and adequacy of the reviews.

Delegation of environmental review to local governments was, as we noted earlier, founded on the principle of expediency, but the president of the Baltimore city council complained before a congressional committee that "cities have paid a heavy price for a little expediency." The reviews, he said, imposed "an administrative snarl of monumental proportions."[18] Environmental assessments for each project and formal environmental reviews for projects with "significant impacts" created a sizable paperwork problem, worsened by many communities' lack of experience. The U.S. Commission on Federal Paperwork found that the review process produced one-fourth of all paperwork in the CD program.[19]

The review procedures also led communities, according to Baltimore's councilor, "to plan projects along the course of least resis-

16. See U.S. Council on Environmental Quality, "Community Development Block Grants and NEPA: Delegation of National Environmental Policy Act Responsibilities to Community Development Block Grant Recipients" (Washington, D.C., 1977); U.S. Comptroller General, *Environmental Reviews*; and U.S. Department of Housing and Urban Development, *CD Second Annual Report*.

17. From 13 pages in 1975 to 16 pages in 1979. See 24 *CFR* 58.

18. Testimony of Walter Orlinsky, U.S. Senate, Committee on Banking, Housing and Urban Affairs, *Community Development Block Grant Program*, hearings, 94th Cong., 2nd sess., 1976, p. 406.

19. U.S. Commission on Federal Paperwork, *Impact of Federal Paperwork on State and Local Governments: An Assessment by the Academy for Contemporary Problems* (Washington, D.C., 1977), 68.

tance, and therefore, those requiring the least environmental study."[20] The environmental review process contained built-in delays for public comment periods, and the delays were certain to be lengthy if a review suggested important environmental effects. Furthermore, some effects automatically brought other federal and state agencies into the project, and often each agency required its own reviews and permits. The more agencies that became involved, the more tortuous the process became. Local governments understandably were wary of creating problems that might ultimately threaten their plans.[21]

BROAD GOALS, SWEEPING RULES

Equal opportunity and environmental review regulations were not the only rules plaguing CD, nor was it the only grant program in which recipients had to deal with troublesome rules. State and local governments faced a long list of regulations that rode piggyback on the programs. The rules were an admission charge for taking advantage of the programs' benefits, and many of the charges had to be paid by the recipients themselves. The complexities of the rules, furthermore, hatched out only as state and local governments tried to follow them. In some cases the rules were vague; in other cases state and local governments did not have a staff trained to deal with them. In yet other cases, certainly, the governments were not predisposed to obey them. Federal agencies dealt with these problems by making the regulations more detailed and by increasing their supervision of how governments complied with them. Monitoring visits became more frequent and more thorough and the certifications became more detailed.

The plethora of programs created a large and varied collection of rules which grant recipients had to obey. In environmental protection, more than seventy different federal agencies drafted regulations explaining the environmental review requirements for their own programs, and the only coordinative body was an advisory agency with-

20. Senate Banking Committee, *CD Program*, 406. See also House Banking Committee, *CD Program*, 58.
21. For some examples, see Kettl, *Managing Community Development*, 64–84. See also Eugene Bardach and Lucian Pugliaresi, "The Environmental Impact Statement vs. the Real World," *The Public Interest*, XLIX (Fall, 1977), 22–38.

out the clout to insure coordination. The result, predictably, was that "there are necessarily wide variations among EIS practices and criteria," the Commission on Federal Paperwork reported.[22] What an environmental impact statement was, and more important, what a "major" federal action was that would require an environmental impact statement, varied by agency and program.

The problem of securing uniform interpretations of broad federal goals carried over into equal opportunity. At least twenty agencies were responsible for administering equal employment opportunity requirements, and the result predictably was inconsistency and confusion.[23] The General Accounting Office, in a 1980 investigation, found that federal agencies were not always certain which programs were covered by title VI of the Civil Rights Act of 1964, the title that extended equal opportunity coverage to recipients of federal aid. Some agencies contended that many programs were exempt, but GAO disagreed. "In their assistance programs," GAO concluded, "agencies have not followed [the Department of] Justice's requirements for enforcing title VI and, as a result, lack reasonable assurance that title VI is being implemented effectively." The problems were varied: agencies lacked adequate regulations spelling out just what procedures title VI required; they had insufficient staff to enforce the rules; the staff they did have was inadequately trained, and the budget available for enforcement was inadequate. GAO investigated in detail two programs operated by what was then the Department of Health, Education, and Welfare—the foster child and health planning grant programs—and concluded: "HEW did not know, and GAO could not determine, if these programs were being administered in compliance with title VI."[24]

The penalty for noncompliance, when discovered, was painful. The city of Chicago, charged with discrimination in employment against women, blacks, and Chicanos, had its general revenue sharing

22. U.S. Commission on Federal Paperwork, *Environmental Impact Statements* (Washington, D.C., 1977), 19.
23. Gary Bryner, "Congress, Courts, and Agencies: Equal Employment and the Limits of Policy Implementation," *Political Science Quarterly*, XCVI (Fall, 1981), 416.
24. U.S. Comptroller General, *Agencies When Providing Federal Financial Assistance Should Ensure Compliance with Title VI* (Washington, D.C., April 15, 1980), Report HRD-80-22, pp. 20, iii.

TABLE 4: DISCRIMINATION COMPLAINTS IN GENERAL REVENUE SHARING

Year	Number Received	Discrimination Findings	Closed	Carried Over
1972	2	0	0	2
1973	27	1	2	27
1974	75	14	26	76
1975	213	8	29	260
1976	229	7	71	418
1977	276	125	142	552
1978	306	156	184	674
1979	330	179	228	776

SOURCE: U.S. Department of the Treasury, *Seventh Annual Report of the Office of Revenue Sharing* (Washington, D.C., 1980), 2.

payments withheld from late 1974 to mid-1976. In February, 1976, a federal district court ordered the city to adopt percentage goals for hiring minorities and women in the Police Department, and only after the court was satisfied with the city's actions was the money restored. The federal government stood ready to use this ultimate sanction for violations of the crosscutting rules.

General revenue sharing is a particularly good case for examining the management of the crosscutting regulations. The program had emerged from Congress bearing close resemblance to Nixon's no-strings approach, and the program provided grants originally to nearly every city, county, township, and state government in the country. The program was young, however, when complaints about state and local operations surfaced, charges that the disadvantaged were being excluded from participating in decisions about how to spend the money and from benefits of the money itself.[25] Charges of discrimination investigated by the Department of the Treasury's Office of Revenue Sharing began slowly but escalated as the program grew older. As Table 4 shows, complaints grew from 2 in 1972, the program's first year, to 213 in 1975 and 330 by 1979. Official findings that discrimination occurred grew just as quickly, from 7 in 1976 to 179 in 1979.

Investigation of civil rights violations was but part of the Office of

---

25. For a discussion of these charges, see Richard P. Nathan, Charles F. Adams, Jr., and associates, *Revenue Sharing: The Second Round* (Washington, D.C., 1977), 8–10.

TABLE 5: GENERAL REVENUE SHARING CASES INVESTIGATED

Area	Fiscal Year 1979	1972–79
Violation of local law	65	842
Violation of GRS financial rules	58	461
Violation of publication rules (planned and actual use)	0	66
Violation of Davis-Bacon rules	58	422
Other	2	30
TOTAL	183	1,821

SOURCE: U.S. Department of the Treasury, *Seventh Annual Report of the Office of Revenue Sharing* (Washington, D.C., 1980), 6.

Revenue Sharing's probe of state and local administration of the program. In the first eight years of the program, the office investigated 842 charges that state and local governments had violated their own procedures in running the program. (See Table 5.) The office's investigators also probed over 400 cases alleging violation of crosscutting rules for financial record keeping and wage standards. The numbers, while large, are but a small share of the nearly 38,000 governments receiving aid. Their importance, however, is not in their number but in their effect. Continuing charges of discrimination and other violation of the crosscutting rules led the Treasury Department to issue new rules specifying in more detail just what general revenue sharing recipients were expected to do. The program that was originally intended to be free of red tape gradually acquired more of it as the federal government viewed the results. Problems encountered by a small number of jurisdictions set the stage for new rules to which all state and local governments were subject.

It is a natural and predictable administrative reaction for federal managers to write more stringent rules to correct state and local mistakes, or even the appearance of mistakes. This reaction, furthermore, is a natural outcome of the climate of discretion in which federal administrators must operate. In its reluctance to specify the details of programs and their procedures, Congress invites administrators to fill in those details themselves. Discretion is a natural part of the administrator's job; indeed, to eliminate it would so hopelessly enmesh Congress in spelling out the precise functioning of govermental agencies that it doubtless would never get more than a fraction of its work done. The consequence of this congressional delegation to administrators is substantial power to write rules interpreting Congress's mandate, "the continuation of the legislative process in administration," as Emmette S. Redford put it.[26]

In federal grant programs, the discretion is double. Federal administrators have the usual measure of discretion in translating broad goals into specific policy. They have the further job of supervising the discretion exercised by the state and local governments that receive the money and that eventually are responsible for what the money buys. Federal administrators have thus had a difficult position, one charged with translating the broad goals of legislation into the details of administration, communicating those details to state and local governments that run the programs, supervising the performance of these governments, and protecting the program from the attacks of outside groups that charge fraud, waste, and abuse.

That position has been especially difficult in dealing with the crosscutting regulations. They deal with broad goals, most of which have very broad support: federal money should not be used in ways that discriminate against minorities, that harm the environment, or that lead to sloppy financial record keeping. Yet in most cases, the goals are so vague as to invite continuing dispute. As one student of federal equal employment opportunity argued, "Congress spent a great deal of time writing, debating, and amending the 1964 Civil Rights Act, yet it was neither really careful to specify some important provisions nor willing to oversee the implementation of the act."[27] Faced with questions of interpretation, charges of abuse, or uncertainty about results, federal administrators naturally turn to their principal tool, regulation, to spell out the policy more clearly. Delegation of management responsibility to federal officials and project administration for state and local officials created a rich climate for the growth of federal regulation.

---

26. Emmette S. Redford, *Administration of National Economic Control* (New York, 1952), 32. See also Kenneth Culp Davis, *Discretionary Justice: A Preliminary Inquiry* (Urbana, Ill., 1971).

27. Bryner, "Congress, Courts, and Agencies," 413.

CHAPTER 4
WHO BENEFITS?

LIKE ALL GRANT PROGRAMS, CD had its own program-based rules. The *Federal Register* spelled out who was eligible for the money, how applications had to be submitted, and what standards HUD would use in reviewing them. The most important of the rules dealt with what projects local governments could fund with their money, important because they were a crucial test of how much discretion the federal government would truly allow communities. As with any grant of money, the donor wondered who would benefit from the largesse. In this puzzle was buried a crucial question of intergovernmental relations: to what degree should communities be free to set their own strategies and decide which local projects to fund? And to what degree is there a national interest in local decisions that requires strong national oversight and control? Federal control brings with it rules, paperwork, and restriction. Local discretion raises the possibility that local decisions might be inconsistent with the national interest, however defined. The New Federalism began with the philosophy of local discretion, but HUD was quickly forced to deal with the dilemma that choice brought it.

HUD's first rules were brief. The agency did little more than reprint the text of the legislation in the *Federal Register* to keep as closely as possible to the New Federalism spirit. Agency managers decided, furthermore, not to provide more detailed guidance to local governments and particularly determined not to produce a program handbook. The urban renewal handbook had become legendary for its size and complexity and a CD handbook, HUD officials decided, would immediately be viewed as a contradiction of their promise of local flexibility. Shortly after the program began, however, the agency faced caustic criticism of its policy of minimal supervision. Interest groups and congressional committees alike complained that HUD's policy allowed local governments to blatantly violate the law. Two areas received the harshest criticism: projects whose benefits ignored the poor and housing plans that ignored local housing needs. The complaints forced HUD into more aggressive supervision of the communities and produced a flood of new regulations.

BENEFITS FOR THE POOR

The three years of congressional haggling that led to the enactment of the CD program produced a complex piece of legislation. The controversy between the House and Senate, in fact, resulted in two pieces of legislation uneasily and inconsistently melded into one. While neither body supported Nixon's original proposals, the House consistently sought to simplify federal reviews while the Senate was concerned with insuring that the program benefited the poor. The House committee report on the 1974 bill set two objectives for the program. One was the continued emphasis on national goals, particularly for equal opportunity, citizen participation, and environmental review. The other was "that the lengthy, burdensome, and generally frustrating process by which HUD approves applications for various community development grants be simplified to the greatest extent possible."[1] The Senate, however, saw the program differently. Its committee declared CD's principal objective to be "the development of viable urban communities through the provision of decent housing, suitable living environments and expansion of economic opportunities, principally for persons of low and moderate in-

1. U.S. House of Representatives, Committee on Banking and Currency, Report 93-1114.

come."[2] There was no easy compromise for two such different views. The House version sought minimal federal involvement while the Senate version by necessity implied a strong federal supervisory role. This controversy froze CD on Capitol Hill for three years, and congressional conferees eventually broke the logjam only by including portions of both bills in the final legislation.

As finally passed by Congress, the Housing and Community Development Act of 1974 was a patchwork of goals. The CD program kept the Senate's "viable urban communities" phrase, but it also contained seven more specific objectives. Four were from the Senate version and contained the clause mandating benefits "principally for persons of low and moderate income." The other three, from the House, listed objectives without the restrictive clause.[3] Local governments were required to certify that their projects either gave "maximum feasible priority to activities which will benefit low- and moderate-income families or aid in the prevention or elimination of slums and blight" or would "meet other community development needs having a particular urgency."[4] The law required HUD to approve local applications unless the department could demonstrate that the recipients were not living up to the certifications.

Buried within this language was a justification for either the Senate or House approach, and for either an active or passive stewardship role for HUD. The key was how HUD would deal with the "maximum feasible priority" clause. In drafting the program's first rules in the fall of 1974, HUD's officials decided to allow communities wide choice in selecting their projects. Projects for the poor would have equal status—and equal eligibility—with other projects that were directed at clearing local blight or meeting urgent local needs. Many of the agency's senior officials had stayed on in the transition from Nixon to Ford and they were still heavily committed to the decentralization strategies of the New Federalism. The rules allowed applicants to certify that their plans met at least one of the three alternatives.

Local governments, however, soon showed imagination that sur-

2. U.S. Senate, Committee on Banking, Housing and Urban Affairs, Report 93–693.
3. Public Law 93-383, Sec. 101(c).
4. *Ibid.*, Sec. 104 (b)(2).

passed federal expectations. Was an animal crematorium eligible for support as a waste disposal facility? Could citizens' band radios be purchased for senior citizens' buses? In one case, HUD ruled that CD funds could be used to build a garden but not for tools or seeds to be used inside it.[5] Many more such questions flooded into HUD's field offices. HUD officials stuck by their decision not to issue a program handbook to spell out just what projects were eligible, but Assistant Secretary David Meeker assembled a group of his staff to review and answer the questions. The responses quickly became known as "Meeker memos" and became the program's working regulations. Distribution of the memos proved irregular, however, and HUD's own field staff sometimes found out about them from interest-group representatives or from city officials. Furthermore, because the Meeker memos dealt with problems as they arose, policy making was ad hoc, leading one area office staff member to complain, "I find it very amusing that we can't make a clear statement about what is eligible and what isn't."[6]

The result was that interpretations of the regulations varied from office to office across the country. The regulations, for example, made public services like child care, drug abuse projects, recreation programs, and public facilities eligible for funding. The Senate bill had prohibited cities from using more than 20 percent of their grants for public services, but the House version contained no such restrictions. The joint conference committee left the provision out but noted that "the conferees expect that not more than 20 percent of any community's grant will be used to finance such services."[7] Some area offices read this phrase as law and put a 20 percent ceiling on public service projects. Other offices ignored the ceiling while some offices allowed no public service projects at all. The problem was especially difficult since these projects were of a type that one of CD's predecessors, Model Cities, had regularly funded. Clever local governments shopped around for an interpretation that favored a project they planned and used that interpretation to convince their own area office. HUD's minimal regulations led to rules that in practice varied

5. 3 *Housing and Development Reporter* 491, October 20, 1975.
6. Interview with the author.
7. Joint Explanatory Statement of the Committee of Conference, S.3066 (1974).

around the country.[8] The "maximum feasible priority" regulation caused the most difficulty. HUD did not define the term and did not establish any measure by which its staff could determine if communities met the rule.[9] What impact the rule had thus depended ultimately on how local governments read it.

As communities wrestled with the problem, several interest groups set to work monitoring local performances. Nearly everywhere they looked, these groups found problems that, they alleged, amounted to violations of the law. The Southern Regional Council published one of the first substantial criticisms of the program, and in its report the council complained that local governments "have been permitted to deviate at will from the national responsibilities that the 1974 Act supposedly places on them." CD, the council said, was a "waste—a squandering of public money." As examples, the council pointed to tennis courts one city built in an allegedly affluent neighborhood. "We must remember the needs of the people who vote," the council's report quoted one local official as saying, and "poor people don't vote." Another city spent some of its CD money for the installation of home security devices purchased by homeowners, a project that one local official said was "nice icing" to replace other proposals that had not been funded. One community decided to upgrade a road that, according to its mayor, was used by "hundreds of people who go to and from the country club section every day."[10] Such projects, the council's director, Peter J. Petkas, later told a Senate committee, were a "flagrant misuse of millions of tax dollars intended to fight urban blight and improve the living conditions of the poor city dwellers."[11]

A coalition of ten interest groups, most of them based in Washington, constituted themselves as the Working Group for Commu-

---

8. For example, see the testimony in U.S. House of Representatives, Committee on Banking, Finance and Urban Affairs, Subcommittee on Housing and Community Development, *Housing and Community Development Act of 1977*, hearings, 95th Cong., 1st sess., 1977, p. 643.

9. U.S. Comptroller General, *Meeting Application and Review Requirements for Block Grants under Title I of the Housing and Community Development Act of 1974* (Washington, D.C., June 23, 1976), Report RED-76-106, p. 6.

10. Raymond Brown, Ann Coil, and Carol Rose, *A Time for Accounting: The Housing and Community Development Act in the South* (Atlanta, 1976), 102, 53, 59, 60–61.

11. Senate Banking Committee, *CD Program*, 25.

nity Development Reform. Based on their own studies, they charged that "funds have too frequently been diverted from low and moderate income persons who need them most, particularly in the wealthier and suburban areas."[12] The working group found support from the other interest groups that had looked at local performance.[13]

Although these stories created substantial bad publicity for the program, two more-detailed studies were far more damaging. These studies, by the National Association of Housing and Redevelopment Officials (NAHRO) and by Richard P. Nathan and his associates through the Brookings Institution, produced more comprehensive evidence on the program's benefits. NAHRO examined where a national sample of communities placed their projects. In 1975, the program's first year, the communities NAHRO studied spent 59 percent of their money in low- and moderate-income census tracts; the amount dropped to 55 percent in the second year, 1976.[14] Brookings' figures for 1976 were similar: 51.9 percent of the money went to low- and moderate-income census tracts.[15]

The monitoring studies of HUD's administration of the CD program during the Ford administration were uniformly negative. After studying the research, the staff of the House Subcommittee on Housing and Community Development concluded: "All of the monitoring studies of the program reviewed by the staff conclude that the low- and moderate-income objectives of the Act are not being met."[16] The

12. See the testimony of Peter Buschbaum for the Working Group, U.S. Senate, Committee on Banking, Housing and Urban Affairs, *Housing and Community Development Legislation of 1977*, hearings, 95th Cong., 1st sess., 1977, pp. 443–44. The working group's report was "Community Development Block Grants—Implementing National Priorities" (Washington, D.C., 1976).
13. The congressional committee hearings on the program are an encyclopedia of such charges. See in particular, Senate Banking Committee, *CD Program*.
14. Robert L. Ginsberg, "Second Year Community Development Block Grant Experience: A Summary of the Findings of the NAHRO Community Development Monitoring Project (January, 1977)," *Journal of Housing*, XXXIV (February, 1977), 80–83.
15. Richard P. Nathan and associates, *Block Grants for Community Development* (Washington, D.C., 1977), 308. Both studies defined low-income census tracts as those with median family income of less than 50 percent of the median family income for the standard metropolitan statistical area, as defined by the Census Bureau. Moderate-income tracts were those with incomes from 51 to 80 percent. NAHRO also calculated the figures based on each city's median family income, a process that produced lower figures: 51 percent in 1975 and 44 percent in 1976. See Ginsberg, "Second Year Experience," 81.
16. House Banking Committee, *CD Program*, 21.

solution, most critics argued, was closer supervision of local governments by HUD coupled with more detailed regulations on what local governments were required to do. The Working Group for Community Development Reform, in a report prepared for the incoming Carter administration appointees in HUD, argued, "There must . . . be some increase in the specificity of the applications" and the rules HUD used to judge them.[17] Senate Banking Committee Chairman William Proxmire (D-Wis.) was more blunt. After thanking witnesses before his committee "for what I think is about as powerful an indictment of an administrative agency that I have ever heard," he blasted Assistant Secretary Meeker. "HUD has clearly gotten this program underway," he began. "What isn't clear is whether the program you have been administering is the program Congress passed." Proxmire concluded that "we are not doing the kind of job we should do to help low income people in this country with this program. . . . It takes a very forceful, advanced position, it seems to me, on the part of this Government in order to achieve it for them. I would hope that you . . . would keep that in mind and will work as hard for the poor and the low income people and minority groups as you can."[18]

HUD issued new regulations to tighten its stewardship of the program. One rule revised existing guidelines to spell out in more detail which projects were eligible: code enforcement and housing rehabilitation were eligible, but community-wide facilities, for which it was impossible to determine precisely who benefited, were not. Another regulation ruled sewage treatment plants ineligible.[19] The Ford administration, however, found it hard to move very hard very fast to make the CD rules more strict. Many of the administration's staff members had worked very hard for Nixon's New Federalism approach to CD and they were reluctant for the federal government to take on stronger oversight of local governments.

Jimmy Carter's new secretary of HUD, Patricia Roberts Harris, had no such reluctance. She told a House committee that "we will

---

17. Working Group for Community Development Reform, "Community Development Block Grants," 2.
18. Senate Banking Committee, *CD Program*, 380, 505, 533.
19. 41 *Federal Register* 2766, January 19, 1976; and 41 *Federal Register* 36898, September 1, 1976.

become the national advocate of cities. We will insist, however, that any unit of Government using funds will use those funds in pursuit of the aims set by Congress." She left no doubt, moreover, how she saw those goals. The maximum feasible priority goal, she said, was the highest priority of the program.[20] Harris backed up her approach with a memo to CD recipients that mentioned the importance of goals for low- and moderate-income persons three times in three pages. She promised, furthermore, a more stringent review of local applications and a closer look at local certifications.[21]

HUD issued new regulations on October 25, 1977, to spell out precisely the department's plans for more aggressive supervision of local governments.[22] The regulations specified that all money had to be used for low- and moderate-income persons, except for any projects attacking slums and blight or urgent community needs. Those exceptions, HUD expected, would amount to no more than 25 percent of the grant. This proposed rule, which quickly became known as the "75-25 rule," changed the foundation of the program. No longer would projects for the poor, slums, and urgent needs be considered equal. In the Carter administration, HUD saw benefits for low- and moderate-income persons as the primary goal, and "maximum feasible priority" of CD funds for the poor became defined as 75 percent of each community's grant.

The proposal provoked more comments than HUD had received on any other proposed CD rule. HUD logged in 1,327 responses. Local government officials on the whole opposed the rule, and they argued that it would take away the very flexibility for which CD had been passed. The proposal, they complained, would generate huge administrative problems and much new paperwork. The interest groups that had attacked the program, however, argued that the regulations needed to be tightened and they applauded the proposed standard.

The most important comments came from Capitol Hill. The

---

20. House Banking Committee, *Housing and Community Development Act*, 8.
21. U.S. Department of Housing and Urban Development, Memorandum to Community Development Block Grant Recipients, April 15, 1977.
22. 42 *Federal Register* 56450.

ranking members of the Senate Banking Committee, William Proxmire and Edward W. Brooke (R-Mass.), wrote Harris "to strongly support the HUD draft regulations." Not only did Proxmire and Brooke believe "it is entirely appropriate that the Department issue regulations requiring this specific numerical figure," but they also argued that "the 75 percent test would have been appropriate under the original 1974 Act." They contended, "Federal resources under this program are simply too meager to permit them to be spent frivolously."[23]

The ranking members of the House Housing and Community Development Subcommittee, however, disagreed both with their colleagues in the Senate and with HUD's proposed regulations. The regulations, they argued, represented an attempt to rewrite the law in a way that the House had opposed in the original 1974 act and in its 1977 revision. "We do not concur in the requirement," they said, and contended: "The placement of one purpose as more primary [sic] than another is neither consistent with the language of the statute nor with the legislative history."[24]

HUD faced a dilemma. After having been under attack through the press, from the interest groups, and in Senate committee hearings, HUD had sought to tighten the regulations. But when it proposed the 75-25 rule, the agency received a quick rebuke from the House subcommittee that accused it of rewriting the law. The attacks from the House led HUD to withdraw the 75-25 rule but to keep the 75-25 split as a broad target. Any community that spent at least 75 percent of its funds to benefit low- and moderate-income persons would be presumed to have met the "principally benefit" standard. HUD pledged to subject all other applications to a stringent review prior to funding to insure that they principally benefited low- and moderate-income persons. The 75-25 split thus was not a requirement, but any community that did not meet it courted close federal inspection.[25]

HUD also attacked the low-income benefit problem by trying to

---

23. Letter to Patricia Roberts Harris, November 17, 1977. HUD Docket File 77-471 on rules proposed October 25, 1977.
24. Letter to Patricia Roberts Harris, November 4, 1977. HUD Docket File 77-471.
25. 43 *Federal Register* 8450, March 1, 1978.

induce communities to concentrate their projects geographically to a greater degree. Communities could designate "Neighborhood Strategy Areas" (NSAs) in which the community planned to produce "substantial long-term improvements within a reasonable period of time."[26] The designation of NSAs was voluntary, but cities that established the areas could fund politically popular public service projects like child care, recreation, and education within the areas. Most communities found the inducements attractive and selected some neighborhoods as NSAs.

The NSA concept represented a strategic shift for HUD. Its first effort was to allow local governments broad discretion in locating projects, but that effort produced the harshest of criticism. HUD found it could not measure well the income of those who benefited from the program. Who, for example, is the eventual beneficiary of a downtown renovation project? HUD consequently sought to guarantee substantial benefits for the poor by influencing where communities located their projects. The NSA process encouraged local governments to identify their neediest neighborhoods and to concentrate, at least to some degree, their projects there. HUD thus moved to geographic location as a proxy for measuring the program's benefits by income level.

Gradual changes in regulations during the Ford years and the major shift toward specific standards during the Carter administration led to a much different CD program from the one Nixon had proposed or Congress had enacted. Gone was the presumption that benefits for the poor was only one of three equal standards or that communities could simply certify their compliance with HUD's rules. HUD moved aggressively first to elaborate on its regulations and then to set benefits for the poor as the program's principal objective. HUD also faced the problem of measuring whether communities met those goals. That problem led to the creation of the Neighborhood Strategy Area and inducements to lure communities toward concentrating more of their money on the poor. New rules defined

---

26. U.S. Department of Housing and Urban Development, *Fifth Annual Community Development Block Grant Report* (Washington, D.C., 1980), xi–2.

both the carrots—the incentives for designating NSAs—and the sticks—the penalties for failure to achieve the program's goals. These regulations came to constrain the freedom of action that CD had originally promised.

THE HOUSING ASSISTANCE PLAN

Before HUD's creation in 1965, federally subsidized housing and urban renewal programs had been run by separate bureaus. Even after 1965, the two functions continued in separate parts of the new department. There had been, as a result, little coordination between HUD's efforts to rebuild communities and to produce new housing. Local officials often complained that they had little to say about the quantity or type of public housing that their communities received.

Congress attempted to correct these problems with the Housing and Community Development Act of 1974. Along with CD, the act created new federal housing aid called the Section 8 program (after Section 8 of Title 2 of the act). The program gave HUD the authority to subsidize new, rehabilitated, or existing housing for the poor.[27] HUD would contract with the owner or prospective builder to guarantee a fair market rent, and the federal subsidy would equal the difference between the market rent and a family's ability to pay. Section 8 was designed to provide the poor with decent housing they might otherwise not be able to afford and to guarantee the builder or owner a fair rent for his property. It was a combined attack on the problem of urban housing: indirect income support for the poor and lessening of risk for the owner.

Congress, furthermore, directly tied the Section 8 program to CD. As part of the CD application, the community had to prepare a housing assistance plan specifying how much Section 8 aid was needed. The plan had to specify the condition of the community's housing stock, the housing needs of the poor, an annual goal for the number of persons to be assisted, and the general location of proposed housing. The housing assistance plan (HAP) gave the local governments

27. Eligible families are those with incomes of less than 80 percent of the area's median income, with adjustments for the size of the family.

the chance to say where federally subsidized housing should be located. Just as importantly, it gave local governments the opportunity to integrate community development projects, like slum clearance or housing rehabilitation, with HUD's housing program.

One thorny element of the HAP was the requirement that communities assess "the housing assistance needs of lower-income persons . . . residing in or expected to reside in the community."[28] The "expected to reside" phrase was both unclear and troublesome. The House, in particular, wanted to insure that communities looked beyond their own residents in setting housing assistance needs.[29] Some communities employed large numbers of the poor but could not or would not provide low-cost housing so the poor could live near their jobs. The result was that some communities bore a much heavier burden of housing and providing services for the poor. The law therefore not only required local governments to plan for the housing needs of their own poor residents but also the housing needs of the poor who might live in the community if decent, low-priced housing were available. Acceptance of subsidized housing was thus not a matter of choice. Congress designed the HAP to force all communities to accept their share of the burden for housing the urban poor; a local government that refused would lose its CD entitlement. More than anything else, it was a strategy to open up the suburbs to housing for the poor.

Neither HUD nor the communities paid much attention to the expected-to-reside requirement during the program's first year. It was a short clause that was subsidiary to the CD program's principal goals. HUD faced large organizational problems in training its field staff for the new less intrusive application reviews and in dealing with thousands of communities new to HUD's programs. Data on which to base the expected-to-reside estimates, furthermore, were not easily available. Few communities knew how many workers would live within their boundaries if adequate housing were available. Indeed, few communities even knew how many workers commuted into their jurisdictions to work. Most local governments com-

---

28. Housing and Community Development Act of 1974, Sec. 104(a)(4)(A).
29. House Report 93-1114.

pleted the forms by extrapolating population figures from the 1970 census. HUD, for its part, gave the "expected to reside" information very little consideration.[30] The interest groups monitoring the program, however, seized on HUD's weak oversight of the HAPs. Detroit's Coalition for Block Grant Compliance, supported by the National Committee Against Discrimination in Housing, argued that the HAPs prepared by some Detroit suburbs did not adequately estimate the number of persons who might be "expected to reside." The committee filed a complaint with HUD in April, 1975, alleging that neither HUD nor the communities were complying with the law. Several monitors examined Livonia, Michigan's application and found further problems. Census data indicated that more than 19,000 workers potentially qualified as persons "expected to reside" in Livonia, but Livonia did not consult the figures. City officials, furthermore, told the Michigan Advisory Committee to the U.S. Commission on Civil Rights that they neither understood the meaning of "expected to reside" nor intended to consider the needs of nonresidents until the needs of residents were met. Although Livonia officials estimated that the elderly made up only 35 percent of those who needed housing, they also decided to use 82 percent of the housing assistance in the first year for the elderly. Housing for the elderly rarely caused the local controversy that other kinds of public housing, particularly for large families, often created.[31]

Assistant Secretary Meeker acknowledged the problems but argued that the data available to estimate the expected-to-reside figures were poor.[32] HUD tried to cope by using the census, but data were available only for cities with populations larger than 50,000 within metropolitan areas of more than 250,000 persons. HUD gave local governments the option of using HUD's figures (which few communities did because the data were poor and the time to submit applications was short), of producing their own estimates, or of outlining

30. U.S. Comptroller General, *Meeting Application Requirements*, 34.
31. Michigan Advisory Committee, *Livonia*, 18–19.
32. U.S. House of Representatives, Committee on Banking, Currency and Housing, Subcommittee on Housing and Community Development, *Oversight Hearing on Community Development Block Grant Program*, hearing, 94th Cong., 1st sess., 1975, p. 17.

steps to produce a better estimate in 1976. During the first year of the CD program, HUD's first priority was to get the program moving, and the department was willing to wait until the second year to tackle the HAP problem.

Some cities, however, were unhappy with HUD's decision. HUD's reluctance to force all cities from the beginning of the program meant that some cities, particularly suburbs, could postpone making commitments to house the urban poor. On August 11, 1975, Hartford, Connecticut, filed suit against the agency in federal district court. HUD had approved the applications of seven suburban towns around Hartford on the promise that they would address the expected-to-reside issue in their next application.[33] Six of the towns had listed a zero "expected-to-reside" figure in their applications; that is, they planned no subsidized housing within their boundaries for nonresidents. Approval of these applications, Hartford argued, was a violation of the law. The federal court immediately enjoined the seven towns from spending any of their CD money.

On January 28, 1976, Judge M. Joseph Blumenfeld held that "HUD acted contrary to the law" when it approved the grants. HUD's approach, the judge ruled, "permits suburban towns to obtain funding under the Act without the *quid pro quo* Congress decided to require—their taking steps to expand housing opportunities for low and moderate income persons."[34] The temporary injunction was made permanent until the communities filed new applications that contained an adequate assessment of the number of persons expected to reside.

The decision forced HUD to issue a series of new regulations to comply with the court's decision. The department's general counsel eventually produced a complex formula with which local governments could compute their "expected to reside" figures for the application. HUD refined the procedures through the pages of the *Federal Register*, and by the end of 1976, communities had a technique that

---

33. The seven towns were: East Hartford, Enfield, Farmington, Glastonbury, Vernon, West Hartford, and Windsor Locks.
34. *City of Hartford v. Hills*, 408 F. Supp. 902 (1976). The decision was reversed on appeal. *City of Hartford v. Towns of Glastonbury* 561 F. 2d 1032 (1976). *Cert denied* 434 U.S. 1034 (1978).

both satisfied the court and produced figures on which they could base their plans for Section 8 housing.

The Carter administration's insistence that a community concentrate the program's benefits on the poor extended to the HAPs and brought a new approach to the "expected to reside" problem. Some staff members were concerned that too many jurisdictions without substantial low- and moderate-income employment were escaping with too low an expected-to-reside estimate. Since companies within their jurisdictions employed few of the poor, the Ford administration's formula produced an expected-to-reside figure that also was low. Secretary Harris' staff believed that many communities were thereby not carrying their share of the burden for housing the poor.

The same March 1, 1978, regulations that set the 75-25 rule also contained new rules for HAPs. HUD abandoned the earlier approach pegged to employment and adopted a new "fair share" formula for calculating the expected-to-reside figure. The "fair share" approach was population based and required all communities within a metropolitan area to accept a minimum number of lower-income households. The formula was a complicated six-part rule. All local governments, by the formula, would be required to bear their share of the housing needs for the region. For example if 25 percent of all households were eligible for assistance, all communities would be expected eventually to house 25 percent of those households. The new formula produced a zero expected-to-reside figure for most central cities (because most central cities already housed large numbers of poor residents), but much higher figures than the old formula for the suburbs (requiring them to shoulder their "fair share" of subsidized housing).[35]

Congress, however, had other ideas about HUD's change in strategy. Members saw it as a departure from the program's attempts to provide local flexibility and, in its 1978 amendments to the CD program, Congress emphasized that it meant to make employment, not population, the heart of the subsidized housing plans. It expanded the language in the original act by requiring local governments to plan for those "expected to reside in the community as a result of existing

35. 43 *Federal Register* 8450, March 1, 1978.

or projected employment opportunities in the community (and those elderly persons residing in or expected to reside in the community)."[36] HUD painfully learned another lesson on the exercise of administrative discretion. The department withdrew its new regulations and eventually published a new formula, based on employment instead of population, with which local governments could compute the number of the poor "expected to reside" in their communities.

The changes in CD regulations forced communities through four major changes in the HAPs in the first five years of the program: HUD's initial strategy to delay the "expected to reside" requirement; new formulas developed as a result of the court decision; the Carter administration's "fair share," population-based strategy; and HUD's retreat back to an employment-based approach. Through it all local governments had to juggle their plans so as not to jeopardize their CD funding while they worked with inadequate data. One local official complained, "The HUD regulations leave all manner of communities with the requirement of doing statistical handstands with data of dubious accuracy. We feel that compliance with the regulation regarding the 'expected to reside' provision of the statute may well frustrate accomplishment of the objective."[37] The result, according to a member of a civil rights interest group, was that "Housing assistance plans are mere paper plans."[38] HUD, its critics charged, placed a low priority on making the plan useful or insuring that its goals were achieved.

Many local governments simply found it easier to put down the figures that HUD's area offices determined for them. An internal HUD memo reporting on a meeting with city officials said, "Most respondents said that they take what the Area Office gives them. First you must submit a set of numbers and 'then you play games'; you put down the bottom numbers and the Area Office divides them up."[39] Raymond J. Struyk, an Urban Institute scholar, concluded that "these problems give rise to a strong sense of powerlessness on the part of

36. 92 Stat. 2080, Public Law 95-557, Sec. 103(c).
37. Orlinsky testimony, Senate Banking Committee, *CD Program*, 406.
38. Statement of Betty Adams, chairperson, Housing Task Force, Leadership Conference on Civil Rights, *ibid.*, 182.
39. Quoted by Raymond J. Struyk, *Saving the Housing Assistance Plan: Improving Incentives to State and Local Governments* (Washington, D.C., 1979), 14.

local officials and create massive disincentives against a strong housing planning process at the local level."[40]

The HAP began as an attempt to integrate housing and community development programs. Local governments, with no direct advice from HUD, would determine what mix of housing would best suit their needs and how it would fit with their CD projects. But with court orders, HUD's attempts to minister to the poor, and congressional guidance, local governments found that they could not meet those lofty objectives even if they were so inclined. The data were poor, the regulations constantly changing. Furthermore, the monitoring groups found some communities that were not inclined to house the poor. The result was that HUD made its regulations more strict, and communities often chose to accept figures for local plans that HUD area offices dictated. The HAP thus went from decentralized planning to central guidance.

DEFINING PROGRAM BENEFITS

The tales of both the "75-25" rule and the "expected to reside" regulations are stories of increasing national control. The CD program began with a promise of local autonomy. That promise came under heavy attack from interest groups, congressional committees, and federal courts for failing to deliver benefits to the poor. HUD in response increasingly sought to define *who* should benefit from the program and, just as importantly, *how* local governments would have to meet their burden of proof. HUD's administration of the program shifted from a presumption that local governments could be trusted with broad discretion to a presumption that communities would have to prove their projects benefited the poor. HUD's regulations, growing in volume and in detail, served as the vehicle to increase its control. Local discretion gave way to the pressures for a straightforward attack on national goals set in Washington.

As the CD program encountered problem after problem, HUD's response was to write new regulations to resolve them. The department insisted that communities demonstrate their compliance with

40. *Ibid.*, 19.

the crosscutting rules as well as the program's goals, and with the passing of time those rules became more lengthy and complicated. Even so, HUD could not directly measure local actions to see if the rules were having the desired effect. There were far too many governments with far too many projects—and far too few HUD field staff—to examine carefully the program's results. The department instead relied on trial by paperwork, seeking to insure compliance by forcing communities to collect and report a wide range of data on their operations.

More than anything else, these regulations drew more power to Washington. HUD wrote rules to prevent CD funds from being used to plant trees along roads leading to country clubs and the poor from being excluded from housing in the suburbs. Communities had to prepare equal-opportunity plans and environmental reviews to the satisfaction not only of HUD but also of a broad assortment of interest groups and congressional committees. As questions arose—and inevitably they did—HUD responded with new and more detailed rules that increasingly left less discretion for local officials.

Even with the rules, local governments probably enjoyed more freedom than they had under the collection of programs that CD replaced. Nevertheless, the steady creep of program-based and crosscutting rules steadily ate away at the discretion that Nixon's New Federalism had promised them. Furthermore, it was an uncertain brand of discretion, for the issuance of new regulations left recipients in a constant state of unease as they wondered what rules might be changed next. It was discretion supervised by a far larger audience than had watched federal grant programs in the past, an audience composed of a broader range of interest groups organized to put pressure on key Washington decisions. It was clear that a new set of forces was at work eroding the good intentions of the New Federalism.

CHAPTER 5
GETTING THE FACTS

HUD's management of the CD program was handicapped more than anything else by its ignorance of what communities were actually doing with the money. When the interest groups complained that communities were wasting the money, HUD could offer no defense because the program's administrators simply did not know how local governments ultimately spent their entitlements. HUD's deliberate strategy of nonintervention during the program's early years left the department naked against criticism. In the spirit of Nixon's New Federalism, HUD chose not to probe communities' plans and intentions. When problems arose, as inevitably they did, and when cries for tighter federal supervision arose, as predictably they did, the department responded with the only tool at its disposal—regulations to make sure the problems did not recur.

HUD's lack of reliable information about the program is part of a fundamental irony of Washington politics. Washington's administrative life is frenetic with the search for information. More issues clamor for attention than any president, legislature, or administrative agency could effectively attack in a century. Information about these issues is critical because it helps the politician and administrator select those problems that require immediate attention and those problems that can comfortably wait. Information about these issues, furthermore, can help politicians and administrators judge just how to deal with a problem. Washington is a city literally awash in information. Administrative agencies publish reports on their activities and problems while congressional committees fill voluminous collections of hearings and reports. Interest groups peddle their own perspectives, supported by special studies and yet more information. And to help make sense of all of these reports, private subscription services produce digests and "insider" reports on what all of the other information really means.

There is a fundamental difference, however, between this information and useful knowledge. Much of the information is incomplete, conflicting, and biased; some of it is simply wrong. Furthermore, there is much more of it than anyone can hope to digest. But which is which? What information is like chaff and what is useful knowledge—knowledge that concisely and accurately tells the administrator what is actually happening to the program he is running? Much administrative activity is simply an effort to obtain useful knowledge on which decisions can be reliably based. Whoever influences the flow of information powerfully influences how administrators make their decisions and, just as importantly, which decisions get made. The struggle for useful knowledge thus affects both the agenda and the content of administrative action.

It is this ironic situation of a flood of information but a dearth of useful knowledge that is both cause and effect of Washington's distance from the rest of the country. As the federal government has defined more problems as national and as those problems have become more complex, it has become more difficult to define just what governmental programs are to do. And as the federal government has pledged to streamline the administrative procedures for each program, it has become more difficult to gather the information needed to gauge the programs' results. The sheer size and volume of the federal government's activities, finally, has created more barriers to gathering useful knowledge. Any skillful administrator can find information that supports nearly any decision. The problem for the administrator is to sift through the mounds of often confusing and conflicting information and to decide what can be believed. Without knowing what the administrative problems are, what approaches are likely to work, and what actual conditions are in the field, effective administration is impossible. In his book on private sector regulation, Emmette S. Redford argued, "Facts—lots of facts—are the *sine qua non* of intelligent public control."[1]

The new programs of the 1960s and 1970s, especially block grants, worsened the problem of gathering useful knowledge about performance. Since the programs gave state and local governments automatic entitlement to federal money and substantially reduced the federal government's review of applications, federal administrators lost much advance control over what grant recipients would do with the money. Federal administrators could have compensated with more retrospective reviews of performance, specifically more monitoring of state and local progress. But as one OMB official explained, "monitoring is always the last thing to be done."[2] There are always higher priorities: issuing new regulations, responding to congressional and interest-group complaints, planning for the announcement of a new program, and simply getting the money out. Measuring local performance—and gathering useful knowledge—got low priority.

THE MEASUREMENT OF LOCAL PERFORMANCE

When asked how much the central office knew about what ultimately happened to CD in the communities, one HUD staffer replied, "Very little. Headquarters is so removed from reality. The opportunities for gathering information are limited, and we consequently spend much of our time shuffling paper. As a result, the monitoring complaints and the newspaper articles take on exaggerated importance because we don't have other sources of information. We knee-jerk a lot to unbalanced criticism because we have such a small staff and relatively few opportunities to get information." "Even in the field offices," another HUD official added, "we find that they don't know what's going on" in the communities.[3]

The reasons lie in the administrative intricacy that afflicts most federal grant programs. In large programs like CD and CETA, money

1. Redford, *Administration of National Economic Control*, 156.
2. Interview with the author.
3. Interviews with the author.

flows to thousands of recipients, each of which manages many projects. In fiscal year 1979, for example, 3,305 communities received CD funds.[4] Each of those communities ran at least several projects, and in a typical medium-sized city the number of projects might easily approach one hundred. The number of projects was so high and HUD's investigation of local activities so weak that the department simply did not have useful knowledge about local administration of the projects. Few local administrators could keep close watch on so many projects, and HUD's field officials found themselves even more handicapped in judging what was happening in the dozen or more communities under their supervision. When that problem multiplied through the ten federal administrative regions and on to Washington, it was little surprise that administrators in Washington had little useful knowledge about what was happening to CD.

Finding out was, at least intially, a very low priority for HUD. Congress passed the program in August, 1974, and HUD wanted to get the money out to local communities by the following summer. The department invested most of its efforts in writing the initial regulations, designing application forms, and perhaps most importantly, drilling its own staff in the administration's hands-off approach. HUD planned initially to keep front-end control, especially by means of the application process, to a minimum. Field officials were to check to make sure that the documents were in order, that the proper assurances had been signed, and that no community proposed ineligible activities. More searching review of communities' progress was to come through performance review. Every grant recipient had to file an annual "grantee performance report" that explained the community's progress in completing the projects planned in the application. HUD field officials also planned to visit annually a sample of the grantees to examine their compliance with the program's regulations and to study their progress. HUD expected the performance reports and field visits to turn up evidence of local problems. Its staff could then concentrate on those communities that most needed help —or that appeared to be violating the program's rules—without having to subject every community to stringent front-end examination.

4. HUD, *Fifth Annual Report*, 1–17.

After a 1978 survey of HUD's management of the program, however, the U.S. General Accounting Office critically concluded, "HUD does not obtain from recipient communities the information needed to evaluate community performance and to assure itself and Congress that CDBG programs are developed in accordance to legislative objectives." Local applications, GAO reported, presented information that "was often generalized and vague." Salem, Oregon, for example, had proposed a $380,000 neighborhood improvement program. Cleveland, Ohio, proposed public works projects in 134 different census tracts but did not explain where the projects actually would be located. Without clearer information about the projects, HUD fell back on using spending rates—how quickly communities spent their entitlements—as an indicator of how well they were performing. GAO concluded, however, that this was "an inadequate measure of progress because it does not relate money spent to accomplishments."[5] The applications, furthermore, described only planned activities. Communities could—and did—change their projects after notifying HUD. That made the original applications even less suitable as a way of gauging local activities.

To make matters worse, the grantee performance reports filed by CD recipients, according to GAO, contained "incomplete or vague data that do not meet HUD requirements." One community, for example, described an activity as "parking lots," did not describe who the lots would benefit, listed the short-term objectives as "provide parking facilities," and noted progress as "central lot acquired and parking structure underway." From the performance report, HUD had no way of knowing where the parking facility (or facilities) was, what benefits the project would have, what legislative objectives the project would serve, or what progress the community was making. Of ten performance reports that GAO examined in one sample, only one community supplied all of the information HUD required about the projects' benefits for low- and moderate-income persons, and this community reported that 12 percent of the benefits of *each* project would accrue to persons of low or moderate income. GAO suggested

---

5. U.S. Comptroller General, *Management and Evaluation of the Community Development Block Grant Program Need to Be Strengthened* (Washington, D.C., August 30, 1978), Report CED-78-160, pp. 3–4.

that it was "questionable" whether every project would produce precisely the same proportion of benefits for the poor.[6] A July, 1977, internal HUD memorandum confirmed GAO's findings: "The data on these forms are not valid and cannot be used as the basis for a performance analysis."[7]

Finally, GAO criticized HUD for giving monitoring a low priority. In 1978, HUD budgeted only about one-fourth of its field staff's time for monitoring, compared with more than three-fourths for application processing and program management. HUD, furthermore, had not spelled out for its field staff what problems to look for or how to help solve them. HUD's monitoring visits consequently became little more than expeditions to check local files. About that, one local official complained: "The regulations always call for having all the information in a file. A file to me is the four drawers out there in a cabinet. But for the field man, a file means one folder. I've had to change my filing system three times. Now, I'm back to the system I used at the beginning of the program."[8] Only rarely did HUD's field staff actually visit a CD-funded project, and then it faced a conflict of interest. Headquarters was interested in getting the program running smoothly—not in uncovering problems in local administration.

The result was that HUD had little useful knowledge about local performance in the first years of the CD program. Its annual reports to Congress were but one sign of the problem. These reports, GAO complained, "provided very little information on the actual use of block grant funds and program progress."[9] And without such knowledge, federal officials were handcuffed in their stewardship of the program. Perhaps the most serious obstacle of all in measuring such performance was in deciding just what *good* performance was. The goals of the program were so broad that communities could begin any of an extraordinary range of projects. "It's hard to get good information on a program like CD when you don't know what it's supposed to do," one OMB official noted.[10] To collect information on all possible goals

6. *Ibid.*, 5, 8.
7. Quoted *ibid.*, 9.
8. Interview with the author.
9. U.S. Comptroller General, *Management and Evaluation of the CDBG Program*, 17.
10. Interview with the author.

would impose enormous costs in paperwork. To collect any less information would run the risk that data would not be available when answers were needed. In CD, HUD officials found themselves awash in information, but equipped with precious little useful knowledge about what was happening to the money they distributed.

HUD's difficulties in collecting useful knowledge were worsened by the fragmentation of responsibility within the department itself. HUD initially decided to operate CD through its large network of field offices, but the department never comfortably settled the difficult question of just what responsibility the field offices were to have. Controversies over interpretation of the regulations and disputes over how to handle the problems of performance rose in Washington, both out of the need to insure uniformity and out of a wish to protect a program that top HUD officials saw as central to the department's mission. When questions reached Washington, responsibility for dealing with them became even more scattered among many special offices. As a consequence, the field offices which were originally to have prime authority found their position seriously weakened, while actual authority became fragmented among Washington-based experts.

The department's field offices were the logical source of knowledge about the program's operations. With thirty-nine offices sprinkled around the federal government's ten regions, the area offices were close enough to the communities to keep tabs on their progress while still remaining faithful to Washington's expectations. Particularly in a program like CD which was to have minimal application review and stronger review of local performance, the area offices seemed the ideal place to concentrate responsibility. HUD's program representative could quickly review the applications to make sure all the documents were in order. Later, armed with knowledge about what activities the communities had planned, the program representatives could review the performance reports and visit the communities to judge how well the local governments were doing. In the federal government's administrative scheme, CD was to have double decentralization: increased discretion for local governments and greater authority for the field staff.

The field offices, however, turned out to be the weakest link in the program's management. Reorganizations had continually upset field operations since the department's creation in 1965. Until 1971, the department had only seven field offices and most funding decisions were made in Washington. As part of the Nixon administration's plans to standardize federal field operations into ten regions, HUD had, just before the creation of CD, vastly expanded its field system to ten regional offices and thirty-nine area offices. Then, with the passage of CD, HUD's headquarters staff delegated the program's principal operating chores to the new area offices. These offices had an extraordinarily difficult time establishing their role. Their personnel had been drawn in part from the staff of previous housing programs, and many CD representatives had little experience with development projects. Nearly all of the field staff were accustomed to a much stronger federal hand, and one of the most traumatic points in the transition from the categoricals to the new block grant in 1974 was the training sessions held for the field staff. A team from HUD's headquarters staff held seminars on both the east and west coasts and preached everywhere the same message to the field staff: keep your hands off of the program. This was to be a locally controlled program, and the last thing HUD's senior officials wanted was interference from the field offices in local decisions. Reactions from the field staff were memorable; the vehemence of their objections surprised even HUD veterans. Headquarters officials insisted nevertheless that field officials take a light-handed role. Applications could be approved in the field, but disapproval could only come from Washington. Field officials were instructed to allow maximum feasible discretion to the communities, and disputes over questions like eligibility had to be referred to the regional offices and ultimately to Washington. Field officials were to play the key federal role, but headquarters officials never trusted the field staff with the discretion needed to make the plan work.

Field officials consequently were unsure of just what their role was to be. The reorganizations had never allowed a stable field structure to develop, and most field officials had come up through the ranks of federal grant programs that had a heavy federal hand. CD itself further complicated their jobs. The program provided very little guidance about where the federal government should draw the boundaries on local discretion or even what the program was to accomplish. The headquarters office initially was reluctant to provide more guidance for fear of trampling on the New Federalism philosophy. Finally, the application reviews themselves proved more complicated than expected, particularly as in later years HUD looked more closely at what activities communities planned and where those activities would be located.

HUD grafted a new and complicated program onto a new administrative system, and much confusion predictably resulted. Because of the huge span of control, communication between Washington and the field often was sloppy. One consultant who examined HUD's field structure in 1976 concluded, in fact, that "no standardized channels of communication—up or down the structure—exist.... We find this an undesirable situation not only in a managerial sense—because the availability of managerial information is virtually nonexistent—but also because no uniform interpretation of programs exists across the country."[11] Alert local administrators in the early days of the program could often inform their field representatives about new interpretations of regulations before the rules reached the field from headquarters. Other skillful local administrators took advantage of HUD's confusion. They consulted with other local officials to discover ways of stretching HUD's interpretation of eligible activities and then used these interpretations on their own area offices. All of these strategies preoccupied field offices and kept them from investigating what communities were doing with the money. They simultaneously worsened HUD's information-gathering enterprise and invited attempts by HUD to set uniform national standards. HUD's problems in managing the field offices set the stage for new regulations.

Fragmentation of responsibility within HUD compounded the knowledge problem. Every national standard produced its own regulations and these regulations in turn produced their own experts. The subject matter was complex, and each rule demanded a team of

11. Coopers and Lybrand, "Recommendations for Near Term Field Organization and Structure" (photocopied report, 1976), 25.

professionals to draft its language, to coordinate it with other agency policies, and to oversee its execution. Environmental review regulations required engineers and biologists. Housing assistance plans needed the attention of housing economists. National equal opportunity regulations created a cadre of equal opportunity specialists trained in the laws and procedures of civil rights and affirmative action. Each special rule required special knowledge and, usually, a special office. Presidents can announce programs, cabinet officials can set broad policy, and assistant secretaries can manage programs. But it is on a complex network of specialized offices that federal stewardship ultimately depends.

In the CD program, local officials complained that the wide latitude HUD allowed its area offices in the beginning of the program produced unclear interpretations of the regulations. Many local officials, according to a report by the staff of the House Subcommittee on Housing and Community Development, questioned "whether or not a highly decentralized program, such as the CDBG program, can or should be effectively administered through a highly decentralized HUD structure."[12] If local officials were to have broad choice, the subcommittee reasoned, the boundaries of that choice had to be clear; when field officials had to check with Washington for definitive rulings, the results were confusion and delay.

The demand was for clearer rules for both crosscutting and program-based requirements. Clearer rules demanded expert interpretation, but this expertise tended to draw power back to Washington from state and local governments, to diffuse it among special offices, and to produce still more regulations. Demands from Congress for stronger national supervision led to a more powerful role for Washington-based officials at the expense of field administrators. It took a skilled economist to determine how the "expected to reside" figure should be calculated, a trained lawyer to assert how equal opportunity standards could be met. These experts worked in Washington and more responsibility flowed toward them for spelling out just what these standards required. The flow of personnel matched the flow of this responsibility. Even though HUD's field staff had most

12. House Subcommittee on Housing and Community Development, *CD Program*, 46.

operating responsibilities and 75 percent of the agency's personnel, HUD's headquarters had two-thirds of all positions graded GS-15 and higher, the most professional and prestigious of the civil service rankings.[13] HUD is not alone in concentrating power in Washington. Since the 1960s, federal employment in the capital has grown at a much faster rate than overall federal employment, as Table 6 shows. The interest groups, not surprisingly, followed suit. In 1971, 19 percent of national associations had their headquarters in Washington. By 1981, the number had grown to 29 percent.[14]

As power shifted to Washington, reponsibility within federal agencies became more diffuse. Within HUD, separate offices supervised the housing assistance plans and the Urban Development Action Grant program, a program of concentrated grants created in 1977. Other offices concentrated on questions of project eligibility. As HUD's central office staff grew by 7.4 percent from 1974 to 1979, the headquarters staff for the Assistant Secretary for Fair Housing and Equal Opportunity increased by 26.3 percent. To help HUD's field offices supervise local environmental reviews, the department increased the field staff for the Office of Environmental Quality by 32.7 percent, while the field staff as a whole grew by only 6.8 percent.[15] This pattern of special offices, furthermore, was not peculiar to HUD. Of the thirteen federal cabinet agencies in 1980, eleven of them had offices for equal opportunity. The only two exceptions were State and Defense, which differed from the rest both in the way they hired their employees and in the services they performed. Seven cabinet agencies had offices for environmental protection.[16] With new regulations came the proliferation of offices to administer them.

Specialization, of course, is the principal virtue of bureaucracy. If every federal employee were a generalist, the federal government

13. Coopers and Lybrand, "Recommendations for Field Organization," 6.
14. Craig Colgate, Jr. (ed.), *National Trade and Professional Associations of the United States and Canada and Labor Unions* (Washington, D.C., 1981), 16.
15. U.S. House of Representatives, Committee on Appropriations, *Department of Housing and Community Development—Independent Agencies, Appropriations for 1981*, Part 8, hearing, 96th Cong., 2nd sess., 1980, pp. 603, 900, 1067; and *Department of Housing and Urban Development—Independent Agencies, Appropriations for 1976*, Part 5, hearing, 94th Cong., 1st sess., 1975, pp. 525, 527, 950.
16. The departments are Agriculture, Commerce, Energy, Housing and Urban Development, Interior, Justice, and Transportation.

TABLE 6: FEDERAL CIVILIAN EMPLOYMENT: PERCENT CHANGE BY DECADE

	Total Employment	Washington Area
1920s	−8	−22
1930s	73	92
1940s	88	59
1950s	22	8
1960s	24	36
1970s[1]	−8	10

NOTES
1. From 1970–1978.

SOURCE: U.S. Bureau of the Census, *Historical Statistics of the United States, Colonial Times to 1970* (Washington, D.C., 1975), 1102; and *Statistical Abstract of the United States* (Washington, D.C., 1979), 279.

could not cope with the complex questions it faces. At the same time, however, the growth of special, expert offices made coordination of the regulations more difficult. The CD program became not one program but several, each defined by the fiefdom within HUD that supervised each regulation. Each fiefdom developed its own regulations for its own turf and each supervised local compliance. Communities were responsible ultimately to HUD's environmental protection office for their environmental reviews, to a housing office for their housing assistance plans, and to another office for the project applications. The program was split into many parts, and communities had to insure their compliance with the requirements of each part. Such fragmentation, as Harold Seidman notes, "atomizes" political power and multiplies the number of interests involved in any administrative decision.[17]

Such atomization of power tremendously complicates the task of coordinating federal programs. Most regulations are not only complex but supervised by fiefdoms where complexity earns a measure of independence. It is difficult for political executives like departmental secretaries or even for specialists from other areas to enter the arcane debate about whether population or employment is the proper base for calculating the "expected to reside" figure. Waging effective battle

17. Harold Seidman, *Politics, Position, and Power: The Dynamics of Federal Organization* (New York, 1980), 319.

on any such question can happen only if an executive concentrates enough time on learning about the issue, and doing so sacrifices attention to other problems. On the other hand, the expertise of expert offices makes it easier for them to resist attempts by outside forces to influence their decisions. The regulatory maze as a result is difficult to penetrate and control. The result, paradoxically, is that the proliferation of specialists has not substantially increased knowledge about program operations. While these experts know much about the technical details of parts of programs, their distance from the program's operations often keeps them in the dark about what eventually happens with the money and how different parts of programs interact. They only reinforce the tendency toward regulation to specify how these technical standards should be administered, a tendency created by the dearth of useful knowledge about program operations.

INTEREST GROUP ANALYSIS

The most powerful sources of information on what ultimately was happening with CD money were not the agency's field offices but the many monitoring groups that kept an eye on local decisions. Their power came through several routes. The monitoring reports contained detailed information that HUD's own statistics could not capture. What were the cities spending money on? Tennis courts? Housing for the poor? HUD collected most of its data from communities' plans and grouped the figures into broad, functional categories like redevelopment, water and sewer projects, housing, and service-related facilities.[18] This information was interesting but not very useful. The categories were so broad it was impossible to be specific about what projects communities were funding, and since the applications listed planned, not actual, uses, HUD did not know into what categories the money ultimately fell. The monitoring reports prepared by the interest groups consequently carried enormous influence: The data arrived in the program's formative months and the tales appeared to bear the power of firsthand observations, two features that made the information impossible to dismiss.

18. For example, see HUD, *Second Annual Report*, 20–21.

The interest groups acquired large influence in the program because they helped federal administrators short-circuit the problems with their own knowledge-gathering efforts. In fact, Lester W. Milbrath argues, "the most widespread and tangible service" that lobbyists give to decision makers is providing information.[19] Unlike field administrators, Washington-based interest groups are not saddled with the pressures of running a program, nor are they thousands of miles away, nor do they disguise their information to protect their performance. Rather, they eagerly share information (at least information that helps their cause) and they appear often in the Congress or in agency offices. Government officials fully recognize that each interest group has its own case to make and that none of the information they peddle is unbiased. But for that matter, none of the rest of the information with which they are deluged is unbiased. Local officials want to make their projects look good and field officials are leery of transmitting bad news. Information from interest groups may arrive more quickly than the information an agency collects from its own field offices, and as an added advantage, it comes free. Lobbyists serve as "listening posts."[20] We most commonly think of lobbyists communicating Washington's decisions to their constituents and arguing their constituents' wishes in Washington. But they argue those points most convincingly when they provide information to decision makers and when they convince the decision makers that their information is to be believed: that the information is truly useful knowledge.

The interest groups' information came in three forms. There were occasional one-time reports of local abuses. Some newspapers, for example, published stories claiming that most CD money was ending up in upper-income neighborhoods, charges that plagued CETA and general revenue sharing as well. Although the charges were rarely investigated further, they created a potent source of distrust among local citizens and congressional committees. A second source of in-

---

19. Lester W. Milbrath, *The Washington Lobbyists* (Westport, Conn., 1976), 307. See also Donald H. Haider, *When Governments Come to Washington: Governors, Mayors, and Intergovernmental Lobbying* (New York, 1974), 227–28; and Raymond A. Bauer, Ithiel de Sola Pool, and Lewis Anthony Dexter, *American Business and Public Policy: The Politics of Foreign Trade* (Chicago, 1972), Chaps. 24, 32.
20. Milbrath, *The Washington Lobbyists*, 164–69.

formation was the nonrigorous field observations conducted by many monitoring groups. The Southern Regional Council's report was perhaps the best known, but the Potomac Institute, the NAACP, the Michigan Advisory Committee to the U.S. Commission on Civil Rights, and the National Urban League conducted similar studies.[21] The reports had a common research technique: an observer would be dispatched to examine a community's CD program and to report back on what was discovered. The rigor of the survey varied by group. Some groups simply collected stories as their observers reported them. Others, like the Southern Regional Council, laid out forty-four questions for the observer to investigate, ranging from "Was the local government reorganized to reflect new responsibility under the community development program?" to "Have there been allegations regarding illegal discrimination and violation of the civil rights laws?"[22] The reports published by all the groups eventually became the grist for harsh examination before congressional committees.

Both of these techniques, however, suffered from the same problems. How could HUD or any other reader be confident about the findings? Perhaps a single charge of abuse in a single city—or even in a few cities—was unique. Perhaps the charge was real but not very significant. Every program, as Arthur M. Okun argues, is like a leaky bucket: some water inevitably sloshes out in the transfer.[23] The important question is not whether a program leaks but how much it leaks. A few problems, after all, were to be expected in any new program with new rules and with many more communities involved.

Some charges might not even have been true. The city manager of Corpus Christi, Texas, responded angrily to a Southern Regional Council allegation that the city was using its CD money to offset

21. See Brown et al., *A Time for Accounting*; Potomac Institute, "The Housing Assistance Plan: A Non-Working Program for Community Improvement?" (Washington, D.C., 1975); Frank DeStefano and Clay H. Wellborn, "Aspects of Community Development Activities in Selected Localities," summary of NAACP findings prepared by the Congressional Research Service of the Library of Congress (Washington, D.C., 1976); Michigan Advisory Committee, *Livonia* and *The Chippewa People*; and National Urban League, "The New Housing Programs: Who Benefits" (New York, 1975).
22. Brown et al., *A Time for Accounting*, 119–25.
23. Arthur M. Okun uses the "leaky bucket" metaphor to discuss the inevitable waste that accompanies any transfer program. See *Equality and Efficiency: The Big Tradeoff* (Washington, D.C., 1975), 91–95.

earlier bond issues. He called the charge "an outright lie," argued that the city had already spent the money raised from the bonds, and was using CD funds to expand its public works program.[24] The New York *Times* seized upon another Southern Regional Council finding, $150,000 for tennis courts in Little Rock, Arkansas, to point to "gross misuse of Community Development money." But the city manager of Little Rock wrote to the *Times* to contest several points. The city planned to use the CD money to acquire land for a park; tennis courts were to be a part of the park and were to be paid for with city funds. And even though an affluent neighborhood lay across the street from the new project, a YWCA and a Boys' Club planned to locate next to the park. The city hoped to use the park to stabilize the neighborhood and to serve residents for other neighborhoods. Furthermore, the city manager reminded the newspaper, "Blacks play tennis too." The Southern Regional Council replied that their complaints were based more on local opposition to the project than on the propriety of building tennis courts. Community residents, the council said, "viewed the project as unresponsive to their needs."[25]

Which side was right in either case is less important than the fact the monitoring groups' charges were often contested. Some local officials complained that the monitors did not understand the projects, the city's situation, or even the program's rules. They also complained that the monitors were biased observers who listened to only one side in the politically charged local disputes over how to spend the CD money. These countercharges, however, never received the same publicity as the original allegations; the charges came to be accepted as fact. The pages of Senator William Proxmire's 1976 hearings on the CD program are filled with such testimony, and those hearings forced HUD to take regulatory action.

One monitoring group, the National Association of Housing and Redevelopment Officials (NAHRO) pursued a third approach. NAHRO wanted to produce a study that could document exactly how much money was going to the poor across the country. NAHRO's principal data came from a survey of the location of CD projects in

24. Letter published in Senate, *CD Program*, 23–24.
25. The New York *Times*, April 12, 1976, p. 28; April 30, 1976, p. 26; and June 9, 1976, p. 38.

eighty-six communities across the country. If a project were located in a census tract with less than 80 percent of the city's median family income, it was assumed to benefit low- and moderate-income persons. By this measure, as we saw in Chapter 4, communities spent only half or less of their money to benefit the poor. NAHRO's evidence seemed to provide the best case for those who suspected local governments of giving the poor short shrift. The poor began, apparently, with only half of all CD funds, and the amount appeared to be shrinking. The other alleged abuses made for good headlines and lively congressional hearings, but NAHRO's findings worried the interest groups, members of Congress, and HUD officials the most. NAHRO had looked at a national sample of applications, analyzed the results by computer, and produced a figure showing limited benefits to the poor. It was powerful information.

It was also data that could not be trusted, for location was not a reliable way of measuring benefits. A housing rehabilitation project might be located in a lower-income neighborhood but not benefit its residents. For example, a community might improve houses only to drive out the poor as rentals increased. On the other hand, a project located in an upper-income neighborhood might benefit the poor. A new fire station might improve fire protection for a larger area than just the census tract in which it was located. Other projects could not be assigned to any census tract at all. In the first few years of the program, HUD's rules allowed city-wide projects like legal service centers. The project might be located in one census tract but serve all city residents. Some of the money, furthermore, was used for program administration for which the income categories did not make sense. In NAHRO's survey, 20 percent of the funds in the first year and 17 percent in the second year could not be assigned to a census tract. In all cases the analysis was made on planned, not actual, uses of the money, and many communities later shifted their plans.

NAHRO's findings, however, confirmed the judgment of most skeptics that the cities could not be trusted with broad discretion. The findings were apparently rigorous in technique and national in scope. NAHRO's reports, when combined with the nonrigorous but consistent tales of abuse supplied by the other monitoring groups, appeared to paint a clear picture: local governments were abusing the program by systematically channeling benefits away from the poor. Even though benefits for the poor were only one of many program goals, the information collected by the pressure groups forced the issue to the top of both congressional and administrative agendas. HUD had no evidence with which to defend itself, and the groups' information became accepted as knowledge.

HUD, like all agencies, was hostage to the knowledge it had about its programs. For small agencies and agencies on the front lines, these problems are serious but usually manageable. But for large agencies, particularly agencies running programs through other levels of government, the problem is acute. Good information about program results is the exception rather than the rule, and getting good information requires careful planning and much hard work. No agency, however, can be effective or protect itself from attack without knowing what is happening with its staff and money. For HUD in CD, the complexity of the program, the discretion granted local governments, the weakness of its own field organization, and its internal fragmentation conspired to keep the department in the dark.

In these conditions, HUD had little choice but to accept the evidence brought forward by the interest groups. Internal information-gathering was weak, and the speed with which the interest groups assembled their information left HUD with little maneuvering room. When the groups took their case to Capitol Hill they were able to push their grievances to the top of the agenda. HUD's defense was to contract with the Brookings Institution for a multi-year examination of the program. Brookings' national network of observers examined the activities of a sample of communities and by 1980 was using a much improved methodology for measuring the program's benefits for the poor. A survey of forty-one communities showed that benefits for low- and moderate-income persons had grown from 54 percent in 1975 to 62 percent in 1978.[26] But as with most scholarly research and many careful policy analyses, Brookings' findings came too late to influence the course of the debate over the program's benefits for the

---

26. Paul R. Dommel *et al.*, *Targeting Community Development* (Washington, D.C., 1980), 160–62.

poor. The report was published in January, 1980, nearly two years after HUD issued its revised regulations on program benefits. HUD in the meantime had been captive to the information provided by the interest groups, a source of knowledge uncertain at best. Any policy study has its biases, and the bias of the interest groups was clear. Knowing in advance what bias a group brings to a study, of course, makes it possible to discount their findings accordingly. But if a program manager has no other sources of information with countervailing biases, the manager has little defense from attacks those groups make with their studies. Many of the interest groups' studies were suspect and many were built on bases of weak expertise and methodology. The interest groups usually operated through untrained observers who had little awareness of the CD program's complex rules or of local conditions. The Southern Regional Council, for example, conducted its survey with student interns. Without being intimately familiar with a program's regulations, the constant changes in the rules, and the nature of local projects, observers risked making sensational but unfair charges. One HUD official explained, "It's hard enough for a rep [field representative] to figure out. Is it any wonder that a citizen group has trouble coming up with a defensible conclusion?"[27] Some local projects the interest groups attacked, in fact, were eligible when first funded but would have been ineligible if begun during the interest groups' investigations. The groups rarely could follow the intricate shifts in the program's regulations and consequently criticized some projects that were legitimate. Many interest groups had a very limited staff so they had to rely on volunteers or low-paid workers to collect their data. But with such workers, the dangers of technical mistakes and unfair charges multiplied. And even when interest groups had expertise, methodological problems sometimes were serious. NAHRO's technique provided questionable results, and the difficulties with nonrigorous research—especially the "horror story" case studies—were even more serious.

The basic questions remained: Were the allegations of program abuse true, or were there reasonable justifications for local decisions? Were abuses where they existed significant or were they relatively

27. Interview with the author.

isolated problems? Without answers to these questions HUD was forced to respond to complaints that came from the interest groups and Capitol Hill. Answers to these questions were shaped by the perceptions of the groups and of the congressional committees, and the perceptions were formed by the charges of scandal that had dominated the congressional hearings. HUD found itself captive to the perceptions that the interest groups' analysis had created, and the agency had no independent source of information with which to combat the prevailing view.

REGULATORY MESSAGES

To short-circuit its information deficiencies, both in communicating downward what behavior would be acceptable and in communicating upward about what results occurred, HUD relied on regulations. If there was a question about which projects were allowed, HUD would specify eligibility in more detail. If the poor seemed to get short shrift, HUD would demand that communities concentrate more of their money on the poor. And if complaints arose about environmental reviews or equal opportunity, HUD would explain how those standards were to be met. In each case, further detail meant more regulations, regulations that limited communities' discretion and drew more power to Washington as officials in HUD's central office defined the program in fuller detail.

This rule making, however, was more than simply clarifying standards or satisfying interest groups' complaints. It was a way of continuing the policy-making process. Regulations simultaneously were the battleground on which decisions were made and the means of signaling who had won. Regulations, in fact, served six important purposes.

1. *Identify beneficiaries.* The CD legislation was vague in specifying just who was to benefit from the program. Congress had set procedural flexibility as an important goal in itself, and communities were to decide themselves who was to benefit. There were many other groups, however—interest groups, congressional committee members and their staffs, potential beneficiaries, and some HUD

staff members—with a stake in how communities made those decisions. The regulations provided a way to define in greater detail who would benefit. Representatives of interest groups, especially those representing the poor, wanted to make sure their members received the fruits of the program's funds. Congressional committee members wanted to keep an eye on where the money went, and some of them wanted to set much stricter standards for who benefited than the legislation did. Some HUD staff members had a vested interest in maintaining strong federal control, for strong control enhanced their own positions. Regulations that defined which projects were eligible, where they could be located, and how to measure beneficiaries were a way of specifying just who was to receive the program's largesse.

2. *Define an agency's posture.* Every program has a wide following (including interest groups, congressional committee members and their staffs, and officials at the White House and OMB) who track a program closely. The pages of the *Federal Register* provide a useful way of communicating to these constituencies just how a federal agency intends to run a program. Will federal stewardship be loose, or will federal officials tightly control what happens with federal money? What questions will receive special attention this year? HUD signaled in 1974 that it would allow communities broad discretion when it did little more than republish the CD program's authorizing legislation as its initial rules. The Ford administration's increasingly strict definition of project eligibility, and later the Carter administration's 75-25 rule, sent out a warning that HUD was going to examine local performance far more closely. As a way of responding to outside complaints, acknowledging an interest group or congressional committee's concern, or signaling a shift in administrative strategy, regulations are useful devices for communicating an agency's posture.

3. *Set standards for local compliance.* Especially when a program's goals are vague, state and local governments are sometimes unsure just what a federal agency expects of them. What kind of records must grant recipients keep? How freely can they reallocate money? Will application reviews or performance reports be impor-

tant tools for federal control? How much attention should grant recipients pay to crosscutting requirements? The natural tendency in a new setting, for a child in a playpen or a horse in a corral, is to test the boundaries. Federal regulations signal state and local governments about the behavior the federal government expects (or at least what it will accept). In CD, more strict standards for project eligibility, location, and benefit signaled increasing federal attention to application reviews in controlling the program.

4. *Communicate with field offices.* Federal field offices are often just as much in the dark about program rules as the state and local governments they supervise—and sometimes even more so because they lack the eyes and ears of Washington-based interest groups. Without clear standards, field operations break down and interpretations of operating rules vary from office to office. Regulations sometimes are most important as a way of communicating from Washington to the field within a federal agency. Especially in HUD, with thirty-nine area offices under a layer of ten regional offices under the Washington headquarters, sending clear signals quickly was usually a problem. The *Federal Register* was sometimes the most timely and effective way for the central office to inform field offices around the country about what they should do: how freely to yield to local requests, what kind of advice to give local administrators, and how carefully to review local plans and performance.

5. *Provide the battleground for intra-agency conflicts.* Only rarely within a federal agency, particularly in its Washington staff, is there a uniform opinion about how its programs should be run. Sometimes that conflict arises among specialists from different offices, sometimes between career civil servants and political appointees with different philosophies about how to run the program. In CD's early days, New Federalism warriors among the political appointees struggled against many careerists' instincts for tight federal control. Later, specialists from different parts of the department argued over whether or not a specific percentage requirement for low- and moderate-income benefits should be adopted. Some groups within an agency win, and some lose, from most regulations, for regulatory

changes mean more power for some administrators and less for others. Drafting rules is often a contentious process within agencies; issuing regulations can signal the victors in the struggle for greater internal influence.

6. *Continue the policy-making process.* Just as intra-agency disputes do not end with the issuance of regulations, broader disputes among policy makers do not end with the passage of legislation. When Senator William Proxmire lost in his effort in the CD conference committee to insist on tighter HUD supervision, particularly of benefits for the poor, he used his committee to generate pressure on HUD to strengthen its oversight and to increase the specificity of the regulations. Later, when HUD attempted to impose the 75-25 requirement, the House subcommittee charged that the regulations were far tighter than the legislation permitted. The rule-making process provides an opportunity to pick up where the legislative process left off. It often contains the same players, fighting over the same issues, in an ongoing struggle for position and advantage.

Regulations thus exist not only as a consequence of a lack of useful knowledge but also as a way of sending signals of their own. They communicate a variety of messages, some subtle and others far more blatant, but all are important to the broad constituency that follows a governmental program. An even more important question, however, is this: who sets the agenda for these regulations?

CHAPTER 6
FRAMING THE AGENDA

FEEDBACK on a program's performance is a powerful force in helping an agency fine-tune its administrative strategies. Every agency wants to know what is going well, what is not, and what can be done to reduce or eliminate problems. The management of a governmental program is thus a dynamic process that never stops. It is, furthermore, a process shaped by an agency's recognition of what its problems are, and whoever controls the information that agency managers use in understanding their problems has a powerful influence on their agenda. In CD, as we saw in the last chapter, the most persuasive and timely (if perhaps not the most accurate) information came to HUD from the interest groups. The groups representing the poor, in particular, were able to focus attention on program benefits for lower-income persons to the exclusion of other program goals because they dominated the flow of information, and thus they captured HUD's agenda.

The interest groups worked through other channels as well to influence the department's policies. Their complaints filled the pages of congressional testimony, while the federal court dockets were peppered with suits challenging communities'—and HUD's—administration of CD. The congressional committees have over the years developed tools ranging from subtle statements in committee reports to well-staged oversight hearings that generate substantial publicity, tools that supplement the ever-present powers of authorization and appropriation. The federal courts, furthermore, have intervened far more aggressively in detailed administrative questions. Crosscutting rules like equal opportunity and environmental protection provide the federal courts with avenues for supervising both federal and local actions, while the broad language and ambitious goals of individual programs have provided the opportunity for judicial supervision—and sometimes for redefinition—of congressional intent. Congressional hearings can place agency administrators under a harsh spotlight, and decisions from the federal bench can force a question onto an administrative agenda in a way no other force can match.

The interest groups played important roles in both Congress and the courts in shaping the administrative agenda. Along with some members of Congress, many of the groups argued that without tighter regulations the poor would suffer. But the interest groups also supplied facts with which to buttress their complaints, facts that proved impossible for HUD to ignore. The interest groups thus forced HUD to deal with the problem, and, through the monitoring they conducted, they provided the information on which HUD made its decisions. To the extent that crucial information comes from forces outside an agency, and to the degree that external forces can influence what becomes defined as an agency's problem, those forces can fix the scope and character of administrative action.

Problems defined by external forces make an agency's actions reactive. In federal grant programs, because the grant programs removed most other controls, these actions have tended to be regulatory. Problems framed by external forces strengthen an agency's tendency to write rules to make sure the problems do not recur: to regulate in self-defense and against the worst case. Warren Butler, second in command of the CD program as Deputy Assistant Secretary for Community Planning and Development in the Ford administration, said, "Whoever is in always has to deal with the fact that you have Congress, interest groups, and the courts looking over your shoulder. The fact that administrators have to answer to outside groups, who are unlikely to act in restrained fashion to instances of local abuse, forces them to act in a protective fashion for themselves and their program."[1] No administrator likes to listen to complaints. But when complaints threaten their agency and their program, administrators find they must act. They can ill afford to lose the support of the "attentive publics" that bolster the agency,[2] or the legislation and appropriations from congressional committees that sustain the agency. Neither can they afford to trifle with federal courts whose decisions can force them to take actions on someone else's terms.

Agencies seek stability first. Tales of administrative aggrandizement are familiar, but agencies at their core, James Q. Wilson contends, "are risk averse."[3] Agency risk aversion leads to regulation in self-defense. Agencies often find that one way to protect themselves against problems—or at least repetition of problems—is to write rules to prohibit them. When communities tried to evade the pressures to concentrate funds by establishing city-wide projects, HUD wrote a regulation prohibiting city-wide projects. When attacked in court for approving housing assistance plans that allowed suburbs to escape the national commitment to public housing, HUD issued detailed rules on how the "expected to reside" figure was to be calculated. As Peter J. Petkas, head of the U.S. Regulatory Council during the Carter administration, explained, "There is almost an institutional instinct [for administrators] to write regulations to explain what Congress meant. It is the desire for certainty and predictability by the federal agencies and by the recipients that leads to regulation."[4] Attack from outside forces leads agencies to regulate in self-defense.

The tendency toward regulation in self-defense leads to a corollary pattern, regulation against the worst case. No agency, having been burned once, wants to take the chance of being burned a second time—even if the first attack came as a result of a single action by a single community. Senator William Proxmire focused national atten-

1. Interview with the author.
2. See Francis E. Rourke, *Bureaucracy, Politics, and Public Policy* (Boston, 1976), 44.
3. James Q. Wilson, "The Politics of Regulation," in James Q. Wilson (ed.), *The Politics of Regulation* (New York, 1980), 377.
4. Interview with the author.

tion on the housing assistance plan of Livonia, Michigan, during a 1976 Senate hearing. Livonia, he charged, had evaded its commitment to public housing and HUD, he suggested, should take administrative steps to insure that no further evasions by other communities could occur. The *Hartford* case, a single case dealing with a single metropolitan area, had meanwhile forced HUD to recast all of its regulations dealing with the HAP. A single case of abuse, or even a single allegation, can force federal agencies to regulate against the worst case. Even if that case might be an isolated instance, no agency wants to risk such close, continued scrutiny.

This double pathology produces two important effects. Regulation in self-defense tends to produce disjointed regulations. Defensive regulation is reactive regulation, with the agenda set by forces outside the agency. Regulations arise as issues make their way onto the administrative agenda, and administrators cannot predict how those issues will arise. The result is that the regulations tend to emerge one at a time, in fragmented fashion, with no promise that what emerges makes coherent sense. Regulation against the worst case, furthermore, imposes costs on all state and local governments for the sins, real or perceived, of a few. To prevent recurrence of cases of alleged fraud, waste, or abuse of program funds, the strong tendency is to write universal rules—even if the case is unlikely ever to be repeated. Rarely is there discussion about whether a potential problem is serious enough to warrant imposing a costly remedy on all recipients of aid. "Federal administrators often used a blunderbuss approach to punishing state and local governments for the mistakes of a relatively small number of communities," explains Carl E. VanHorn.[5] The result is an increase in costs for aid recipients without any assessment of whether the regulations will eliminate the problem at hand.

This is a pattern that has been repeated across the gamut of federal grant programs, particularly in CETA, general revenue sharing, and the safe-streets block grant. It is part of the "creeping categorization," the steady development of regulation, that afflicted many grant

---

5. Carl E. VanHorn, *Policy Implementation in the Federal System* (Lexington, Mass., 1979), 148. See also Sundquist and Davis, *Making Federalism Work*, 271.

programs during the 1970s.[6] In each of these programs the pattern was similar. Questions of local mismanagement or outright fraud would arise, and those charges would produce unpleasant headlines, complaints from interest groups, and sharp questions from Capitol Hill. The agency would react with regulations. The agency's reactions, however, were conditioned on those initial charges and it often had no way of weighing the complaints to see if they were substantial or even real. HUD's information-gathering machinery was weak and it found itself, consequently, dependent on outside sources for the management information it needed to run the program.

This is not to say that federal agencies cannot shape their own agendas. New presidential administrations often bring policy changes, and HUD Secretary Harris and Assistant Secretary Embry undertook a broad revamping of the CD program in 1977. The key question is whether the new rules that shaped the CD program during the Carter administration came principally from the administration's pledge to provide greater benefits for the poor. Put another way, would HUD under a Ford administration have done what Harris and Embry did? There is no question that HUD under Secretary Hills and Assistant Secretary Meeker was moving to tighter controls through more detailed regulations and applications. New regulations steadily were tightening loopholes in eligibility requirements and the housing assistance plan. A continued Ford administration undoubtedly would have seen a direct attack on the problem of benefits for the poor. It is also clear, however, that the attack would have been different from the Harris-Embry approach. During the Ford administration, HUD's strategy had always been much closer to the House's insistence on local flexibility than on the Senate's concern with benefits for the poor. For Harris and Embry, the questions were reversed; they agreed with the Senate that who benefited was more important than procedural reforms. The Ford administration would not likely have attempted the Carter administration's percentage-based approach, but it nevertheless would have faced the same demands for tighter federal supervision of local projects.

6. U.S. Advistory Commission on Intergovernmental Relations, *The Intergovernmental Grant System: Summary and Concluding Observations* (Washington, D.C., 1978), 8–9.

Even during the Carter administration, however, the regulations did not come solely from aggressive administrators. The interest groups representing the poor had easy access to HUD during the Carter administration, and one coalition of interest groups—the Working Group for Community Development Reform—even actively helped HUD Assistant Secretary Embry draft new regulations. Members of the Working Group held about forty meetings with Embry that ranged from suggestions for legislation to detailed discussion of individual regulations, particularly the proposed rules on citizen participation, grantee performance reports, and the program's benefits for the poor. "The Working Group has played an unusual role," the group's head, Andrew Mott of the Center for Community Change, explained. "This is one of the few times that a coalition representing non-governmental organizations has been allowed to get involved in the interstices of a government agency."[7] No interest-group influence could be stronger than taking a hand in drafting new regulations.

In one sense, federal administrators of grant programs hold the final card. They both distribute the money and write the rules that govern it, and it is upon these factors that the eventual impact of any program rests. But at the same time, congressional committees and the federal courts—supported by the interest groups—have come to fix the administrators' agenda. They define many of the questions on which administrators must take action and they provide much of the basic information that shapes the administrator's response. Federal administrators have prime responsibility for managing federal grant programs, but the issues upon which that stewardship rests tend to be defined by external forces. Such a method of framing the agenda only increases the tendency toward reactive, escalating regulation of federal grant programs.

INTEREST GROUPS

Interest groups date from days even before Madison's warnings in Federalist 10 of the "mischiefs of faction." Such groups are neither peculiarly American nor particularly political. But the American po-

---

7. Interview with the author.

litical system provides a special focus for group interests. Government spends money, regulates behavior, and manages programs that affect individuals and the groups they form. Government, especially federal government with numerous places to influence governmental action, is thus an especially attractive target for interest-group activity. Before the New Deal, however, intergovernmental lobbying was rare. This was a reflection more of the nature of the intergovernmental system than of the pressure groups. The principal questions revolved around the proper division of state and federal functions, and there were few aid programs to catalyze group interest. As the country grew, there had been demands for more federal support for education and for highways. But it was not until the Depression and the New Deal that interest groups became important forces in intergovernmental relations.

The development of intergovernmetal lobbying, Donald H. Haider argues, came in three steps that paralleled the shifting administrative strategies of aid programs discussed in Chapter 2.[8] The first step, lasting from the New Deal to the early 1960s, came through the first efforts of public officials, especially mayors and governors, to organize and make their voices heard more clearly in Washington. The big-city mayors were particularly active, for the burdens of the Depression fell at first unevenly upon the cities. Demand for relief grew as local revenues shrank, and the New Deal programs helped to stabilize local governments perhaps even more than they aided the poor. More important, the New Deal programs increased the scale of grant programs and established the pattern of direct federal aid to the cities. Federal aid united many of the new interest groups in their search for federal support, but it also established a pattern of competition between the states and their local governments for the fruits of federal grants.

The Great Society brought a second phase that lasted through the 1960s. More federal aid in more categories created many new claimants, and many of those claimants themselves organized to press their interests in Washington. Much of the aid bypassed the states on

8. Haider, *When Governments Come to Washington*, 48–64. Haider is concerned with lobbying by state and local executives, but his discussion characterizes intergovernmental lobbying in general.

its way to local governments and that created competition between state and local officials. Furthermore, since many new programs were competitive project grants, the contest for assistance sometimes brought intense struggles among local officials. State and local officials soon began to recognize their common financial link to federal aid, however, and they began to work together more actively toward more attractive federal support. That work culminated in the passage of general revenue sharing in 1972 and led to the third phase, Nixon's New Federalism in the 1970s. A broad coalition of interest groups, composed principally of elected officials from all levels of government, worked hard for revenue sharing, CETA, and CD. After their successes, the groups lay back to consolidate their gains by strengthening their staffs and honing their lobbying activities. But during their regrouping, other groups like the Southern Regional Council and the NAACP struggled to gain greater influence over who benefited from the programs. These groups became competitors with the public officials for control over the programs.

By the end of the 1970s, three different kinds of interest groups had arisen to influence federal grant policy. One kind was the traditional interest group that sought to steer federal decisions toward benefiting its members. In hearings on federal housing programs, for example, representatives from the Mortgage Bankers Association of America, the National Association of Home Builders, and the Manufactured Housing Institute all appeared to argue for more federal support for home-building. The goal of such traditional interest groups is governmental action, administrative and legislative, that either serves the individuals they represent or at least does not hurt them.

Popular usage has obscured the distinction between the other two kinds of pressure groups, since both are known as public interest groups. One kind, with the emphasis on *public*, is composed of the groups whose members are public officials. Known as PIGs, these groups include the U.S. Conference of Mayors, the National League of Cities, the National Association of Counties, and the National Governors Conference. I will refer to them instead as "public officials' groups." They are of two types. Some, like the U.S. Conference of Mayors and the National League of Cities, are composed of elected officials, while others, like the National Association of Housing and

Redevelopment Officials and the National Community Development Association, are trade guilds formed by appointed administrators. The public officials' groups seek benefits not so much for their members as for the jurisdictions they govern. The third kind, with the emphasis on *public interest*, includes groups like the Sierra Club, the NAACP, and the Southern Regional Council. They do not so much seek to benefit their members as to seek the commonweal, at least as they see it.[9] I will refer to these groups as "public interest groups." (The confusion over the names exists even in Washington, a city that usually resolves such problems with intricate acronyms. Part of the confusion stems from historical accident, for the public officials' groups predated many of the public interest groups. Part of the problem undoubtedly also stems from the unusual attractiveness of the name. No group wants to renounce its claim to speak for the public interest.)

Although lobbying is most commonly considered as a part of lawmaking, the administrative process is a powerful lure for interest groups. As Congress has delegated more power to administrators, interest groups have become more concerned with how administrators exercise that delegated power. Nowhere has interest been keener than in the rule-making process, and the CD program is no exception. Twenty-two groups actively participated in rule making for the program.[10] The groups ranged broadly from the mammoth AFL-CIO to small groups with tiny staffs. (See Table 7). One group, the Coalition for Block Grant Compliance, was an ad hoc group formed to probe charges of local malfeasance. The one thread uniting this disparate collection of interest groups was their concern for how the CD program was run and who received its benefits.

---

9. The definition is from Jeffrey M. Berry, *Lobbying for the People: The Political Behavior of Public Interest Groups* (Princeton, 1977), 6.

10. Nineteen of the groups commented on more than one "controversial" CD proposed rule. The controversial proposals are defined here as proposed regulations that drew more than twenty-five responses during the public comment period. (Under the Administrative Procedure Act, proposed regulations must be published and opened to public comment before being made final.) The eleven controversial rules are, with the date of publication in the *Federal Register*: original CD rules, September 17, 1974; housing assistance plan rules, January 15, 1976; changes in project eligibility, March 1, 1976; changes in project eligibility, October 4, 1976; program management, November 15, 1976; grant administration, November 30, 1976; changes in project eligibility, Janu-

TABLE 7: INTEREST GROUPS ACTIVE IN CD RULE MAKING

	Year Founded	Number of Members	Number of Staff Members
TRADITIONAL GROUPS			
AFL-CIO	1955[1]	13,600,000	600
Association of Rehabilitation Facilities	1969	1,000	20
Nat. Assoc. for Retarded Citizens	1950	275,000	65
Nat. Easter Seal Society	1919	1,124	80
United Cerebral Palsy Assoc.	1949	277	100
PUBLIC OFFICIALS' GROUPS			
Nat. Assoc. of Counties	1935	1,825	120
Nat. Assoc. of Housing and Redevelopment Officials	1933	9,100	33
Nat. Community Development Assoc.	1969	350	7
Nat. League of Cities	1924	900	125
U.S. Conference of Mayors	1932	830	105
PUBLIC INTEREST GROUPS			
Center for Community Change	1968	([6])	57
Coalition for Block Grant Compliance[2]	N.A.	N.A.	N.A.
Leadership Conference on Civil Rights	1953	149[4]	4
League of Women Voters	1920	125,000	55
NAACP, Special Contribution Fund[3]	1909	450,673	125
Nat. Citizen Participation Council	1972	300[5]	18
Nat. Committee Against Discrimination in Housing	1950	43	20
National Urban League	1910	50,000	2,000
Potomac Institute	1961	([6])	4
Rural Housing Alliance	1975	2,500	50
Sierra Club	1892	183,000	325
Suburban Action	1969	([6])	7

NOTES
1. Date of merger.
2. Ad hoc organization.
3. Part of the national NAACP, for which the dates here are given.
4. The Conference is a coalition composed of other interest groups.
5. These members organizations represent approximately 15,000 individuals.
6. Non-membership organization.

SOURCE: Denise S. Akey (ed.), *Encyclopedia of Associations*, Vol. I. (Detroit: Gale Research Co., 1980); and information provided by the groups themselves.

Two things accounted for the growing role of these groups. First, the 1960s and 1970s brought, in the words of Samuel H. Beer, "the rise of new centers of influence in the public sector."[11] The profusion

---

ary 17, 1977; general revision of the rules, October 25, 1977; and environmental review regulations, October 10, 1974, May 16, 1977, and October 19, 1978.
11. Beer, "The Adoption of General Revenue Sharing," 129.

of new programs expanded the number of people and groups that benefited from federal largesse. This, in turn, created a large and vocal clientele for continued funding of old programs and support for new programs. And with more state and local governments making more decisions about these programs, the groups had many more places to take their case. Second, the costs of access became lower.[12] The national media devoted more attention to the interest groups' complaints of discrimination against the poor or destruction of the environment, and this in turn led to an explosive growth in the number of interest groups. Of a sample of eighty-three public interest groups studied in 1977 by Jeffrey M. Berry, 63 percent had been founded after 1960 and 47 percent had been founded between 1968 and 1972.[13] The result was an unusual collection of private interests, elected and appointed public officials, and groups seeking broader goals, all working to influence governmental—and especially regulatory—decisions.

Each of the groups came to governmental decisions with different motivations. The traditional groups shared a commitment to insuring that the CD program benefited their members. The AFL-CIO had for decades led the support for social programs, and the organization argued that CD funds ought to be used to benefit the poor. The group issued an early warning that "national objectives are unlikely to be fulfilled unless HUD's guidelines to local applicants are very explicit and HUD's monitoring and enforcement policies are implemented aggressively."[14] Social program goals, the organization worried, would not be met without a strong guiding hand from Washington. Other HUD regulations stipulated which neighborhood facilities were eligible for CD funding. Groups representing the handicapped worked hard to guarantee that communities could use CD funds to build and run centers for their members.

The public officials' lobby, on the other hand, argued for greater financial support for CD and greater flexibility for its recipients. The National League of Cities and the U.S. Conference of Mayors com-

12. See Wilson, *The Politics of Regulation*, 385.
13. Berry, *Lobbying for the People*, 34.
14. Letter from Henry B. Schechter, director, AFL-CIO Department of Urban Affairs, HUD Docket File 74-292 on rules proposed September 17, 1974.

plained that the proposed 75-25 rule for lower-income benefits would "unduly complicate, restrict, and seriously undermine successful programs in scores of cities."[15] The National Community Development Association concurred, contending that the "imposition of percentage requirements is clearly inconsistent with the intent of the block grant concept."[16] The public officials battled to protect the flexibility of the CD and other New Federalism programs that they had worked so hard to win.

For the public officials' groups, however, questions of regulatory flexibility were much less important than the reliable flow of cash. "Tax politics," Haider contends, "tends to be the most pervasive and inescapable political pressure operating upon state-local chief executives."[17] As economic downturns and regional shifts in industrial growth plagued the cities, intergovernmental aid became a fiscal lifeline. Local officials as a result placed first priority on the continued flow of money. But since, as Suzanne Farkas puts it, "the federal government does not give money; it 'gives programs'" which in turn channel money,[18] the public officials' groups spent much of their time in Congress trying to protect the big-ticket grant programs. One HUD official rated a single issue at the top of the public officials' concerns: the continued flow of money as free as possible from restrictions on how to spend it. He complained, "In our discussions, we can't get the [U.S.] Conference [of Mayors] and the [National] League [of Cities] to think about urban problems. They think about whether CETA or the CD block grant will pass. We can't get the Conference or the League to spend two seconds on other problems."[19]

The most natural constituency to oppose further regulation of the CD program—the public officials who had to deal with the rules—thus rated regulatory issues relatively low on their agendas. They

15. Letter from Alan Beals, executive director of the National League of Cities, and John J. Gunther, executive director of the U.S. Conference of Mayors, November 24, 1977, HUD Docket File 77-471 on rules proposed October 25, 1977.
16. Letter from Nicholas P. Retsinas, president of the National Community Development Association, November 23, 1977, HUD Docket File 77-471 on rules proposed October 25, 1977.
17. Haider, *When Governments Come to Washington*, 77.
18. Suzanne Farkas, *Urban Lobbying: Mayors in the Federal Arena* (New York: 1971), 241.
19. Interview with the author.

cared more about the flow of money than the package in which the money arrived. To be sure, they kept a careful eye on regulatory changes and regularly filed opinions on each proposal. They saved their powder, however, for the big and important battles, the debate over the authorization of new programs and the level at which they would be funded. The result was that there was no strong constituency to oppose the regulatory changes many other groups, particularly the public interest groups, wanted.

The strongest weapons in the regulatory skirmishes were the studies produced by the public interest groups. These studies universally contended that the communities were misusing the program, to the detriment of the poor and occasionally of the environment. The groups found it easiest and most effective to concentrate their work in Washington. Organizing to influence the decisions of thousands of local governments, each of them making scores of CD decisions, was a task that lay beyond the capacity of even the largest public interest groups. They were better situated to influence administrative decisions in Washington, and they sought regulations to pass those decisions on to each community. The public interest groups, furthermore, deeply distrusted local governments' commitment to the poor and the ability of the poor to make their voices heard. As a leader of one of the groups said, "If you have a totally decentralized program without tough standards, you are asking for a political program and for the scattering that comes with it. Those that have power will get the money."[20] Centralizing power through regulation gave the interest groups more power over who in the end benefited from the money.

For all groups, the central goal was getting their substantive concerns on the federal agenda. There is no influence without access, and policy makers' agendas were crowded with competing claims. Few policy makers could deny that the handicapped needed special centers, that the poor deserved better housing, or that local officials struggled with inadequate revenue. But no program can answer every demand, no matter how deserving. Which groups win relief is determined more by who wins a place on the agenda, who succeeds in attracting notice for his claims, than by any other factor. The changing

20. Interview with the author.

shape of federal aid shifted the battle for this agenda. The struggle of the public officials' groups for more predictable funding led to more formula grants, but the formula grants in turn shifted more of the important questions about who benefits to the regulatory arena.

Complicating each interest group's task was its two constituencies, its members and the other groups in Washington with whom it must interact. The views of these constituencies often do not coincide, and thus every group faces the delicate task of balancing support from its members with building coalitions with other Washington-based groups. "You listen to your constituency," one Washington lobbyist explained, "but only with rare exceptions can a single group in this town go it alone. You have to find issues on which you can agree."[21] Broader coalitions carry more weight than narrow ones; they assemble the force of more members around the country as well as stronger organizational resources in Washington. The groups thus eye each other as much as they do Congress and the administrative agencies. Other groups are important sources of information about likely congressional action or administrative decisions. They provide cues on what stand is reasonable on any given issue and which other groups are likely to be allies. Since much of Washington's activity is set by those who set the agenda, the interest groups can influence the agenda by how they interact. Combined press conferences or lobbying efforts can add force to an individual group's arguments. Negotiated truces can prevent some issues from reaching the boiling point. Finding those coalitions, however, can be difficult. Each organization has its own mission and the missions of different interest groups often conflict. Hot issues naturally lead to differences but influence can come only through consensus.

The coalitions that do form are ad hoc and unstable, coalescing around the issue at hand and shifting with the next issue. As Beer contends, "it is the program that creates the lobby, not the lobby that creates the program."[22] Proposed rules on eligible activities drew many letters from legal aid societies, day care centers, recreation programs, and other social service agencies whose funding rested on the

---

21. Interview with the author.
22. Beer, "The Adoption of General Revenue Sharing," 160.

definitions HUD adopted. On the other hand, proposed rules on CD program management attracted comments principally from local officials. Groups like the National Easter Seal Society and the United Cerebral Palsy Association entered the lists only when HUD's proposed rules threatened funding for neighborhood centers. The interest groups involved in any administrative decision tended to be those with an immediate stake in the outcome and those with the staff to monitor regularly the *Federal Register*.

The groups often disagreed with each other. In particular, the public interest groups often found themselves in battle with the public officials' groups. "Both of us are interested in the continuing flow of money," the head of one group lobbying for the poor said,[23] but past that the groups agreed on little. The public interest groups struggled for stricter CD rules on benefits for the poor, public housing in the suburbs, environmental review, and equal opportunity. The public officials' groups, on the other hand, argued against any change that would restrict the operating flexibility of their members. At the core of the dispute was a set of assumptions that the public interest groups held: that local governments had neither the will nor the capacity to concentrate benefits on the poor or to deal with the broader issues of environmental review and equal opportunity; and that ultimately local governments would not be responsive to the needs of their citizens, particularly their poor citizens. Past federal programs, the public interest groups believed, emphasized procedural guarantees like citizen participation without giving citizens power. The route to empowering citizens—the ultimate form of decentralization—was, they ironically argued, to withdraw discretion from local officials. Strict federal rules, they concluded, protected the poor. "If you have a totally decentralized program with tough standards," the head of one Washington lobby for the poor said, "you are asking for a political program and for the scattering [of funds around the city] that comes with it. Those that have power will get all the money."[24]

The sharp disagreement between the public interest groups and the public officials' groups was irreconcilable. The former urged tight

23. Interview with the author.
24. Interview with the author.

controls on the money while the latter wanted funds as free from federal strings as possible. The battle was joined on questions of regulatory policy. The public officials' groups struggled to keep the issue off the agenda altogether. The evidence that the public interest groups had collected, from newspaper headlines alleging fraud to broader surveys showing little money was going to the poor, was persuasive stuff. The public officials' groups were worried that the attacks might not only increase the restrictions on how their members could use the money but that they also might ultimately endanger the programs themselves. But the public interest groups skillfully used a collection of tools to attract attention: newspaper stories, detailed monitoring reports, broad surveys, and congressional testimony. The result was that they won the battle for the agenda. After they forced HUD to recognize their charges, the department had little choice but to tighten the rules.

Complicating interest-group politics was a further problem. Washington-based interest groups tried carefully to balance the needs of their own members with the pressure of holding together coalitions with other interest groups. They relied on their members for financial support and information; after all, their reason for existence was to serve the members in the field. Members often disagreed among themselves, and the struggle to maintain internal cohesion sometimes proved difficult.[25] But Washington-based interest groups relied heavily on other groups as well to build their influence. Keeping the support of both constituencies often proved troublesome, especially for the public officials' groups. Local elected officials feared that the public interest groups' campaign for tighter regulations would sharply reduce their flexibility in running their programs. At the same time, the public interest groups' evidence was hard to ignore and impossible to avoid. The public officials' groups had to face that evidence in transactions with other interest groups and in questions from congressional committee members. The National League of Cities and the U.S. Conference of Mayors trod a difficult middle ground between these two constituencies. The public officials' groups,

---

25. See David B. Truman, *The Governmental Process: Political Interests and Public Opinion* (New York: 1971), esp. Chap. 6.

one public interest lobbyist explained, were "being forced into more of an advocacy role [for the poor] than I think they want. They can't afford to take an out-front position that would appear to be against poor people."[26] Despite complaints from some of their members that the new regulations were eroding the program's promised discretion, fighting the rules too hard would have weakened the public officials' groups in dealing with other interest groups and HUD.

Furthermore, in any group so varied as local government officials, anything near unanimity on any issue is impossible. Cities have widely differing problems, ranging from too little growth to too much growth. No one program nor any single stand by their national organizations is likely to receive universal support. Some local officials, for example, are increasingly conservative fiscally and question the federal government's strong financial role in local affairs, a stand that goes against the very philosophy of the intergovernmental lobby's existence. Not all local officials *want* more federal aid, and those who do want the aid want it in different packages. Washington-based organizations do not always find it easy to speak for their members because their members often speak with different voices.

The public interest groups handled both constituencies the best. They enjoyed strong internal support from their members for their campaign toward stricter regulations, and they found many other groups with whom they could join. With their massed resources they could organize a coalition—the Coalition for Block Grant Compliance—to press for their demands and to gather information to support them. With that information they were able to confront HUD with apparently irrefutable evidence of local misuse of the money, to attract substantial publicity at congressional committee hearings, and to press their cases in court. They were thus able to capture the agenda for the program.

CONGRESS

Most members of Congress have little taste for administrative details. As David R. Mayhew has persuasively argued, most members

26. Interview with the author.

of Congress have reelection as their primary goal, and that goal shapes the way members spend their time: they tend to seek chores in which they can claim credit and to shun jobs that promise little public attention. The result is that members of Congress concentrate on constituency casework and pork-barrel politics.[27] Solving constituents' problems—from a senior citizen's difficulty in getting a social security check to a mayor's struggles with a federal agency over a grant program—gives members of Congress the opportunity to demonstrate to constituents both their effectiveness and their responsiveness. The growing popularity of formula grant programs in the 1960s and 1970s, furthermore, gave more members of Congress a chance to roll the pork barrel. The formula grants were particularly porcine because they gave all members of Congress a chance to bring home federal dollars to their districts. As party leadership in Congress weakened, guaranteed distributions by formula became the glue that held coalitions for grant programs together. The formula grants also gave individual members of Congress the chance to bring the bacon home.

Congressional legislation for grant programs consequently emphasized distribution over performance. One of the leading questions in the CD program's original passage was which cities would receive how much money, and the question became sharper in the program's 1977 renewal when a second formula emerged to give northeastern and midwestern cities larger grants than they otherwise would have received. Questions of performance were more difficult to define and even more difficult to measure. Congress tended to deal with them by writing vague goals and broad standards—and by passing detailed questions on to the rule-making process. Vague legislative language eased the path to compromise. The CD program's controversy over strict federal supervision versus broad local discretion was ultimately left to HUD. Congress concentrated its attention instead predominantly on how the money was to be distributed.

The crosscutting requirements, furthermore, gave members of Congress an opportunity to take positions on many policy questions. Congress could help protect the environment by voting to require all recipients of federal aid to examine the environmental effects of their

---

27. Mayhew, *Congress*. See also Morris P. Fiorina, *Congress: Keystone of the Washington Establishment* (New Haven, 1977), 46.

projects. In civil rights Congress could prohibit discrimination in the distribution of program benefits. Members of Congress could insist that all federally funded projects be accessible to the handicapped. The requirements allowed a member of Congress to take a well publicized stand on an important issue and to stake out a broad area of public concern. Their very breadth, however, also freed Congress from having to face hard choices of strategy. What environmental effects are important? What does "accessible" to the handicapped mean, and how much should the country pay for accessibility? Both the administrative problems and the financial costs, furthermore, were passed on to state and local governments. The crosscutting requirements hence provided a splendid opportunity for Congress' taking a public stand while transferring ultimate responsibility for performance.

At the same time, these standards, no matter how broad, also provided the grounds on which members of Congress could intervene in administrative decisions. Congressional oversight of administration is perhaps both the most powerful yet most irregularly used method of influencing administrative activity. Close budgetary review is the essence of the appropriation committee's existence, but administrative oversight has a low priority for the legislative committees. It is hard work to examine the intimate workings of a program and it is work with few electoral rewards. Just as important, there is no routine that leads a committee to examine regularly a program's management. When it does occur, oversight is more likely to be a quick skirmish than a comprehensive review. Members of Congress simply find that oversight has fewer payoffs than other uses of their time.[28]

Congressional oversight of administration, consequently, is haphazard. Congress' predisposition against oversight, however, can disappear when—as in the CD program—the scent of scandal wafts through the air.[29] With federal grant programs—and particularly the New Federalism programs—tales of abuse were legion. Furthermore,

---

28. Congressional scholars agree that oversight receives low priority. See Seymour Scher, "Conditions for Legislative Control," *Journal of Politics*, XXV (1963), 526–51; Joseph P. Harris, *Congressional Control of Administration* (Washington, D.C., 1964), Chap. 9; Morris S. Ogul, *Congress Oversees the Bureaucracy: Studies in Legislative Supervision* (Pittsburgh, 1976), 20; and Lawrence C. Dodd and Richard C. Schott, *Congress and the Administrative State* (New York, 1979).

29. Seidman, *Politics, Position, and Power*, 74.

the interest groups involved in the program were arrayed on competing sides that made conflict inevitable. Groups representing the poor urged Congress to force stronger supervision upon HUD while groups representing local officials continued to argue the benefits of local discretion. A few members of Congress—especially the ranking members of the legislative committees that had originally drafted the program's legislation—followed the debate closely. The tales of abuse found interested ears on Capitol Hill, especially in members who began with great skepticism about Nixon's New Federalism approach. Carefully staged hearings gave the interest groups a stage upon which they could present their information, and they provided a forum in which the committee members could transmit a clear message to HUD. The agency could not ignore such strong pressure and criticism, especially when it came from the committees that authorized its programs. The hearings forced a variety of issues onto HUD's agenda.

Central to the committees' oversight of HUD's administration were the members of the committees' staff. They gave the CD program closer and more sustained attention than any member of Congress could. Staff members were in regular contact with HUD's administrators as well as with the staff of the major interest groups—part of the "issue networks" that, as Hugh Heclo explains, dominate national politics.[30] The committee staff thus knew intimately the complaints and the evidence that the interest groups had and the strategies that HUD planned to try. This shared knowledge was crucial. Committee hearings rarely if ever produced surprises, because the players knew in advance what other participants were likely to say. One committee staff member furthermore noted matter-of-factly that the staff usually tried to settle potential problems without having to bring them to the committee members' attention.[31] Staff members scheduled the witnesses, framed the questions, and even occasionally led the interrogations at committee hearings. Committees dominated congressional oversight of administration, and staff members dominated the work of the committees.

30. Hugh Heclo, "Issue Networks and the Executive Establishment," in Anthony King (ed.), *The New American Political System* (Washington, D.C., 1978), 87–124.
31. Interview with the author.

The committee hearings themselves thus were typically opportunities not so much to answer questions about agency performance as to send signals about congressional (that is, committee) feelings about an issue. The signals might be to HUD to increase its review of applications or to alter regulations, or they might be to interest groups to show Congress' concern about a problem. But whatever signals the hearings sent out, they were messages that no federal administrator could ignore. Displeasure about a regulation or administrative decision could translate itself into changes in a program's authorizing legislation, funding levels, or even into termination of a program itself, as the Department of Labor discovered about its CETA program. As Francis E. Rourke explains, "however lightly some congressmen may regard their role as overseers, executive agencies themselves tend to look toward the Hill with considerable anxiety."[32] Congressional committees, and especially their staffs, carefully orchestrated the hearings to send the desired messages to administrators and interest groups alike. Here, the interest groups' information provided the raw material with which the committees crafted those messages.

The sanction of subjecting a top official to harsh questioning (and thus harsh publicity) also gave committee staff members easy access into the early stages of agency decisions. This is especially true with the growth of various kinds of congressional vetoes of administrative actions.[33] The CD program became the target of such a strategy during the program's 1978 reauthorization. Members of the House Housing Subcommittee, in particular, were upset with HUD Assistant Secretary Embry's attempt to force communities to spend 75 percent of their money to benefit the poor. Both the subcommittee's chairman, Thomas Ashley, and its ranking minority member, Garry Brown, believed that the proposed 75-25 rule violated the program's block grant spirit and its legislative requirements. Brown was particularly angry, and introduced the legislative review as an amendment on the floor of the House. "If they [HUD] do not like the way the law reads," he complained to his colleagues, "they change its effect by regula-

32. Rourke, *Bureaucracy, Politics, and Public Policy*, 65; see also Herbert Kaufman, *The Administrative Behavior of Federal Bureau Chiefs* (Washington, D.C., 1981).
33. For a discussion of legislative vetoes, see Louis Fisher, "A Political Context for Legislative Vetoes," *Political Science Quarterly*, XCIII (1978), 241–54.

tions and then administer it the way they think it should have been written."[34] HUD, Brown alleged, was among the worst offenders in abusing the discretion Congress granted.

The 1978 amendments required HUD to submit semiannually an agenda of proposed regulations to the House and Senate housing committees. Under this review process, either committee can express an intention to review any regulation during the first fifteen days of the session; HUD then is required to submit a copy of the regulation in its final form. Furthermore, HUD must submit every proposed regulation to the committees for their comment fifteen days before publication in the *Federal Register*. Both of these requirements give the committees a chance to head off any troublesome regulation before publication. In addition, no HUD regulation can take effect until twenty days after publication in the *Federal Register*. If neither committee voices an objection to the rule within the twenty-day period, the rule takes effect. If either committee objects, however, the regulation is delayed ninety days to allow Congress to act if it so desires.[35]

In the legislative review's first three years of existence, Congress used it only once. HUD had proposed insulation standards for housing construction that the masonry industry opposed on the grounds the rules would be too costly. The industry's lobbyists convinced a majority of members of the House Housing Subcommittee, which voted to oppose the rule on the eighteenth day. The resolution, however, was not delivered to the clerk of the House until after the twenty-day waiting period had expired, and HUD contended that the subcommittee had not met the terms of the legislative review. The federal court agreed, but the victory was short-lived. Congress later changed the law to uphold the masonry industry's position.

But even if the legislative review's formal procedures have been little used, they nevertheless have had important effects on the HUD administrators who write CD rules. The legislative review made it more difficult to put regulations in place because only days of contin-

34. *Congressional Record*, June 29, 1978, p. 19472.
35. For a description of the origin and features of this legislative review, see Grace Milgram, "Legislative Vetoes in Housing," report of the Congressional Research Service of the Library of Congress, October 22, 1979; printed in U.S. House of Representatives, Committee on Rules, Subcommittee on Rules of the House, *Studies on the Legislative Veto*, committee print, 96th Cong., 2nd sess., 1980, pp. 515–59.

uous legislative session count in the twenty-day period. As Grace Milgram of the Congressional Research Service points out, HUD's authorization acts tend to be adopted in the last days before congressional recess. Because the acts often alter legislative requirements and hence demand regulatory changes, HUD often finds itself with two choices. On the one hand, the department can hurriedly write new rules before Congress adjourns without giving the rules full study. On the other hand, it can wait until Congress comes back into session and risk criticism that it is dragging its feet in meeting congressional guidelines. Furthermore, the waiting periods make it impossible to propose any new regulation when Congress is in recess. Milgram concluded that "it seems difficult to see what has been accomplished by the review process other than a further ruffling of HUD's not-always smooth operation."[36]

The review process has also had a more subtle influence in strengthening the role of congressional committees and subcommittees in administrative rule making. The process gives the relevant committees extensive authority to review and comment upon regulations before HUD issues them. The very existence of the review, however, induced HUD officials to consult informally with the majority and minority staffs of the committees and subcommittees in the initial stages of drafting new regulations. Harsh Senate committee hearings and the legislative review forced HUD officials to scout out any possible opposition before issuing new rules. The congressional message was clear: the committees did not like the way HUD was administering the program; even though each committee had a different view of how that program ought to be run, each committee was determined to see that HUD followed its own guidance in writing rules. As one HUD official explained, "when we get clear signals against a regulation from either committee on the Hill, we will usually withdraw it before publishing it."[37]

The most important effect of the legislative review was thus the creation of an informal, hidden network for the drafting of regulations. To adopt a new rule, one HUD official noted, "You need waiv-

36. Milgram, "Legislative Vetoes in Housing," 523.
37. Interview with the author.

ers from both the majority and the minority members of both committees."[38] The waivers insure that no member of Congress important to the agency will oppose a new rule. In practice, this process requires HUD's staff to consult extensively with the majority and minority staffs of the House and Senate committees long in advance of formal publication of a proposed rule: What language should be used? What kind of projects should be eligible? How should HUD supervise the rule? Does the committee have any objection to this proposal? Members of the House and Senate committee staffs thus gained an early and authoritative entrée to HUD's decision making.

The congressional committees played a powerful role in setting HUD's agenda by the messages they sent through their hearings. In these hearings, the interest groups had a crucial role. They provided testimony with which the messages could be sent, and often their own investigations prompted committee concern in the first place. The interest groups' own messages were received by the committee staff members who then structured the hearings. The hearings provided a crucial path to HUD's regulatory agenda, and the legislative review provision built into the CD statute gave committee staff members important influence on how HUD eventually made its decisions. These factors only increased HUD's natural tendency toward reactive regulations directed in self-defense and against the worst case.

THE FEDERAL COURTS

Especially since the 1960s the federal courts have been an important and independent route for influencing administrative action. One student of federal grant litigation, George D. Brown, estimated that there are "hundreds—probably thousands—of federal court decisions concerning the award or administration of federal financial assistance."[39] More legal challenges were made during CD's first year, James A. Kushner discovered, than in the previous decade of urban renewal and other categorical programs.[40] Grant programs in gen-

38. Interview with the author.
39. George D. Brown, "The Courts and Grant Reform: A Time for Action," *Intergovernmental Perspective*, VII (Fall, 1981), 6.
40. James A. Kushner, "Litigation Strategies and Judicial Review under Title I of the Housing and Community Development Act of 1974," *Urban Law Annual*, XI (1976), 98.

eral—and CD in particular—invite controversy. They distribute large amounts of federal money through nonfederal agents. Particularly in block grant programs that leave recipients broad choice, there are large numbers of local proposals not funded for every project that receives support, and every loser is a potential litigant.

Access to the federal courts increased for complainants during the 1970s for three reasons.[41] First, federal courts recognized broader rules of standing in grant cases, a trend that ran against more restrictive standing in many other areas. Standing is, simply, the ability to bring suit. It depends on a plaintiff's demonstration of harm, evidence that the harm was caused by the defendant's conduct, and indication that the court's intervention can help redress that harm. The Supreme Court showed itself through the 1970s willing to entertain more liberal concepts of injury and redress, including requiring only that a favorable ruling be likely to benefit the plaintiff. More liberal concepts of standing have led to more suits being filed by more, disparate interests—and more decisions against federal agencies administering grant programs.

Second, the courts during the 1970s increasingly read grant statutes as granting an "implied right of action" to parties denied the benefits promised by the statute. The federal courts, furthermore, applied these benefits broadly. They included both the crosscutting rules that affected a grant program, such as rights of equal opportunity and of equal protection, and the requirements of individual programs, such as the promise of benefits for the poor. Third parties (from interest groups to neighborhood associations) who stood to benefit from these standards could sue grant recipients if they believed the recipients were not meeting the standards. On numerous occasions, the federal courts sided with the third parties and provided further access through the judicial system for those who disagreed with how state and local governments spent their money.

Finally, third parties challenging state and local grant decisions have relied on what have become known as "Section 1983 actions," after 42 U.S.C. 1983:

41. See Brown, "The Courts and Grant Reform," and Thomas J. Madden and Patrick R. Harkins, "New Block Grant Program Faces Period of Adjustment in the Courts," *National Law Journal*, IV (March 8, 1982), 29–31.

> Every person who, under color of any statute, ordinance, regulation, custom, or usage, of any state or territory, subjects, or causes to be subjected, any citizen of the United States or other person within the jurisdiction thereof to the deprivation of any rights, privileges, or immunities secured by the Constitution and laws, shall be liable to the party injured in an action at law, suit in equity or other proper proceeding for redress.

Some groups argued that Section 1983 covered federal grant programs, and in 1980 the Supreme Court in *Maine* v.*Thiboutot* agreed, holding that third parties are entitled to sue state and local governments that deny them intended benefits of a grant program.[42] Although subsequent decisions diluted the impact of *Thiboutot*, the federal courts nevertheless showed themselves willing to entertain complaints by groups alleging a denial of benefits promised either by a grant program or by attending crosscutting regulations.

No example is better than the *Hartford* case. The federal district court ruled that the city had standing because if it won the case it would be eligible to receive a share of the funds denied to the suburbs. The court also granted standing to two lower-income residents of Hartford who had argued on the "expected to reside" issue that they would be injured if the suburbs did not provide federally subsidized housing for the poor. The district court agreed with the plaintiffs, a decision that froze the suburb's CD grants and that forced HUD to assemble quickly a new data base on which to calculate the "expected to reside" information for *all* cities. That the federal circuit court later reversed the lower court's judgment only emphasizes the powerful role that courts can play in the administration of federal grants. A plaintiff does not have to defeat governmental agencies in court to win the case. Threats of litigation, many opportunities to sue, and the lengthy process of appeal force administrators to stand constantly on guard. A single court decision, even if in a lower court and even if later reversed, can force sweeping national changes in program administration.

The crosscutting regulations, especially the equal opportunity and affirmative active rules, provide more opportunities for litigating

---

42. 100 S.Ct 2502.

differences in court instead of settling them administratively. The civil rights laws suggest numerous avenues for raising questions of equal protection and discrimination.[43] Opponents of CD projects who believe they might create environmental problems, furthermore, can file suit to stop action on a project. A single citizen armed with the right data can stop a multi-million-dollar project.[44] Court injunctions can force grant recipients to take specified actions, prevent them from doing other things, and ultimately block the flow of federal money altogether.

The potential for judicial involvement in administrative decisions is enormous, and many disgruntled citizens have turned to the courts when their complaints to state and local officials went unsatisfied. The courts, moreover, have given interest groups influence over when and where the courts will intervene in the administrative process.[45] More liberal rules on standing have given interest groups the opportunity to pick the jurisdiction in which they will contest a policy and when that suit will be filed. The rules on standing have also substantially lowered costs of access to the system to the price of a good lawyer and the bill for constructing the case. If a plaintiff wins, the courts can force an issue onto the administrative agenda. And even if the plaintiff eventually loses, the mere threat of suit can force federal, state, and local administrators to exercise extra caution. The courts, for their part, have shown no reluctance to involve themselves in the minutiae of administrative decisions at all levels of government. Judicial actions have become a powerful force in shaping the administrative agenda and have tethered administrative discretion with the rope of judicial oversight. And much of that force has been shaped in turn by the increased influence of interest groups.

REGULATING COMMUNITY DEVELOPMENT

Congress, and especially congressional committees, played a crucial role in the increasing regulation of the CD program. Members of

43. Kushner, "Litigation Strategies," 51–58.
44. Ibid., 90–97. See also Bardach and Pugliaresi, "The Environmental Impact Statement."
45. See Karen Orren, "Standing to Sue: Interest Group Conflict in the Federal Courts," American Political Science Review, LXX (1976), 723–41.

Congress who had serious reservations about the Ford administration's approach used the hearings to publicize the interest groups' charges, and in doing so they sent messages about the preferred direction for the program. For the interest groups themselves, this congressional role meant increased influence. As policy became more fragmented, as administrative decisions became more detailed and technical, interest groups vested with skilled staffs enhanced their positions. It was less a case of massing their constituencies for a show of power than of marshaling evidence to prove their points. In the growing size and professionalism of congressional committee staffs, the interest groups' staffs found natural allies. The interest groups' information and the congressional committee staff's growing role nicely complemented each other, and together they became forces with which HUD's administrators had to deal.

At the same time, the federal courts became more receptive to the interest groups' contentions. Court challenges proved even more effective a route for forcing issues onto HUD's agenda. The department had little choice but to comply with a court order, and the specter of judicial action kept HUD's staff on guard. Regulations were drafted with an eye to eventual court challenge, but HUD's defenses were always weak. A single case in a single jurisdiction could breach the department's plans, and a defense that the case was not representative of national conditions was a weak defense.

HUD thus found itself under constant scrutiny. CD administrators were uncertain in advance of where problems would arise, and the program's weak information base offered few trustworthy clues about where the trouble spots were. Complaints about the program's administration came sometimes from unpredictable directions. In most cases, problems popped up in unsystematic ways—concern about housing assistance plans, eligibility requirements, equal opportunity regulations. These problems only increased the tendency toward reactive regulation. When problems arose, HUD naturally wrote rules to insure they did not recur. When a single city's housing assistance plan could be subjected to close congressional scrutiny, as was the case for one Michigan city before the Senate committee, or to court order, as was true in the *Hartford* case, HUD's regulations sought out the least common denominator: regulations to prohibit the worst case likely to occur.

In managing the CD program, HUD thus found its agenda largely shaped by outside forces. Because of the unpredictable way in which those forces acted, HUD's regulatory response was often haphazard as well. Regulations became more intrusive than they otherwise might have been because of HUD's instincts to protect the program. And as access for these outside forces increased, the pace of regulation escalated.

CHAPTER 7

UNCERTAIN BRIDES

THE PROBLEMS posed by reactive, escalating public sector regulations scarcely went unnoticed. Critics of the grant system complained about federal intrusion on state and local decisions and about the administrative morass that hundreds of different grant programs created. Still, only rarely did observers of American politics couple "regulatory reform" with "federalism." Regulation was, in the popular view, something imposed by the federal government on industries or individuals. The few attempts presidents made at regulatory reform left intergovernmental grants largely untouched. In fact, presidential efforts to reform private sector regulation did not begin until the 1970s and did not receive sustained attention until the Ford administration. First Gerald Ford and then Jimmy Carter attempted to increase presidential control over the way federal agencies wrote rules and the content of the rules themselves. The prime concern of both administrations was that many federal regulations imposed costs far in excess of their benefits, costs that included excessive federal control over private decisions and that increased financial burdens on a strapped economy.

Both Ford and Carter tried hard to force regulators to consider the benefits, costs, and cheaper alternatives for the rules they wrote. On November 27, 1974, Ford issued Executive Order 11821 requiring all federal agencies to review the inflationary impact of all proposed federal regulations. Two years later, he revised the order to require a full economic study of all proposed federal regulations that carried compliance costs of more than $100 million. To monitor the executive order, Ford also created the Council on Wage and Price Stability (CWPS) to review agency studies and to conduct its own analyses of selected rules. Although most of CWPS' studies dealt with private sector rules like airline deregulation and workplace safety, CWPS occasionally ventured into public sector rules, including requirements for day care programs and accessibility of public transit to the handicapped.

On March 23, 1978, Carter issued Executive Order 12044, which expanded on Ford's strategy. Carter created a semiannual calendar of proposed regulations to provide an early warning system for controversial proposals as well as to give some coherence to the rulemaking process. The executive order also pressed agencies to provide more advanced notice of proposed rules to allow greater opportunity for public comment, and required cabinet officials to review the regulations their agencies published to guarantee their consistency with agency policy. It launched major efforts to reduce duplicative regulations and to write rules in plain English. Finally, the executive order required agencies to conduct a "regulatory analysis" of the costs of proposed regulations and to consider alternative strategies that would achieve the same purpose more cheaply. Two organizations, a new Regulatory Analysis Review Group (RARG) and CWPS, were to supervise these guidelines. RARG would review the economic impact of about twenty rules per year, would press agencies to reconsider rules that seemed too costly for the results they produced, and would take its case to the president if it had no success with the agency.

These initiatives were important first steps in controlling the tide of regulation, but their effects on public sector rules were limited. They were directed principally against the "big ticket" private sector rules that had captured the headlines, such as standards for cotton dust and auto emissions. Few public sector rules had such large impact or such political salience. Because there was no real constituency for reform of the public sector rules, it was hard to press these issues onto the reform agenda. There were no good estimates of the cost federal rules imposed on state and local governments, and state and local governments had few incentives to measure them. The rules came as part of a package of federal assistance that few governments could afford to decline, and the federal government paid the cost of compliance with some of the rules anyway. The greater concern of most state and local officials lay with the steady flow of cash and not with its accompanying rules. Especially when compared with private industry's loud and continuous complaints about the federal government's rules, few persons—whether regulator or regulated—could muster much excitement about the promise of reform. Public sector rules consequently escaped sustained attention during the Ford and Carter administrations.

Ronald Reagan was the first American president to succeed in firmly establishing a public image of states and cities as regulated governments. In his first two years in office, Reagan made the reorganization of American federalism a top priority of his administration. He had little more success than his predecessors in creating broad public support for intergovernmental reform, but he did succeed in creating a new partnership between the federal government and the states and cities.

REAGAN'S NEW PARTNERSHIP

Reagan set recasting the intergovernmental system as an early and important goal of his administration. In his inaugural address, he announced his intention "to curb the size and influence of the Federal establishment and to demand recognition of the distinction between powers granted to the Federal Government and those reserved to the states or to the people."[1] He stressed the Tenth Amendment to the U.S. Constitution, the reserved powers clause that gives to state governments all powers not explicitly delegated to the federal government. Reagan, of course, was not the first president to suggest that

---

1. U.S. Office of the Federal Register, *Weekly Compilation of Presidential Documents*, XVII (January 26, 1981), 2.

the federal government had intruded excessively into state and local operations. In his 1971 State of the Union Address, Richard Nixon contended, "The time has now come in America to reverse the flow of power and resources from the States and communities to Washington, and start power and resources flowing back from Washington to the States and communities and, more important, to the people all across America."[2] But while Nixon succeeded in launching an era of new grant programs with more flexibility—notably general revenue sharing, CETA, and community development—he never reversed the flow of power from the states and cities to Washington. The new programs gave state and local governments much more leeway compared to the categorical programs they replaced, but these new programs also became the vehicles for carrying increasingly more demanding requirements into the nation's state houses and city halls. Furthermore, because these programs went to nearly all state and local governments, the breadth of federal regulatory involvement became greater.

Reagan came into office with a much more explicit agenda—budget cuts—and offered state and local governments an explicit *quid pro quo*—fewer regulations in return for less money and a swap in responsibilities. State and local officials quickly agreed to the first part of the deal. In the rising tide of Proposition 13 and Reaganism, many of them suspected the cuts would come anyway and they were eager to secure them on their own terms. Along the way, however, the promised trade never quite materialized. As the budget's red ink spread, the cuts in intergovernmental aid grew. Meanwhile, Congress proved not nearly as eager as the president to renounce federal controls over federal money.

As a result, the promise of less money but more freedom became even less money coupled with only a limited cut in federal rules. Federal expenditures for intergovernmental grants shrank from $94.8 billion in 1981 to $91.2 billion in 1982, and to a projected $81.4 billion in 1983.[3] This made state and local governments even more wary of the

2. U.S. Office of the Federal Register, *Weekly Compilation of Presidential Documents*, VII (January 25, 1971), 92.
3. U.S. Office of Management and Budget, *The Budget of the United States Gov-

swap in responsibilities Reagan proposed in 1982: state assumption of the Aid for Dependent Children (AFDC) welfare program for federal assumption of the quickly growing Medicaid program. State and local governments became uncertain brides in the marriage they had consummated. Along the way, they collected something old, something new, something borrowed, something blue.

SOMETHING OLD

Reagan continued the Ford and Carter approaches, but with a somewhat greater emphasis on public sector rules. OMB conducted a painstaking effort to identify, consolidate, and where possible eliminate the welter of crosscutting regulations. One rule that underwent particular scrutiny was OMB's circular A-95, a standard dating from the Great Society that required governments applying for federal aid to submit their applications to area-wide clearinghouses. Federal officials had discovered during the 1960s that intergovernmental grants sometimes duplicated existing services yet left other needs unmet. The clearinghouses studied each application, compared it with existing and planned services in the region, and reported to the federal government on whether the application fit the region's needs. Critics complained that A-95 rarely worked; it often became one more layer of red tape with which grant applicants had to comply, and federal officials seldom took the clearinghouse's studies seriously. As one OMB official said, the process "is detailed and descriptive and requires a lot of paperwork, with no distinction between important and unimportant subjects. It is so weighty that state and local governments were not able to get good comments in, and the federal government agencies were not paying that much attention."[4] OMB greatly simplified the requirements and gave state governments the primary responsibility for deciding how federal governments would be coordinated in metropolitan areas.

In the agencies, federal officials tried to streamline the administrative process and to roll back regulations from previous admin-

---

ernment, 1983, *Special Analysis H: Federal Aid to State and Local Governments* (Washington, D.C., 1982), 3.

4. Quoted by Douglas B. Feaver, "Another Great Society Milepost Falls," Washington *Post*, May 27, 1982, p. A25.

istrations. New political appointees in HUD criticized the Carter administration's management of the CD program: "Over the past few years, HUD has imposed additional administrative requirements which have tended to reduce the freedom of localities to decide which activities to fund and have increased administrative costs."[5] HUD announced early in 1981 a series of new policies to counter the Carter administration's requirements. The department said it would presume that information submitted by local governments was accurate in the absence of information to the contrary. It would grant waivers to nonstatutory regulations more often. Additionally, it revoked the explicit standards to which local governments previously had been held in providing benefits to the poor. HUD also made it far more difficult to impose extra conditions on grants.

Such attempts to streamline regulation are nothing new. Whereas for the first time rules affecting state and local governments gained a central place in presidential policy, simplifying rules and reducing costs through administrative means is part of an effort that began in earnest in the Ford administration and carried on through Carter's term. That brand of reform was attractive to previous administrations seeking leverage over federal spending—and over the federal officials who ran the programs. Equally old is the problem of marshaling support for administrative improvements. Such reforms are important but they do not naturally generate enthusiasm or create broad political support. While state and local governments welcome reduced restrictions, they care far more about the amount of funds sent by the federal government. But in the way that the Reagan administration pursued these reforms there was something new that changed the way public sector rules were written.

SOMETHING NEW

Reagan was determined to make regulatory reform a high priority on the national agenda. Just nine days after his inauguration he froze the effective date of 119 new regulations for three months. Three weeks later, he issued Executive Order 12291, which applied benefit-cost analysis to major rules. The order specified that:

5. U.S. Department of Housing and Urban Development, Community Planning and Development Notice 81-5, May 15, 1981.

Regulatory action shall not be undertaken unless the potential benefits to society for the regulation outweigh the potential costs to society;

Regulatory objectives shall be chosen to maximize the net benefits to society;

Among alternative approaches to any given regulatory objective, the alternative involving the least net cost to society shall be chosen; and

Agencies shall set regulatory priorities with the aim of maximizing the aggregate net benefits to society.[6]

The spirit of the benefit-cost approach had been at the heart of the Ford and Carter initiatives, but for the first time, Reagan made it mandatory for rules with an anticipated cost to the economy of $100 million or more. To enforce the order, the president named OMB to set guidelines for the analyses, to review the analyses, and to examine the regulations themselves. This was substantially different from the Ford and Carter approaches. In those two administrations, OMB, CWPS, and RARG became involved only after the publication of a proposed rule (and usually after the rule had already generated some political heat). Reagan gave OMB primacy in the rule-making process by requiring advance clearance of rules through OMB *before* their publication in the *Federal Register*.

The president also created a Task Force on Regulatory Relief chaired by Vice President George Bush and supported by OMB's staff. The task force was charged with identifying existing regulations for careful review and revision. By the end of 1981, the Bush task force had issued three lists of regulations for review, and for the first time public sector rules occupied a prominent place on the "hit lists." Of the one hundred regulations identified by the task force, twenty-five primarily affected state and local governments. These rules ranged from pre-treatment of sewage waste, access for the handicapped, and equal opportunity to community development, highway design, and environmental impact statements.

Strict benefit-cost analysis is always problematic, particularly for

---

6. 46 *Federal Register* 13193 (February 19, 1981).

many of the social regulations with which state and local governments must deal. How much is it worth to improve equal opportunity or to review the environmental impact of proposed projects? What is the value of insuring that a specified amount of a grant goes to the poor or that a federally funded project is accessible to the handicapped? Such analysis is fraught with technical difficulties, and the very burdens of preparing the analysis may not be cost-beneficial. Regulatory analysis, furthermore, does not often result in many regulations being sent back to the agencies. Of 2,715 regulations reviewed by OMB in 1981, 2,412 were found consistent with President Reagan's executive order, 78 were exempt, and 134 were found consistent with minor changes—more than 96 percent of the total. Only 91 rules were returned to or withdrawn by the agencies.[7]

The task force's attention also led to changes in existing rules. The Department of Education withdrew the Carter administration's regulations requiring bilingual education, an action estimated to save from $900 million to $2.95 billion in initial costs and from $70 to $155 million in recurring costs. Revised Department of Transportation rules removing the requirement that existing mass transit systems be made accessible to the handicapped saved, according to the task force, $1.7 billion in initial costs and $95 million per year thereafter.[8]

In fact, regulatory review proved less a technique to analyze the impact of rules than a device to slow the pace of regulation. The number of pages in the *Federal Register* fell 27.5 percent during 1981 while the number of rules dropped 16.5 percent, compared with 1980.[9] As one official of an urban interest group explained, Reagan's war on regulation created a new "regulatory aroma" in Washington.[10] By the end of 1981, there was indeed a new ethic that argued for eliminating regulations where possible, for not writing new rules whose costs exceed their benefits, and for not making needed regulations any more intrusive than necessary. It was the era, as one HUD

7. Presidential Task Force on Regulatory Relief, "Media Advisory," December 20, 1981.
8. *Ibid.*
9. Derived from Felicity Barringer, "Rulebook," Washington *Post*, January 18, 1982, p. A9.
10. Interview with the author.

official said, of "minimalist" regulations. Reagan's executive order greatly enhanced OMB's authority. "This is brute power," one OMB official said. "It gives the president or his surrogates the power to influence these off-budget or non-budget items that they never had before."[11] By requiring agencies to submit copies of proposed regulations to OMB before publishing them in the *Federal Register*, the executive order got OMB into the game early and enabled the agency to make its will known before the lines were drawn. In the first months of the Reagan administration, OMB tried to restrict the scope of regulations as much as possible. "There is a tremendous impetus from OMB not to put anything in the regulations that is not in the legislation," one official at the U.S. Conference of Mayors remarked.[12]

The stage for Reagan's attack on regulation had been set at the end of the Carter administration with the passage of the Paperwork Reduction Act of 1980 (PL 96-511). The act's charge seemed, as is the case with many management improvements, platitudinous and not very exciting: it required OMB to reduce the government-imposed paperwork by one-fourth before October 1, 1983. Few observers of governmental behavior could dispute that government-imposed paperwork was a heavy burden or that it should be reduced. And on the surface, the charge of reducing it by a quarter within three years seemed a job few agencies would desire. OMB, however, fought hard for the bill and for the responsibility of overseeing it for subtle yet important reasons. OMB's budget examiners had for years enjoyed leverage over departmental finances, but officials on the management side—the "M" in OMB—had great difficulty in gaining leverage over agency actions. The Paperwork Reduction Act provided that leverage. No governmental agency can function without paper: forms for prospective recipients of services to complete, reports to list the results of governments grants and contracts, accounts to certify compliance with federal regulations. Just as armies move on their stomachs, governments move on paper, and in gaining control over the amount of paper a federal agency could employ OMB gained crucial influence over federal operations.

11. Interview with the author.
12. Interview with the author.

The act gave primary responsibility for controlling paperwork to a new OMB Office of Information and Regulatory Affairs. The office prepared an annual Information Collection Budget that first counted and then allocated to federal agencies the work (measured in hours) that their forms could impose. This work in turn formed a natural base from which to supervise the implementation of Reagan's executive order. The office reviewed proposed regulations, before agencies published them, for compliance with the executive order and, more important, for their fit with the administration's insistence on "minimalist" regulations.

Both policies greatly strengthened OMB's hand in dealing with governmental regulations. More of OMB became involved earlier in the rule-making process. Instead of having to wait until the publication of a proposed regulation, as was the case during the Ford and Carter administrations, OMB's prepublication review gave the agency a chance to suggest changes before printed proposals in the *Federal Register* set the battle lines. OMB and White House officials had often previously found that once agencies published proposed regulations, political debate became so polarized over the suggested language that their influence was minimal. Furthermore, the executive order and the paperwork act gave OMB officials concrete authority. They could demand that the agencies make changes, and they could rely on the order and the act to back them up. This authority in turn gave even mid-level OMB officials instant access to top administrators, like assistant secretaries, with whom communication had often been scanty in the past. If nothing else, this increased responsibility improved morale in OMB's management branch. As one official explained, "This [administration] has been the most activist crowd in terms of getting results. It makes it exciting to work here."[13]

OMB's new role thus changed the context in which the executive branch made intergovernmental policy. Central review became stronger and the pace of regulation slowed. Some existing regulations were revised while new rules were subjected to the "minimalist" test. For state and local governments, some relief was immediate. OMB officials reported that the paperwork burden would be reduced

13. Interview with the author.

by one-fourth during fiscal year 1982.[14] In its first two years in office, the Reagan administration succeeded in creating something new in presidential oversight of intergovernmental regulation.

SOMETHING BORROWED

The central element of Reagan's initial strategy for loosening federal controls on state and local governments was the block grant: consolidation of several related programs into a single program to provide recipients with greater freedom in deciding how to spend the money. The idea was a relatively old one; block grants date from the Partnership for Health Act passed by Congress in 1966. With the passage of CETA and the community development program in the early 1970s, block grants became an important part of the intergovernmental grant system. With Reagan's proposal, however, a president for the first time explicitly linked greater flexibility for the grantees with cuts by the grantor. Reagan borrowed the block grant concept to help him on his path to budgetary retrenchment.

Reagan proposed in 1981 to consolidate eighty-five categorical grants (out of a total of about five hundred) into seven block grants. In the mammoth reconciliation bill that contained the disparate parts of Reagan's first year accomplishments, Congress created nine block grants that consolidated fifty-seven categorical programs and authorized $7.6 billion for the new programs in fiscal year 1982, a 25 percent cut from the previous year.[15] The new block grant programs were a varied lot: maternal and child health care; health services; alcohol, drug abuse, and mental health; primary care (becoming effective in fiscal 1983); social services; low-income energy assistance; community services; education; and the community development program for small cities.

But despite their variety, OMB set nine uniform requirements

14. U.S. Office of Management and Budget, *Information Collection Budget, Fiscal Year 1982* (Washington, D.C., 1981), 1.
15. As one sign of just how complicated the system and attempts to reform it are, sources differed on just how many grants Congress combined into the nine block grants. Most Reagan administration sources counted fifty-seven categorical programs, but the U.S. Advisory Commission on Intergovernmental Relations listed seventy-seven. (See David B. Walker *et al.*, "The First Ten Months: Grant-in-Aid, Regulatory, and Other Changes," *Intergovernmental Perspective*, VIII [Winter, 1982], 5–22.) I will use fifty-seven here.

that regulations for all of the programs were to meet. Each rule was first to be minimal, extending as little as possible past the legislation. Second, rules were to be free-standing and were not to require the voluminous supporting documents that some past regulations had. Third, rules were to require minimum paperwork; grant recipients could report their intended use and performance in whatever form they found most appropriate. Fourth, rules were to be without prescription; grant recipients could determine themselves how to comply with them. Fifth, rules were to be devoid of the cross references that in previous rules had sent state and local officials scurrying through volumes of crosscutting requirements. Sixth, rules were to have formal yet simple due process. Seventh, where cabinet secretaries had discretion, such as in grants to Indian tribes, that discretion was to be specified in the rules. Eighth, the rules were to clarify state, local, and federal roles. State auditing practices would prevail in financial management, for example, while OMB would waive its own management regulations. Finally, the rules were to be "silent in other respects to permit States to make their own interpretation of the statutes and administer the programs appropriate to their own needs."[16]

When the first regulations emerged for these new programs, they were brief as the administration had promised. Many were only one or two pages and few went beyond the text of the legislation that created them. OMB set a conscious course to keep the rules as lean as possible to make clear the administration's commitment to transfer power to state and local governments, and it relied on the executive order and the paperwork to make that commitment real. One Carter administration official noted that he detected "a passion of Federal officials to prove they will not interfere."[17] The new programs indisputably cut the volume of regulations attached to federal grants. They also put the states in the center of debate about federalism for the first time since the 1950s.

The changes actually wrought, however, proved in the end not very substantial. Two of the new block grants were in fact recon-

16. OMB, *Information Collection Budget*, 17.
17. John Herbers, "Block Grant Programs Assumed in Most States," New York *Times*, November 3, 1981, p. A14.

structions of old block grants. Four of the new programs continued only one previous categorical program and thus did not broaden any grant categories. In the other programs, Congress attached strings to insure that recipients spent the money in about the same way as they had in previous categorical programs. Among the restrictions were prohibitions on certain uses; requirements for states to match the federal contribution; maintenance of previous effort (that is, no cuts in programs previously receiving aid); and mandatory pass-through of aid from the states to local governments.[18] The new programs thus did not broaden state and local choices as their advocates had promised, and the conditions that remained left doubts that recipients could save enough in administrative costs to compensate for the budget cuts.

SOMETHING BLUE

The promise of less federal red tape proved irresistible to the nation's mayors and governors in 1981, but in the budget cuts they got more than they bargained for. "There was too much of a good thing this year," an analyst at the National Governors Association explained during Reagan's first year. "The governors are concerned that block grants will be linked too closely with budget cuts."[19] Many state and local officials feared that the new programs created too many responsibilities supported with too little money. They also worried that regulatory relief through block grants had become too closely tied with budget cuts. Biagio DiLieto, Mayor of New Haven, Connecticut, acknowledged, "Cities are partly responsible for not recognizing that they might lose the money"; but, he argued, "the federal government is responsible for creating the need [for the added services]. It has to live up to the expectation."[20] Reagan's budget, with its sharp cuts in federal aid, made plain that the president planned to lower substantially the old expectations.

Federal grants were naturally an inviting target for the budget cutters. As perhaps the largest area of controllable spending in an in-

18. Quoted *ibid.*
19. Interview with the author.
20. William L. Bulkeley, "Cities Fear 'New Federalism' Will Further Pinch Budgets Already Hit by Tighter Government Aid," *Wall Street Journal*, March 2, 1982, p. 50.

creasingly uncontrollable budget, federal aid reductions had a natural lure, and the promise of fewer strings traded for less money seemed a fair deal to the nation's mayors and governors. It quickly became evident, however, that it was far easier to cut dollars than rules. Dollars spent on programs are easy to find and can be decreased through the annual appropriations process. Regulations, however, are far more difficult to find and even harder to eliminate. Many rules have staunch defenders among interest groups and congressional committee members, and these factions are often far less willing to loosen a rule than is the president. The result was an imbalance between budget cutting and regulatory reform, leaving some observers wondering if the mayors and governors had been left holding the bag.

WHO CONTROLS THE DOWRY?

Most attempts to reform the intergovernmental system, and especially the complex network of intergovernmental regulations, have been piecemeal. Presidents since Richard Nixon have engaged in trench warfare to pare back the controls in a few areas by seeking to streamline some regulations and, more importantly, by combining existing programs into block grants promising state and local governments more flexibility. Results during the 1970s fell short of even these limited objectives as proposals ran into a buzzsaw of opposition on Capitol Hill and with the interest groups. Reformers who sought to eradicate apparently irrational rules found most of the requirements had strong political support that gave them a rationality all their own. Federal controls once set proved extraordinarily difficult to loosen. If there was to be a new partnership among the nation's federal, state, and local governments, deciding who controlled the dowry turned out to be a thorny problem.

Nowhere was this more true than in the regulations promulgated in 1981 to turn the small cities portion of the CD program back to the states. The same act that in 1974 created the CD program also established a competitively awarded grant for small communities not automatically entitled by formula to federal aid. (For the most part, these were communities with populations of less than 50,000.) HUD solicited applications from small cities, ranked them according to a complex rating formula, and awarded grants to the highest-ranked communities. The program accounted for only about one-fourth of the $4 billion appropriated for CD, and the average grant of $463,000 was only about one-tenth of the amount the typical entitlement community received. The small cities portion of the CD program, however, accounted for two-thirds of the 2,900 grants HUD made to local governments in fiscal year 1980.[21]

As part of the Reagan block grant reforms of 1981, Congress turned administration of the small cities program over to the states. The states were to be free to decide which communities received the money, how much they got, what they could use the money for, and to what review standards they would be held. HUD in late November, 1981, drew up brief rules for the program that fit OMB's nine block grant guidelines and promised to give "maximum feasible deference to the State's interpretation of the statutory requirements." The states could define just who "low- and moderate-income families"—the program's principal beneficiaries—were, and each recipient was required only to "maintain such recordkeeping requirements as the State shall deem appropriate." Performance reports were to be "in such form and contain such information . . . as the State shall deem appropriate," and HUD announced it would accept these reports "in the absence of independent evidence."[22] Faced with a decision of whether to list the crosscutting regulations and laws that applied to the program, OMB even insisted that the states could look them up themselves. OMB put heavy pressure on HUD to keep the regulations terse and to allow the states as much flexibility as possible.

The nation's governors understandably were enthusiastic about the program in its proposed form. The National Governor's Association announced its complete support and asked only "that the regulations be promulgated by the Department in their present form as quickly as possible."[23] The National League of Cities, whose mem-

---

21. U.S. Department of Housing and Urban Development, *Sixth Annual Community Development Block Grant Report* (Washington, D.C., 1981), 20–33.
22. 46 *Federal Register* 57256 (November 20, 1981).
23. Letter from Governors Christopher S. Bond and William F. Winter, January 19, 1982, HUD Docket File 81-940 on rules proposed November 20, 1981.

bers would be the most affected by the new rules, was considerably less happy. The lack of a specific definition of low- and moderate-income persons, NLC worried, would "undercut the primary objective of the Act," and the vagueness of the record-keeping language "provides no real guidance to states." NLC was most concerned that the broad language would open the path to subsequent findings that grant recipients had violated the program's goals, to disruptions as state and local governments struggled to change their practices, and to more regulations to spell out new standards.[24]

The public interest groups, however, were enraged by the proposed regulations. The Working Group for Community Development Reform found the rules "seriously defective" and complained about HUD's failure to specify who should benefit or how recipients would report their performance. "It is inconceivable," the Working Group said, "that HUD would permit States to choose themselves what to report on, given the fact that there is national legislation, with a national objective and specific eligible activities, as well as mandates in civil rights and environmental impact, among others."[25] The National Housing Law Project agreed, arguing to HUD that "your present interpretation fails utterly to carry out Congress' purposes and intent."[26]

Some members of Congress felt the same way, especially the members of the House Subcommittee on Housing and Community Development. The members and staff were unhappy with HUD both for the substance of the regulations, which they saw as too vague, and with the process by which HUD had written the rules. The legislative review the committee held over HUD's regulations, known as 7 (o) after the provision of the authorizing legislation, gave the subcommittee fifteen days to review any proposed regulation. HUD had delivered an early version of the rules to the subcommittee, but the department later made several changes in the rules before sending them simultaneously back to the subcommittee and to the *Federal*

---

24. Letter from Alan Beals, executive director, January 19, 1982, HUD Docket File 81-940 on rules proposed November 20, 1981.
25. Letter from Paul Bloyd, project director, January 19, 1982, HUD Docket File 81-940 on rules proposed November 20, 1981.
26. Letter from Frances E. Weiner, staff attorney, January 8, 1982, HUD Docket File 81-940 on rules proposed November 20, 1981.

Register for publication. The subcommittee staff telephoned HUD to complain that by not giving them another fifteen days to review the revised rules, HUD had violated the law. HUD's general counsel, John J. Knapp, fired back a letter to the subcommittee's staff director that contended he could "find no support for the position taken by your colleagues in the language of Section 7 (o) and even less in its intent." He concluded, "I can hardly think of anything that would be more discouraging and counterproductive" than the subcommittee's position.[27]

HUD meant to demonstrate its intention—and OMB's as well—to get the program moving swiftly with as few regulations as possible, but HUD's quick actions in violation of previously understood procedures angered the Democratic members of the subcommittee and of the full committee. Just a few days after receiving Knapp's letter, Fernand J. St. Germain (D-R.I.), chairman of the House Committee on Banking, Finance and Urban Affairs, and Henry B. Gonzalez (D-Tex.), chairman of the Housing Subcommittee, joined in scolding HUD Secretary Samuel R. Pierce, Jr. "We can only surmise that the Department intentionally violated Section 7 (o) procedures," they wrote, and they demanded assurance that HUD's procedures were "an aberration and will not be repeated in the future."[28]

To drive home the point, Gonzalez called a hearing of his subcommittee and lectured Knapp and HUD Assistant Secretary Stephen J. Bollinger. "I view these regulations," he said, "as an attempt to do by administrative fiat what the administration could not achieve through the legislative process." He continued:

> We are concerned that the regulations violate the intent of Congress, and that they have the likely result of making the small cities community development block grant program ineffective in reaching its purposes, subject to endless abuse, and reduce it to a general revenue sharing program. . . . Under this absence of guidelines, a partisan-minded Governor could literally turn the program into a slush fund to reward the loyal and punish the opposi-

---

27. Letter from John J. Knapp to Gerald R. McMurray, November 20, 1981.
28. Letter from Fernand J. St. Germain and Henry B. Gonzalez to Samuel R. Pierce, Jr., November 24, 1981.

tion. . . . If ever there were a more open invitation to fraud, waste, and abuse than this, I have not seen it.

. . . The lack of any meaningful program guidelines and the absence of any accounting standard simply means that this program will break down in administrative chaos.[29]

In addition to the procedural problem of 7 (o), the hearing concentrated on four complaints: that HUD did not define just who was low- and moderate-income, that the rules did not define the purpose or eligible use of the funds, and that HUD had set no uniform accounting standard. Most importantly, members of the subcommittee complained that HUD's pursuit of "maximum feasible deference" to state decisions meant, as Stanley N. Lundine (D-N.Y.) put it, "simply that the States can do anything they want."[30] Gonzalez concluded by threatening HUD with a resolution of disapproval unless HUD rewrote the rules.

Supported strongly by OMB, HUD refused to make any changes, but HUD Secretary Pierce suggested that HUD might alter the rules in response to public comments when the comment period on the rules closed in late January. As the period drew to a close, however, the subcommittee learned that HUD planned to finalize the rules as they stood. The subcommittee's staff prepared a resolution of disapproval in the knowledge that such a resolution would send the whole process back to the start—and that thousands of communities waiting for funds might be denied support until the next fiscal year. The subcommittee nevertheless stood firm in demonstrating its concern over the proposed rules.

A Republican member of the subcommittee eventually convinced HUD and OMB officials that not only was a congressional resolution of disapproval likely but that it would also receive bipartisan support. HUD agreed to a compromise that would emphasize the program's concentration on the needs of the poor and the elimination of slums and blight. The new rules defined low- and moderate-income persons

29. U.S. House of Representatives, Committee on Banking, Finance and Urban Affairs, Subcommittee on Housing and Community Development, *Community Development Block Grant—Small Cities Regulations*, hearing, 97th Cong., 1st sess., 1981, pp. 1–2.
30. *Ibid.*, 21.

by the previous standard of 80 percent of an area's median income, set basic standards for review and record keeping, and identified the applicable laws with which the states would have to comply.[31] The subcommittee had made its point that the Reagan administration needed to administer the program as Congress wanted it run, but the resulting regulations were little more detailed than the original ones to which the subcommittee objected. Indeed, if there was a winner in the dispute, it was OMB, which insisted that HUD write the rules to the administration's position instead of the subcommittee's wishes. OMB did not win all that it wanted, but the agency did succeed in winning most of its points and, more importantly, in forcing both HUD and members of Congress to acknowledge its new role in rule making.

The dispute highlighted the serious problems of attempting to pare back regulations through centralized control. Is OMB's staff adequate for the task? Will Congress go along? Will such minimalist rules withstand judicial scrutiny? And does a closely held process of central review create problems of fairness in the rule-making process?

OMB'S STAFF

OMB's new role did not spring full-blown from the first seeds planted by the Reagan administration. The Ford and Carter administrations had been deliberately maneuvering OMB into a stronger role in overseeing federal regulations, a role capped by the passage of the paperwork act. Reagan's executive order was only the next step in strengthening central management, although it was a stronger step toward mandatory benefit-cost analysis than his predecessors would likely have pursued. OMB's stronger role in turn made it more difficult to write regulations, itself undoubtedly a goal that all three administrations sought. For HUD, rule making meant first passing a proposed regulation through the appropriate program officers and legal officials and then around to each of the department's sections for review and comment. Obtaining internal clearance proved a lengthy process but only the first step. OMB reviewed proposed regulations for their impact on the federal paperwork burden, for their compli-

31. 47 *Federal Register* 15290 (April 8, 1982).

ance with the executive order if the regulation had large effects, and for their fit with the administration's block grant guidelines. Congressional committee staffs reviewed the rules as part of the 7 (o) procedures. It consequently was harder to get rules out, not only for HUD but for all federal agencies and departments that had to follow similar steps.

But particularly at OMB, finding adequate numbers of skilled staff to review regulations comprehensively was difficult. In the agency, the "M" side has traditionally been the weak sister of the "B" side, and the agency devoted only a small portion of its staff to regulatory review compared with the budget officials who examine departmental budgets. OMB could not launch its own views of which regulations made sense and which did not. Instead, it fell back to compiling "hit lists" by asking interest groups, industries, and state and local governments which regulations they would like to see simplified or eliminated. Occasionally, OMB could also take on an important rule like the small cities standard. There is nothing wrong, of course, in responding to the most salient problems. But without an independent ability to develop its own agenda, OMB risked missing chances for more comprehensive reforms.[32] Indeed, as we shall see later, there is a danger that such haphazard review may simply create a greased path for special interests at the expense of public participation.

Coupled with the problem of setting the agenda for review is the difficulty of marshaling the facts to conduct it. Because of its own limits, OMB must fall back upon information supplied by agencies. Thus, a strategy designed to strengthen central management and control may ironically make central managers more dependent upon those officials in the agencies they are trying to control. In an era of retrenchment, agencies have limited incentives to sharpen the sword with which they may be attacked, and even if they wanted to comply, they could find their analytical staffs depleted by budget cuts.[33] OMB can unquestionably have an enormous impact on the regulatory process, particularly in selected cases, but its capacity for continuous or

32. See George C. Eads, "White House Oversight of Executive Branch Regulation," in Eugene Bardach and Robert A. Kagan (eds.), *Social Regulation: Strategies for Reform* (San Francisco, 1982), 177–97.
33. *Ibid.*

comprehensive review is nonexistent. Even in the first year of Reagan's executive order, OMB had to let most new rules slip through to concentrate on a handful of regulations important to the administration. The agency might be able to pick off a few of the more politically odious rules, but numerous small rules are likely to sneak through.

CONGRESS

As the small cities' case demonstrated, different actors have different stakes in regulatory decisions. For Congress, and especially for congressional committees, the stakes lie in control of administrative discretion. The authorizing legislation for the state-administered small cities program was a typically vague congressional mandate. Congress, to be sure, vested substantially greater responsibility in state governments for the program's administration, but the goals and standards for the program looked much the same as previous laws. In the small cities rules, HUD ironically stirred up a hornet's nest by not elaborating upon the legislative language, an ironic development in an age filled with complaints about administrators exceeding their authority. Members of Congress cared less about how far agencies' interpretations of the law ranged from congressional intent (for that intent proved usually to be a dynamic and evolving concept) than that a mechanism existed for Congress and its committees to intervene selectively. As Congress proved in the small cities controversy, that mechanism exists through committee action.

Block grants, and especially the Reagan block grants, threatened that mechanism. Since the mid-1960s, these grants have had as a principal goal the decrease of federal administrative power and the increase of state and local authority. This in turn meant the diminution of congressional power, for it removed Congress several steps from the critical decisions about who benefits. Despite the attractiveness of grant programs that automatically entitled thousands of governments in every congressional district to federal aid, block grants proved inherently unstable instruments. Widespread and automatic distribution of money was important in developing a legislative coalition to pass the programs, but the promised transfer of authority threatened congressional power centers in the committees. The committee members, and more particularly their staffs, had spent years developing contacts in the agencies and honing strategies for occasional intervention in administrative decisions. Automatic grants weakened the power of federal administrators, but they at least retained some operating authority to review state and local performance. Reductions in federal oversight of state and local activities much more sharply reduced the power of congressional committees and their staffs, and this has made the block grant an inherently unstable instrument.

The Reagan block grants threatened congressional power even more because they made OMB into a key player. Executive branch agencies gained a new defense against congressional demands; they could argue that they might not like the regulations either, but that they had been forced into issuing them by OMB. Local governments discovered years ago that federal agencies learned to use that gambit themselves. OMB's intermittent involvement in regulations brought presidential attention to bubbling controversies and made it far more difficult for congressional committees to influence departmental decisions. Finally, OMB's interest in some regulatory questions helped to fragment the mutually supportive issue networks on which the professionals on congressional committees relied for their influence. High-level OMB involvement in intergovernmental regulation thus short-circuited existing patterns of power, and in doing so the agency weakened Congress' position in the policy-making system. It also diminished congressional enthusiasm for developing more power to state and local governments.

COURTS

Shortening federal regulations about how state and local governments could use intergovernmental aid did not end the questions about who benefits or what the money buys. Since most of the money went to the states but was likely to end up in the hands of local governments and nonprofit contractors, the states faced the task of creating their own regulatory machinery to obtain compliance, with both state goals and federal mandates, from those who finally spent the money. Furthermore, most of the crosscutting regulations remained. State and local officials still had to comply with regulations governing civil rights, environmental protection, and pay levels. The regulations accompanying the new grant programs typically said nothing about how state and local officials were to meet the rules. The result predictably was that the states adopted many different strategies.

Vague federal regulations and the different state interpretations that follow inevitably invite challenge in the federal courts. Where federal statutes impose conditions, state and local governments are bound to meet them regardless of how detailed federal regulations might be. Furthermore, third parties who believe that Congress intended them to benefit from a grant program and who contend that state governments have denied them those benefits can cite these implied rights in a federal suit. A federal "hands-off" attitude does not diminish the basic contractual relationship between the grantor and the grantee, nor does it eliminate an aggrieved party's right to sue.[34] Minimal regulations that promise maximum discretion for state governments thus ironically make program administration more difficult. Without federal rules that specify just what performance is required and how that performance is to be reported, the natural tendency is to keep extensive records in self-defense—just in case federal policy should change, citizens or federal administrators probe local actions, or the government face judicial challenge. The alternative is to risk being caught without needed information. Without knowing what will be needed, the choices are to collect more than is likely to be required or to take chances that no problems will arise. Either way, the costly result is administrative risk taking.

The problem lies in giving the states and cities broad new responsibilities while holding them to certain federal requirements and failing to spell out just what performance is expected. When rules are vague, an official at the U.S. Conference of Mayors wondered, "How do you avoid being slammed in an audit?"[35] If criticism mounts, how can a federal agency defend itself without some standards for performance and some system of measurement? Without answers to such questions, the trail is clear for judicial challenge. Judicial decisions,

---

34. Madden and Harkins, "New Block Grant Program Faces Period of Adjustment."
35. Interview with the author.

when they come, tend to come haphazardly. An agency may discover, as HUD did in the *Hartford* case, that it needs to tighten up its rules in one area; some parts of a program thus remain relatively unregulated while standards increase in other areas. The changes come not as a result of a policy decision but as a consequence of who files suit on which issues. Broad and simple regulations that govern complex programs issue engraved invitations for court challenges.

SUNSHINE

OMB's new role as overseer of regulations, even though exercised selectively, quickly created a new regulatory underground. As the process of drafting regulations became longer and more complicated, and as regulators needed to check with more interested parties before issuing the rules, the opportunities for unsupervised contact between administrative officials and lobbyists grew enormously. OMB decided early in the Reagan administration not to log conversations between its officials and representatives of interest groups.[36] Some observers worried that OMB's new authority and its willingness to keep such ex parte conversations confidential would take important policy decisions out of the sunshine and hide them from public view. "Now more than ever," wrote Washington lawyer William Warfield Ross, "it can be expected that the race will be to the swift, to the enterprising and those with access to the levers of power, not only in the Congress and the regulatory agencies, but also in the presidential office."[37] The concerns were two: for fairness, that some individuals might gain access to important decisions denied to others; and for openness, that some decisions might be made without those affected knowing about it.

Constitutional scholars, furthermore, worried about ex parte contacts between the White House and the agencies. Morton Rosenberg contends that Congress intended "to deny the President formalized, substantive control over administrative policymaking."[38] Thus, Ro-

---

36. See Kim Masters, "OMB Asserts Contacts Need Not Be Logged," *Legal Times of Washington*, June 22, 1981, p. 1.
37. William Warfield Ross, "New Rules for 'Major' Rulemaking: Living with Executive Order 12291," *National Law Journal*, III (April 27, 1981), p. 19.
38. Morton Rosenberg, "Beyond the Limits of Executive Power: Presidential Con-

senberg concludes, Reagan's executive order is unconstitutional. Although this argument is certainly open to contest (and indeed Justice Department lawyers examined it and dismissed it in preparing the order), ex parte contacts between the White House and executive branch agencies do raise serious constitutional questions. Can the president and his agents interpose themselves in an agency's exercise of congressionally delegated power? And what would Congress' reaction be if such contacts occurred in secret? Rosenberg contends that "such unrecorded and unreviewable communications threaten to deprive individuals of due process and to distort the APA's [Administrative Procedures Act's] provisions for judicial review and public participation."[39]

At the very least, the growing network of congressional vetoes and presidential review mechanisms creates an underground rulemaking process. Agency officials do not publish new regulations without sending the relevant congressional committees an advance copy, and Reagan's executive order requires agencies to supply OMB with a copy of all proposed rules before publication. Interest group officials, furthermore, keep in close touch with agency actions and know the general shape if not the exact language of pending standards. When problems surface, they often are resolved before publication of the rule in the *Federal Register*, and usually at the staff level. Thus, publication of a proposed rule, intended in the Administrative Procedure Act to be the first step toward development of a final rule, typically represents a compromise among the interested and well-connected parties. This was not true, of course, in the small cities regulations. A large part of the subcommittee's pique, though, arose precisely because HUD had violated the norm of advance notice.

AN UNSTABLE MARRIAGE

Reform of the regulatory process has become more difficult because more players have more stakes in rule making. In large part, the stakes lie in exclusive access to policy decisions out of the public

---

trol of Agency Rulemaking Under Executive Order 12,291," *Michigan Law Review*, LXXX (December, 1981), 195.
    39. *Ibid.*

view. The rule-making process has developed two tracks, one influential, dominated by professionals with ties to the issue at question, and hidden from public view; the other public, open, but far less important. This subterranean rule-making process enormously complicates the regulatory process and makes it far harder to untangle and devolve authority. Congressional committees have a vested interest in supervision of an agency's plans. Interest groups value their privileged access to the policy debate (and occasionally even to the drafting of regulations). OMB busily is trying to enhance presidential supervision of regulation as well. With so many players with an interest in influencing decisions in Washington, there is a natural constituency for re-centralizing programs like block grants that attempt to spin power off to the nation's state and local governments.

Few serious observers of federalism disagreed that the system needed overhaul in the 1980s, but the uncertain brides in the relationship—states, counties, and cities—increasingly feared that attempts at reform were born more out of political convenience than a desire to recast the partnership. Reform, furthermore, raised sticky questions about where responsibility for change ultimately rested. As one National Governors' Association staff member said of Reagan's initiative, "Regulatory reform to some extent passes the buck from where it really belongs. Most of these regulations have a statutory base."[40] Presidential reform efforts were thus a shot in the skirmish between the executive and legislative branches over who controlled domestic policy. Reforms that attempted to strengthen presidential control threatened congressional prerogatives, while block grants found themselves in the middle of continuing debates over national versus local and congressional versus executive power. Such measures proved inherently unstable and subjected state and local governments to unsettled winds of constant change.

40. Interview with the author.

CHAPTER 8
LOOSENING THE REGULATORY STRINGS

FEDERAL GRANTS to state and local governments have proved at least since the 1930s an attractive strategy for domestic programs. Interest groups that could not gain a voice in the nation's state houses and city halls could often be more persuasive in the halls of Congress. The federal venue thus provided a different route for influencing state and local politics and for providing the muscle of federal money to strengthen that influence. Federal grants, furthermore, provided an administrative mechanism for doing many things the federal government could not or would not do on its own. Building the interstate highway system or launching a war on poverty would have proved impossible—or at least extraordinarily difficult—if the federal government had tried to run the programs itself. For their part, state and local governments could pursue projects they might not otherwise have been able to afford, without having to worry about raising the cash. It proved a cozy marriage but only sharpened the basic problem: which piper calls the tune when one government raises the money and another spends it?

Efforts to solve this riddle have been cyclical.[1] Complaints about

---

1. Herbert Kaufman, "Administrative Decentralization and Political Power," *Public Administration Review*, XXIX (1969), 12.

excessive federal control tend to be followed by proposals to shift more power to state and local governments. Then, when problems arise in state and local administration—and problems inevitably arise when any organization tries to administer anything—demands for closer federal supervision and tighter federal control follow. New regulations chart federal goals more carefully. Critics in time view these growing controls as dangerous, and they demand more discretion for state and local governments. As one OMB official explained, the cycle moves on:

> As you free up controls, there is always an accretion of controls back on, prompted not only by federal officials but also by the states. The regulatory branch will get loaded and the branch will break. We chopped off a few of the limbs, but there is a natural tendency to put controls on, both by the grantees and by the grantor. The grantee likes an umbrella to hide behind, definitive guidance to protect the project managers in audits. And no one gives money away without putting a string on it. It's a law like Newton's law.[2]

Thus it has been with federal grant policy and thus will it ever be. These cycles, however, have not been simply repetitive. Three trends have crept into the cyclical flow of centralization and decentralization. First, as the size of government and the scope of its interests have grown, the pace of the cycles has quickened. Second, the cycles have, since the early 1970s, involved more players. The passage of general revenue sharing brought the states and all general purpose local governments into the grant arena. Any perturbations in the system consequently are felt more broadly than was the case even during the 1960s. Finally, the system has become more fundamentally regulatory. Program-based regulations arose to dictate the operation of individual programs while crosscutting rules exploded in number during the 1960s and 1970s.

The regulatory explosion during the 1970s has clear roots. State and local officials—and their Washington representatives—put a premium on formulas that guaranteed entitlements to aid and broad-

2. Interview with the author.

ened the distribution of money. Although they always favored reduced federal control, they cared more about the predictable flow of money than the package it came in. Guaranteed funding by formula removed the most useful federal control over the money—advance approval—and Washington political forces (interest groups, members of Congress, and federal administrators) fell back upon regulations to recapture influence they had lost to the formulas. Whether the question concerned which income groups received the benefit of federal money or how fast that money was spent, the regulatory process proved a ready route for Washington-based forces to influence decisions in cities around the country. The regulatory process proved as well to be attractive for piggybacking a wide range of goals, from civil rights to environmental review, onto the program's fundamental purposes.

Within the Washington community, those regulations emerged from information provided and agendas shaped by parties at interest. Stories of program abuse, true or not, proved impossible to ignore, especially when federal administrators had little reliable information to the contrary. Interest groups from the NAACP to the Sierra Club produced tales that caught congressional attention, and heavy pressure from the interest groups and congressional committees proved too heavy for HUD to ignore. An earlier era might have left the department with more options, but the CD program's guaranteed entitlements made the rule-making process its best, perhaps its only, card.

Even the supporters of federal aid agreed by the late 1970s that the expansion of federal control had imposed heavy costs. Some of the costs were financial, although most of the efforts to put a dollar figure to those costs produced wildly varying and in the end unreliable estimates. More serious was the erosion of state and local administrative flexibility and political autonomy. There certainly is a case for some federal regulation, but even the most loyal supporters of the programs agreed that the overall pace of public sector regulation had quickened to a dangerous gallop. The Reagan administration tried to pare back many of these rules, and in fact it succeeded in several cases. The administration, however, never developed a scheme for applying federal controls in those areas where continued federal involvement was inevitable.

The Reagan approach, in fact, was more antiregulatory than deregulatory, and it pointed out sharp changes in Washington politics. During the 1960s, the debate on federal aid was filled with discussions about how state and local governments—and especially state and local administrative officials—played the grants game with finesse. Grantsmen worked with federal grant administrators to create what the U.S. Advisory Commission on Intergovernmental Relations called a "vertical functional autocracy"—an alliance of federal, state, and local administrators who dominated decisions about which governments got funds for which purposes.[3] That autocracy, critics charged, seized power at the expense of citizens, elected officials, and groups with different interests.

The regulatory era that began in the 1960s and reached its peak in the 1970s, by contrast, marked the growth of horizontal power in Washington at the expense of vertical relationships among administrators, of Heclo's "issue networks" at the expense of the "vertical functional autocracy." The tales of increasing regulation of the CD program are remarkably bare of some of the key players: state and local elected officials and most of the important administrators' interest groups. Interest groups representing the poor, the environment, the disabled, or minorities provided the key information and dominated the agenda. This is not to say that officials and administrators from local governments were not heard. Officials from the U.S. Conference of Mayors and the National League of Cities regularly appeared before congressional committees. They kept in close touch with HUD administrators and their members filled HUD's files with comments on the regulations. They saved their powder, however, for the issues of most salience to them: reauthorization of the program and the level at which the federal government would fund it.

The grant-by-formula process left a broad range of Washington politicos—interest groups, congressional committee members and their staffs, federal administrators in the departments and in OMB—with the greatest voice over administrative issues. They used the dynamic rule-making process as a way of developing and using politi-

3. See U.S. Advisory Commission on Intergovernmental Relations, *Urban America in the Federal System* (Washington, D.C., 1969).

cal power, and they used that power to reach deeply into the decisions local officials made. Public sector regulation is thus far more than an administrative issue. It is an essentially political question, a question about who gains influence over decisions at different levels of the American federal system and where that influence lies.

Rule making in federal grant programs during the 1970s thus served a host of purposes. It provided a mechanism for federal administrative control once automatic entitlements robbed federal discretion over who received how much money. It provided a way for the burgeoning collection of issue networks to reclaim power from the coalition of administrators who had dominated the federal aid system, to shift power from a vertical coalition to a horizontal, Washington-based network. And it provided a dynamic system in which that network could extend its influence into the minutiae of decisions made around the country. Public sector regulation thus proved far more than an administrative device. It was a strategy for shifting political control.

The issue of public sector regulation boils down to two interlocking questions. First, what should the federal government do and what should it leave to the state and local governments? The New Deal, Great Society, and New Federalism all enormously expanded the federal government's role and the power of those who held sway at the federal level. For their part, state and local governments scarcely proved shrinking violets in lusting after federal cash. Some things might best be left to state and local governments, and some things the federal government might best handle. The key to unlocking the problem of regulation is to separate them.

Second, if we can establish a corral for federal activities, how can the federal government best administer them? Regulation might be appropriate for some problems, and different administrative approaches for other problems. Not every federal problem demands a regulatory answer, but every federal question is essentially a political one. Different administrative strategies advantage some political forces at the expense of others, just as grants-by-formula advantaged the players in Washington's regulation game. But there are administrative, as well as political, costs and benefits to alternative strategies, and seeking relief from regulatory burdens means weighing all of these issues in the dynamic balance of intergovernmental politics.

THE CASE FOR FEDERAL CONTROL

The federal government has always insisted on its supremacy, at least in limited areas, over state and local governments. That supremacy has played itself out, Arthur W. Macmahon observes, in two important roles: umpire of disputes over the allocation of intergovernmental power and guarantor of constitutional rights.[4] At the heart of the problem is delegation, both congressional delegation of administrative discretion to federal agencies and federal delegation, through administrative decentralization, of operating flexibility to state and local governments. Delegation in turn means the "creation of agents,"[5] and Congress, supported by the federal courts, has acted to arbitrate the distribution of power. The federal government, in both the judicial and legislative branches, has also sought to insure that its agents meet the increasingly expansive definitions of constitutional rights. By willingly enlisting in federal programs (even though they scarcely could afford not to), they subject themselves to federal review of basic principles.

At the most basic level, the federal government seeks to insure that recipients of its money adequately account for how they spend it. No grantor cherishes the prospect that a grantee might spend money for a project other than the one intended or that money might be spent corruptly as bribes. A grantor can legitimately expect a grantee to keep an honest set of books through which its use of the money could be traced. Even basic standards of accounting, however, have tremendous political importance, for the power to dictate how books must be kept gives the federal government tremendous leverage over and information about state and local activities. Indeed, financial requirements associated with the general revenue sharing

---

4. Arthur W. Macmahon, *Administering Federalism in a Democracy* (New York, 1972), 17.
5. Barry M. Mitnick, *The Political Economy of Regulation: Creating, Designing, and Removing Regulatory Forms* (New York, 1980), 327.

program led some local governments to conduct the first audits in their histories.

At a higher level, a grantor might legitimately expect to be assured that a project built with its money provides at least a basic level of service. The federal government could legitimately examine highways built in the interstate highway system to insure that they are strong enough to support cars and trucks, and that bridges carry their cargo to the other side. Houses rehabilitated with federal money ought to be fit to inhabit and sewage disposal systems ought to work. This much is easily granted. The job of surveying services, however, becomes much more difficult as a project's goals become mushier. A job training program ought to provide trainees with employable skills and day care centers ought to provide safe, stimulating environments for children left there by parents. But how to be sure a trained worker has employable skills, or that children at a center are well cared for? The job of evaluation is difficult although, as we shall see shortly, there are some strategies for tackling it. Even in the broadest of grant programs, the federal government has legitimately insisted that its grantees use its money productively.

Finally, a grantor can use its money as leverage to induce grantees to change some of their basic social or economic practices. The federal government has attached civil rights and environmental review strings, as well as many others, across all grant programs. As part of its umpire function, the federal government has insisted localities control pollution problems they might otherwise be inclined to pass on to other jurisdictions. As guarantor of basic rights, the federal government has intervened in state and local administrative practices that might be (and in fact often had been) used to discriminate against minorities. Similarly, the federal government has stipulated that a certain share of its money go to the poor (defined as the federal government chose) or that subsidized housing be located in specific areas.

This last point goes beyond basic financial and programmatic control. Indeed, regulations in this category have in the past usually attempted to substitute national political outcomes for those that would have occurred at the state or local level. Still, as supplier of the money the federal government retains the right to insist that recipients meet its standards. For their part, state and local governments have the right to refuse, but that refusal of course costs them dearly. By offering a choice that is in fact no choice, the federal government has extended its role deeply into state and local decisions.

MEASURING PERFORMANCE

Through public sector regulation, the federal government has come to insist on primacy over a broader range of state and local behavior. The federal government has sought not only to regulate basic financial accountability and the productivity of its money, but also how state and local governments conduct their programs. It has insisted on control over process in addition to—and sometimes instead of—control over substance. Federal rules specify the number and method of advertising public hearings instead of the nature of public input; the location of federally funded projects instead of who they benefit; the forms required in a grantee's application. American federalism has become a government by process,[6] intolerant of error. The sins of a few governments, or even of one, can become the basis for costly regulatory burdens imposed on all governments. Sometimes, in fact, the sins can be alleged by accusers unaware of the motives, commandments, or actions of the alleged sinner. Yet the emergence of a Washington-based network of issue specialists has led to increased emphasis on the details of policy, to an emphasis on process and attempts to dictate it through regulation.

Regulation is undoubtedly appropriate for minimum financial standards. Regulation can be useful as well for setting criteria for a project's basic efficacy, like the thickness of concrete on a highway or electrical standards for rehabilitated houses. Furthermore, regulations can prescribe fundamental economic and social goals like nondiscrimination and protection of environmental resources. Clear rules can set these goals firmly and unequivocally. And not only is regulation an appropriate strategy for these purposes; it is doubtful that the federal government would want, or that the disparate interests represented there would allow, the transfer of federal aid without these conditions.

---

6. See Lowi, *The End of Liberalism.*

Regulation furthermore sometimes serves more subtle purposes. In the dynamic, politically charged environment in which administrators write regulations, the rules themselves are both political trophies and communication devices. They signal who wins and who loses, and what behavior is expected of the regulated. At the same time, however, federal administrators, members of interest groups, and staffs of congressional committees have been frustrated by their inability to make states and cities dance at the end of the regulatory strings.

Some of this frustration has in turn led to federal efforts to regulate state and local governments' overall performance and to measure that performance by process standards. It is not a far step from dictating financial record keeping to regulating how the money can be used; from setting fundamental service levels to regulating where governments locate projects; from establishing minimum civil rights standards to regulating who should benefit from these projects. There is only a short conceptual jump from fixing basic standards to regulating performance, but with that jump comes fundamental administrative problems.

Federal efforts to regulate performance have usually led to process measures, and no process measure has proved more attractive to regulators than the rate at which grant recipients spend their money. Federal grants have often proved surprisingly difficult to spend. Pressman and Wildavsky examined a development program in Oakland that after four years had produced few jobs and no completed projects. Their conclusion was that implementing a federal program can prove extremely difficult, and even "technical details" can cause more delays than critics or supporters of a project can often predict.[7] The problem is not confined to federal grant programs. Even in the Defense Department, which has a procurement system second to none in the civilized world, delays in negotiating contracts have often led to spending shortfalls that have embarrassed presidential efforts to show American determination for a strong military.

In 1976, Congress created an emergency anti-recession public works program to pump $6 billion into the economy. Federal admin-

---

7. Pressman and Wildavsky, *Implementation*.

istrators at the Economic Development Administration obligated all of the money to local governments by the end of the fiscal year, a remarkable accomplishment in itself. Yet despite special federal requirements designed to force communities to get the money out quickly, local governments managed to spend only half of the money in the program's first year. The recession was over before most of the money was spent. In EDA's regular public works program, local governments had not spent two-thirds of fiscal 1978 money by January, 1980.[8] In 1976, a House subcommittee worried that nearly $2 billion of CD grants lay unspent.[9]

HUD administrators came to use spending rates as a proxy for program performance; the CD program's goals were vague and broad, and even if they had been more specific, HUD had not marshaled its field staff to examine local performance very closely. Federal administrators looked to the spending rates to identify state and local governments that lacked administrative expertise or political support for its projects. Members of Congress saw the spending rates as signals for programs whose authorizations could be cut (and this naturally made federal administrators all the more anxious to make sure the money got spent). At the very least, as some policy analysts have pointed out, spending rates can act as a thermometer, symptomatically suggesting the places where problems might exist.[10]

There were some very valid uses to which spending rate measures could be put. For anti-recession programs designed to pump money quickly into a sick economy, delays in spending meant both that the programs did not have their desired effect and in fact that they might put money into the economy as it was improving, only to fuel a new round of inflation. And in publicly funded projects, just as in privately funded projects from plant expansion to production of nuclear power plants, inflation drove up the costs of delayed projects. As Pat

8. Pat Choate, *As Time Goes By: The Costs and Consequences of Delay* (Washington, D.C., 1980), 4.
9. U.S. House of Representatives, Committee on Appropriations, Subcommittee on HUD—Independent Agencies, *Department of Housing and Urban Development—Independent Agencies, Appropriations for 1977*, Part 6, hearing, 94th Cong., 2nd sess., 1976, pp. 756–57.
10. John P. Blair, "Spending Rates as Evaluative Tools," *Evaluation Review*, V (1981), 712–19.

Choate contended, "The diversion of capital to finance the cost of delay—interest charges and replacement of inflation ravaged funds—is a major contributor to the rising levels of inflation and the loss of productivity in the U.S. economy."[11] But perhaps the most important reason why federal officials relied so heavily on spending rates was that they were easy to gather. Compared with the tough work of visiting and examining a community's performance, federal administrators could simply check how much of its entitlement it had spent.

Slow spending in the CD program resulted from several problems. HUD was slow in issuing its first regulations for the program, and communities had little time to plan their early projects. Furthermore, when HUD did begin the program, it initially kept with the Nixon administration's "new federalism" policy of minimal federal control. For local governments, many of whom were new to the community development game, this also meant minimal federal help and little technical assistance. Finally, some local governments undertook unusually ambitious projects like attempting to rebuild their decaying downtowns, projects that inevitably took a long time to plan and that often sputtered when problems developed. In these cases, spending rates were a casualty of the ambition that the CD program stimulated.

HUD adopted in 1977 more objective and explicit standards to induce local governments to spend their money more quickly. Regulations defined the spending rate as a measure of a community's "continuing capacity" to continue in the program. Sanctions for slow spending included warning letters, instructions to reprogram money into new activities, reducing the grant amount, and "conditioning" the grant with restrictions. HUD, for example, might approve a community's grant subject to revisions in the application or demonstration of progress that HUD's field officials deemed adequate. The unexpended funds continued to grow, however, to $6 billion by the end of fiscal year 1978, a level that the House Appropriations Committee viewed with alarm. In June, 1979, the committee noted its concern with the size of the unexpended balance and promised to "continue to monitor this situation carefully."[12]

---

11. Choate, *As Time Goes By*, v.
12. U.S. House of Representatives, Committee on Appropriations, *Department of*

The message was unmistakable, and HUD aggressively set out to increase the program's spending rate. HUD officials worried not only that the slow pace of spending signaled that communities were having major problems running the program but also that continued slow spending would lead Congress to reduce CD appropriations. They stepped up the pace of "conditioning," and by 1980 HUD had set 495 conditions for 247 grantees, nearly 40 percent of all entitlement communities. Half of the conditions stemmed from problems HUD had uncovered in reviewing the communities' applications (problems that ranged from eligibility of projects to preparation of the Housing Assistance Plan). The other conditions applied to communities that were not making adequate progress, in HUD's opinion, toward completing their projects.[13] The most famous case was Houston, which by July, 1979, had spent only $41 million of $97 million awarded to it since 1974. HUD threatened to cut Houston's grant by $3 million as a sanction, but the department's threat created a furor. Houston's representatives in Congress complained that the city was being treated unfairly and they vigorously protested the proposed reduction. Houston eventually agreed to make management changes to speed some projects along and HUD relented in its threat, but not before attracting national attention to the department's "use it or lose it" sanction.

That emphasis on spending money as an indicator of performance, the General Accounting Office worried, "creates the potential for ineffective and inappropriate use of such funds." Communities chose processes and projects designed to get the money out quickly, but that sometimes violated the program's standards. Some local governments drew down their grants and, in violation of federal guidelines, earned interest on the money. (The federal government does not like to have to borrow money itself so that state and local governments can earn interest, so it requires money be spent within a few days of receipt.) Other communities charged ineligible costs to the program or failed to engage in competitive bids.[14] Communities, furthermore, found they could spend money in some projects more quickly than in

---

Housing and Urban Development—Independent Agencies, Appropriations Bill, 1980, House Report 96-249, 96th Cong., 1st sess., June 7, 1979, p. 10.
    13. HUD, Sixth Annual Report, 93.
    14. U.S. Comptroller General, Analysis of Community Development Block Grant

others—in housing rehabilitation rather than downtown renewal, for example—and tended to shift their projects accordingly. HUD's pressure to spend money thus affected the very decisions it was trying to measure, and in some cases affected those decisions adversely.

Spending the money, furthermore, did not guarantee that the projects would work well. GAO discovered many housing rehabilitation projects that suffered from defects ranging from poor workmanship to payments to contractors for work not done well, or not done at all.[15] The problem of measuring quality through quantitative measures like money spent, of course, extends far past intergovernmental programs. The Defense establishment annually spends billions of dollars, yet soldiers in Vietnam suffered with guns that regularly jammed and the Carter administration's Iranian rescue mission failed because of helicopters that could not fly. Defense procurement has been plagued by planes with weak wings and anti-tank missiles that require a soldier to stand exposed to enemy fire as he guides the missile to its target.[16]

Attempts to gauge performance by measuring process ultimately contribute to the instability of block grants and the intergovernmental system. The control over process, accompanying the promise of more freedom for the states and cities, has ironically only encouraged regulation. Process measures are particularly nasty, for they not only dictate how state and local governments are to do what they are doing, but eventually they begin to drive the very choices they seek to measure. Instead of controlling the programs as the federal government desires, such regulations have only created new problems for which federal administrators must devise new regulations.

THE DECENTRALIZATION ALTERNATIVE

Stopgap reforms would certainly ease the regulatory burden that the federal government imposes on state and local governments. One

---

Program Drawdown Rates (Washington, D.C., August 20, 1980), Report CED-80-137, pp. 16, 13–14.

15. *Ibid.*, 15.

16. For example, see James M. Fallows, *National Defense* (New York, 1981); and James Canan, *War in Space* (New York, 1982).

promising candidate is a recasting of the categories of federal aid. With 90 percent of federal grant programs accounting for only 10 percent of the money, there are numerous opportunities for writing rules with small stakes and for imposing burdens with few compensating benefits. It is doubtful that the country needs sixteen air pollution programs or seventy different programs for elementary and secondary education.[17] One way to streamline the intergovernmental system is to combine such closely related categories into fewer programs. Another is to shift responsibility for some functions back to state and local governments altogether. Tampering with existing programs, of course, interferes with the existing patterns of power among Capitol Hill professionals, interest groups, and departmental administrators. Furthermore, the chronically weak condition of many state and local governments limits the number of functions they can perform. Still, sorting out the existing programs would help reduce the regulatory burden that they impose.

More fundamentally, the federal government needs better administrative mechanisms for reviewing state and local compliance with the rules that do exist, and for examining performance in ways that escape the process measure trap. If federal programs are to remain and if they are to carry federal goals—and federal programs will always have at least some basic federal goals—federal administrators must have some way of informing state and local officials about what is expected of them and of measuring how well they perform. As one HUD official put it, "Performance review has to become more important because that's all there is."[18]

Such programs live in a world of dilemmas. No program can be administered solely from a nation's capital, for each area of a country inevitably has special circumstances that require special treatment. Development programs must be tailored for the special needs of New York and Topeka and Tucson. But national policy must be uniform if it is to be truly national. Federal administrators must assure the citizens of New York and Topeka and Tucson of equal and fair treatment

17. U.S. Advisory Commission on Intergovernmental Relations, *A Catalog of Federal Grant-in-Aid Programs to State and Local Governments: Grants Funded FY 1978* (Washington, D.C., 1979).
18. Interview with the author.

(or the federal courts will instead). Federal administrators cannot deal with the problem by writing rules for every circumstance and every community; this only vastly multiplies the number of rules and subjects all state and local governments to rules intended for a few. Overly specific rules, furthermore, rob needed flexibility for fitting national goals to local conditions. On the other hand, rules so broad as to fit all conditions are so broad as to provide no guiding hand. Ultimately, no set of rules can adequately guide and measure performance.

The ageless alternative to centralization is decentralization, and in modern American federalism that means reliance more on not only states and cities but also the federal field administration. More than 90 percent of all federal employees work outside of the Washington area, and the accelerating pace of federal regulations has weakened their positions as much as it has robbed state and local governments' flexibility. Federal field officials are in a unique position in the intergovernmental system. They are representatives of the federal government and thus owe their loyalty ultimately to federal policy, but they are close enough to the action to observe it firsthand. By visiting the sites of federally funded projects they can directly measure and observe results. Do rehabilitated houses meet adequate standards? Do job training programs train, and do highways meet engineering minimums? Simply by engaging in more monitoring—firsthand observation of program results—federal field administrators could go a long way toward reducing the torrent of regulations produced by communications failures. Midway on the bridge between state and local governments and national policy makers in Washington, federal field officials can avoid reading tea leaves by long distance, tea leaves like spending rates or local governments' own reports on their progress.

This proposal is scarcely new, for decentralizing more responsibility to field offices is one part of the centralization-decentralization cycle that has traditionally run throughout American government.[19] The objections to it are familiar. The quality and competence of field administrators has been a constant source of concern for officials at headquarters (who of course believe themselves to be not so afflicted).

---

19. See James W. Fesler, *Area and Administration* (University, Ala., 1949).

Just as common is the suggestion that field administrators have little time to escape from paperwork at the office to go out in the field and perform their most important function: to judge firsthand the results of national policy.

One way out of this bind is to reduce application reviews and regulatory controls and to place more emphasis on firsthand reviews of performance. Less time spent by federal field officials reviewing paper leaves more time for monitoring of program results. Effective federal control ultimately requires careful supervision of those things the federal government judges to be important and selectively applying incentives to improve the performance of the slow or reluctant. Field officials are in the best position to do this without simultaneously imposing a universal regulatory burden.

A more serious impediment to stronger field administration and monitoring is government's continuing impetus toward reorganization. Reformers tend to see organizational structure as the culprit in most government problems. Decentralization is the usual prescription for troubled centralized systems, centralization for decentralized ones. The result, as HUD has demonstrated since its founding, is more often confusion than improvement. The department began in 1965 as the department of the nation's cities and initially most responsibility remained in the hands of field officials. Four years later, in 1969, a presidential policy memorandum directed all federal agencies to set up ten uniform regional offices. Secretary George Romney drew new regional boundaries and further decentralized the department's structure by creating the area offices. The new area offices took on the day-to-day operations of HUD's programs, while the regional offices were to evaluate and monitor the department's programs, provide technical support for the field offices, and allocate program funds. These changes were to give responsibility to those officials closest to the local programs, the area office directors. The CD program was to use this structure with the area offices making the key program decisions. Area offices could approve communities' applications (although disapprovals had to be sent to the regional offices), and decisions about which projects were eligible were left to area office review. Later, review of local governments' performance was to be a key area-office function.

It did not take long, however, for questions to arise about what individual regulations meant and for different answers to emerge from different area offices. At first a special headquarters group reviewed the problems and issued memoranda to the field designed to answer the questions, but later as attacks on the program became more severe and questions of interpretation became more complex, HUD resorted to guidance through the pages of the *Federal Register*. With increasing regulation came the steady erosion of power from the field offices and the gradual accretion of power in the Washington issue networks. The more questions of interpretation flowed to Washington, and the more regulations emerged in response, the more the power of the field offices shrank.

The reorganizations and regulations scrambled HUD's structure of authority. The rules removed much operating authority from the area offices while the regional offices' position degenerated into confusion between their actual and intended roles. The regional offices found the temptation irresistible to retrieve responsibility from the area offices. The central office in Washington, meanwhile, asserted a strong hand in resolving disputes and questions of interpretation. Decisions tended to percolate up out of the area offices, and to be resolved ultimately by regulation.

Strong field offices thus raise several problems. The stronger field offices become, the harder it is for the central office to keep control of a program. Furthermore, strong field offices often produce inconsistent interpretations of similar policies that invite national intervention. This, however, is a different way of putting the central problem of national policy. National policy does not require uniform interpretations of every question, but only on those questions requiring umpires and guarantees. Indeed, attempts to enforce even wider uniformity often rob state and local governments of the discretion that federal programs promised them.

This, however, is the heart of the problem. A galaxy of political forces has become powerful enough in Washington to reverse political decisions in the states and cities. The result has been a strong and growing obsession with federal control of administrative minutiae, of defining all problems as national and attempting to regulate them. This tendency has become a powerful centralizing force in American policy, a force promoted by congressional committees and interest groups and federal administrators because decentralization removes from their grasp the levers of power.

The biggest barrier to stronger performance monitoring and field administration is thus the powerful surge toward centralization. Increased national control through the regulatory process has only created new problems that in turn require more regulation. Regulations have focused administrative attention on the details of each program, on individual trees while the forest often is lost. Only ironically by renouncing the obsession with controlling administrative detail can federal control over those matters truly of national importance be strengthened.

THE CENTRALIZATION MAELSTROM

Reforming intergovernmental relations and the regulations that accompanied them, one OMB official told me, was like steering a supertanker. Once moving in a certain direction, regulations respond only slowly and sluggishly to attempts to change direction. Yet they can be turned if the pilot knows the direction in which he wants to go. It is the direction of intergovernmental relations that has so plagued federalism, and the pressures on the tiller have been conflicting. There has been through the history of the republic, and especially through Nixon's and Reagan's grant reforms, a powerful rhetoric advocating state and local autonomy. At the same time, there has been a growing tide toward a stronger federal role, even in decisions that once were the predominant province of state and local governments. The new federal interest began with the identification of certain programs as national objectives and grew into efforts to pursue a wide collection of social goals.

Most of the administrative confusion and political controversy surrounding federal grant programs since the 1930s has rested on the irresolvable dilemma of federal control and local discretion. Many programs became mired in disputes over which goals they should advance. Highway programs, critics charged, developed the suburbs at the expense of central cities while urban renewal, others complained, benefited developers at the expense of the poor. These struggles continued into the 1970s with many critics alleging that the new breed of federal grant programs systematically discriminated against the poor. The experience of the 1960s and 1970s, in particular, suggests that *who* makes intergovernmental decisions is far more important than what policy is alleged to be at the core of the decisions. The heavy reliance upon administrators during the 1960s, the delegation of substantial discretion to state and local governments during the 1970s, and the growing power of the issue networks affected intergovernmental programs far more than statements of presidential objectives or legislative intent. Who makes decisions dictates who wins and who loses, and often that determines the outcome of the programs themselves.

The pattern of public decisions from the 1930s through the 1970s was increasingly regulatory, and the decisions in growing numbers were made in Washington. Some public sector regulation is not only inevitable but also a necessity. The federal government has a continuing national interest in insuring that those who spend its money keep at least minimal standards. But attempting to regulate performance neither succeeded in guaranteeing that programs worked nor protected those basic federal goals. More effective federal control paradoxically can be achieved only by more decentralization, a decentralization in which federal field officials more closely monitor the results of federal programs.

Every recent effort to enhance decentralization, however, has foundered in the centralization maelstrom, the turbulent whirlpool of national politics that draws power to Washington. Most often that maelstrom is fed by the irresistible lure of federal grants and the assumption, based on old prejudices, that state and local governments have neither the administrative capacity nor the political will to serve their citizens on their own. There is little evidence, though, that state and local officials are any more venal than federal administrators or members of national interest groups. Furthermore, administrative capacity does not exist as an absolute. It is not a state of being so much as it is a process. Capacity cannot be instantly created; nor can it simply be argued not to exist. Rather, it must be developed, and it can only be developed in an atmosphere of trust. The climate of regulatory federalism has not only steadily drawn power to Washington but it has also robbed from state and local officials the opportunity to develop their own capacity to perform some functions. Fear of state and local capacity has thus become a self-fulfilling prophecy.

Cracking the regulatory veneer of American federalism depends ultimately on halting the incessant tendency toward pulling all decisions of import to Washington. Stopping that tendency, of course, would do great damage to a generation of vested power and subtle folkways that have grown up in the capital. It also requires greater acceptance than Washington officials usually show for the wide variety of decisions that state and local officials will make if left more to chart their own courses. But within these problems are buried lasting principles. American government is dedicated to the concept of federalism and is administratively constrained by the impossibility of running all programs from Washington. At the same time, American government holds at least some goals as indisputably national. Two decades of growing public section regulation has demonstrated that attempting to regulate state and local decisions from the capital only makes those goals that are truly national more difficult to identify and to achieve.

In the end, we will have to bring our goals back within our reach, to limit our search for national goals to those goals we can reasonably achieve. To do otherwise means we may create more problems than we solve. It is naturally this question of goals, though, that is the most intractable. David B. Truman argued with prescience in 1940, "The problems of centralization-decentralization . . . are a result of the dynamic forces of a changing society and are among those problems for which a final solution has never been found."[20] Nor is any solution likely ever to be found, for the forces at work are strong and conflicting. We can, however, hope for temporary accommodations that achieve at least a short-term balance between fundamentally irreconcilable objectives. This balancing depends ultimately on the problem of accountability—whose values will prevail, through which methods. The nature of this balance speaks volumes about national goals and about who controls the central strategy of national domestic policy.

20. David B. Truman, *Administrative Decentralization* (Chicago, 1940), 204–205.

EPILOGUE
RIDING THE TROJAN HORSE

RONALD REAGAN'S AMBITIOUS 1981 new federalism demonstrated the enormous difficulty of loosening the regulatory strings. Despite the highly principled rhetoric of Reagan's plan to return power to state and local governments, its real objective was to help the "true fiscal math of the Reagan Revolution" add up, as David Stockman put it.[1] The promise of fewer federal constraints proved in reality a Trojan horse within which to disguise budget cuts. In limited measure, the administration's deregulation program did in fact untie some procedural snags, although this only worsened many of the knottiest administrative problems of intergovernmental regulation. Meanwhile, though, the sweeping reach of these mandates stretched unabated into new areas, worsened by the lack of money to enforce or pay for them. The result was an intergovernmental system even more entangled in regulation and the problems that accompany it.

REGULATION OF PERFORMANCE

On the surface, the pace of regulation seemed to slow during the Reagan years. In the CD program, for example, Congress simplified

---

1. David Stockman, *The Triumph of Politics* (New York: Harper and Row, 1986), 215.

the detailed application form and eliminated most citizen participation requirements. At the same time, HUD lowered its expectation that local governments concentrate benefits on the poor and allowed recipients maximal discretion in using the money. Furthermore, HUD officials simply accepted the information on performance reports submitted by local governments, despite a record of suspect information in the program's early years. When a local group complained to HUD about the way a community spent its money, HUD just forwarded the complaints to the community for response, did nothing to follow up, and simply mailed back to the complainants any response received from the community. Stuart Sloame, HUD's assistant secretary for community planning and development, explained: "Our primary focus is on technical assistance to the cities, to disseminate the money as Congress intended, to benefit low- and moderate-income people. It's a positive approach"—compared with what he called the "gotcha policeman technique" of the earlier years.[2] But without rules forcing communities to concentrate their money on the poor, one neighborhood representative argued, they could "kiss community development goodbye" in hundreds of neighborhoods around the country.[3] One official in Chicago was more blunt, charging that "CDBG is the mayor's cookie jar."

With Reagan's new federalism, it was impossible to tell how the money was being spent, since HUD abandoned close supervision of performance as part of the political price for budget cuts in the CD program. As a result, CD program expert Paul R. Dommel concluded, "No one is currently accountable for the way the program works."[4] Similar problems accompanied the new block grants enacted in 1981. They left both the form and the content of reports to the discretion of state and local governments. A U.S. General Accounting Office report worried that little common data would be available to discover the results the grants produced. It was unlikely, GAO concluded, that

2. Neal R. Peirce and Robert Guskind, "Reagan Budget Cutters Eye Community Block Grant Program on Its 10th Birthday," *National Journal* 17 (January 5, 1985), 14.
3. U.S. House of Representatives, Committee on Banking, Finance, and Urban Affairs, *Effects of Budget Cuts and Deregulation on Low- and Moderate-Income Groups in Cities*, hearings, 97th Cong., 2nd sess., 1982, p. 32.
4. Peirce and Guskind, "Reagan Budget Cutters," 16, 13.

there would be any authoritative source of national information about grantees' performance.[5]

In the new block grant programs, and in the Reagan administration's implementation of old ones, the link between federal aid and federal regulation was broken. More federal programs allowed state and local governments to write their own rules, and the administration was less vigorous in enforcing those rules remaining on the books. HUD, now aloof about most substantive details, concentrated on insuring procedural flexibility. As Garland Yates, an official from the Center for Community Change, put it, cities interpreted the new CD rules to mean "you can spend the money any way you want to."[6]

Budget cutting had submerged all other issues, and the deregulation of federal aid was but a tactical move in the administration's larger domestic-policy strategy. But in uncoupling federal rules from federal aid and reducing its supervision, the federal government lost important leverage over state and local performance as well as the ability to measure what these governments were doing with the money. Deregulation thus did not end the most difficult administrative problems of earlier grant programs, the tasks of producing good information and promoting good performance.

CHANGING FORMS OF REGULATION

The growth of other intergovernmental regulations further complicated the regulatory puzzle. In addition to the crosscutting and program-based regulations discussed in Chapter 1, two other forms of federal intergovernmental regulation grew in prominence. One is the crossover sanction, which threatens the reduction or termination of aid in one program unless the requirements of another program are met. This has been the federal government's principal weapon in enforcing the uniform 55-mile-per-hour speed limit. While it has no power to set a speed limit for the states, the federal government could—and did—make setting the speed limit at 55 a condition for receiving federal highway aid. Such crossover sanctions have been in

---

5. U.S. Comptroller General, *Lessons Learned from Past Block Grants: Implications for Congressional Oversight* (Washington, D.C., September 23, 1982), Report IPE-82-8, p. 73.
6. Peirce and Guskind, "Reagan Budget Cutters," 13.

effect since 1965, when the federal government (through the Highway Beautification Act) threatened to withhold 10 percent of a state's highway construction funds if it did not comply with new federal billboard requirements.[7]

The other form of regulation is partial preemption, in which the federal government sets national standards preempting state and local ones but delegates administration of the standards to state and local governments if they adopt similar guidelines. The premier example of this mechanism is the Clean Water Act of 1965, which established what one analyst called the "if-then" approach: if a state does not write rules conforming to federal standards, then the federal agency will do so instead; and if a state does not enforce these regulations, then the federal government will assume jurisdiction instead. Since 1965, the Clean Water Act has grown into probably the most expensive of federal mandates.[8]

The burdens of these regulations have weighed heavier on localities as federal aid has shrunk. In mid-1986, for example, officials in St. George, Utah, worried that they might face fines of up to $25,000 per day for failing to meet clean water standards. The city was building a new sewage treatment plant; city officials hoped to receive a grant from the federal Environmental Protection Agency to fund 75 percent of the plant's $13 million cost, and spent $100,000 trying to qualify. The Reagan administration, however, was attempting to eliminate the grants. "We've been chasing after EPA dollars for years," said Larry Bulloch, St. George's public works director. "It's like a carrot on a string; we just never catch up with it."[9]

Congress has scarcely become less eager to impose new regulations as federal aid has grown tighter, and the federal courts have not restrained the increasing regulatory burden. The courts have often spoken with widely different voices, and the Supreme Court's occasional pronouncements on intergovernmental issues have, for the most part, passively allowed regulations imposed by the legislative and executive branches to grow. The Advisory Commission on Inter-

---

7. U.S. Advisory Commission on Intergovernmental Relations, *Regulatory Federalism: Policy, Process, Impact and Reform* (Washington, D.C., 1984), 9.
8. Ibid., 9, 253.
9. W. John Moore, "Mandates Without Money," *National Journal* 18 (October 4, 1986), 2366.

governmental Relations contends that "the Court has been a cautious institution," choosing to adhere to precedents established long ago when grants were relatively few and their conditions relatively slight.[10] The result has been a tacit judicial endorsement of expanding federal regulatory activity at the expense of state and local discretion.

UNCOUPLING MONEY AND MANDATES

As federal money has become tighter, federal regulations have become ever more attractive as policy instruments. "The booming message coming out of the mandate field right now is the widespread fear on the part of state and local policy makers that Congress will now try to do with mandates what in the old days it did with grants, and force states to carry out national priorities," noted ACIR expert John Shannon.[11] The uncoupling of federal regulations and federal aid—new mandates with no aid, old mandates with less support—is the most striking aspect of intergovernmental regulation in the 1980s. Federal grants were the lures that brought state and local governments into the federal government's tent and helped blur the lines, political and administrative, separating the levels of government. With the precedent for federal regulation thus established, it is the residue that remains as the money diminishes.

The federal government has used intergovernmental regulation also as a strategy for solving its fiscal problems. In 1986, for example, Congress mandated Medicare coverage for all state and local employees hired after April 1, 1986. The law allows the federal government to collect an extra $500 million over three years to help shore up the Medicare trust fund and adds an extra $250 million to state and local costs. At the same time, Congress was considering similar proposals for bringing all remaining state and local employees into Medicare, which would have cost at least twelve times as much, and into Social Security as well.[12]

Thus, the principal issues of domestic politics have found their way into the intergovernmental debate. Federalism has become part of nearly every facet of domestic American politics, and vice versa.

10. ACIR, *Regulatory Federalism*, 251.
11. Moore, "Mandates Without Money," 2368.
12. Ibid.

(Indeed, state and local governments have moved increasingly into international affairs as well. The states, especially California, have been ahead of the federal government in taking punitive action against apartheid in South Africa, and few states have failed to develop economic foreign policies of their own.) The fiscal, administrative, and political connections have become inescapably intertwined.

The challenges are great. The transfer of responsibilities without accompanying resources has created fiscal problems that are especially difficult for the many local governments that are struggling under the substantial costs of meeting federal mandates. There is deep irony in this reverse redistribution, for many federal programs originally were created to channel federal aid to the governments in greatest financial need. Some of the challenges are administrative: With the deregulation that accompanied many of Reagan's block grants, state and local officials became responsible for achieving federal goals with far less federal supervision. At the same time, they became responsible for pursuing a wide range of other goals attached to federal aid. The situation provides a golden opportunity to discover just how much state and local administrative capacity has grown since the beginning of LBJ's Great Society in 1964.

Perhaps the biggest challenge of all is political: Although the uncoupling of aid and regulations has diminished the federal government's role as senior partner in the intergovernmental system, its regulatory role keeps it in a place of prominence as the agenda-setter, and the federal courts sit as final arbiter of intergovernmental disputes. But, as the federal government lost the leverage it had exercised through the aid process, state and local governments won more maneuvering room in meeting the terms of federal rules, and the growing political and administrative muscle of state and local governments has made them into stronger powers.

The federal courts, Congress, and federal agencies will, of course, have much to say about the variations that will inevitably result from these changes. Indeed, these variations, with perhaps, in time, even a stronger federal fisc, may lead to a reassertion of the federal role. In the interim, though, the regulatory aspect of federalism has taken center stage. The leveling off of federal aid has substantially changed the game, but the sweeping implications of the regulation of American federalism remain.

APPENDIX

CROSSCUTTING REGULATIONS

SOCIOECONOMIC POLICY REQUIREMENTS	AGENCY CHARGED WITH RULE MAKING
A. Nondiscrimination	
NONCONSTRUCTION ACTIVITIES	
1. Civil Rights Act of 1964, Title VI (race, color or national origin), 42 U.S.C. 2000d et seq. E.O. 11764 gives the attorney general responsibility for effective implementation.	Justice
2. Age Discrimination Act of 1975 (42 U.S.C. 6101).	HEW
3. Title IX of the Education Act Amendments of 1972, as amended by P.L. 93-568, 88 Stat. 1855 (20 U.S.C. 1681 et seq.).	HEW
Housing	
4. Title VIII of the Civil Rights Act of 1968, P.L. 90-284, 82 Stat. 73 (18 U.S.C. 245).	HUD
Handicapped	
5. Sec. 504 of the Rehabilitation Act of 1973, P.L. 93-112, and Rehabilitation Amendments of 1974, P.L. 93-516; E.O. 11914 delegates coordination to HEW.	HEW

SOURCE: U.S. Office of Management and Budget, *Managing Federal Assistance in the 1980's* (Washington, D.C.: U.S. Government Printing Office, 1980), pp. 20–26.

6. Architectural Barriers Act of 1968, as amended, P.L. 90-480 (42 U.S.C. 4151 et seq.). — ATBCB*

Alcoholics

7. Comprehensive Alcohol Abuse and Alcoholism Prevention, Treatment, and Rehabilitation Act of 1970, P.L. 91-616 (42 U.S.C. 4581). — HEW

Drug Abusers

8. Drug Abuse Office and Treatment Act of 1972, P.L. 92-225, as amended (21 U.S.C. 1174). — HEW

CONSTRUCTION ACTIVITIES

9. E.O. 11246, September 24, 1965, Part III (race, color, creed or national origin). — Labor

B. Environmental Protection

10. National Environmental Policy Act of 1969, as amended, P.L. 91-190 (42 U.S.C. 4321 et seq.). — CEQ
11. Sec. 508 of the Federal Water Pollution Control Act Amendments of 1972 (Clean Water Act), P.L. 92-500 (33 U.S.C. 1251 et seq.). E.O. 11738, 9/12/73, provides for administration of act with respect to contracts, grants, or loans. — EPA
12. Title XIV, Public Health Service Act, as amended by Sec. 1424(e) of the Safe Drinking Water Act of 1974, P.L. 93-523 (42 U.S.C. 300f to J10). — EPA
13. Conformity of Federal Activities with State implementation plans under the Clean Air Act Amendments of 1977, Title I, Sec. 129(b). — EPA
14. Sec. 306 of Clean Air Act, as amended by the Clean Air Amendments of 1970, P.L. 91-604, 84 Stat. 1707. — EPA
15. Endangered Species Act of 1973, P.L. 93-205 (16 U.S.C. 1531 et seq.), as amended by P.L. 95-632. — Interior
16. Floodplain Management, Executive Order 11988, May 24, 1977. — Water Resources Council
17. Protection of Wetlands, Executive Order 11990, May 24, 1977. — Water Resources Council
18. National Flood Insurance Act of 1968, as amended by Flood Disaster Protection Act of 1973, P.L. 93-234, Sec. 102 and 202. — HUD

*Architectural and Transportation Barriers Compliance Board

APPENDIX / 183

19. Fish and Wildlife Coordination Act of 1934 (16 U.S.C. 661 et seq.). — Interior
20. Sec. 106 of the National Historical Preservation Act of 1966, P.L. 89-665, as amended (16 U.S.C. 470), 84 Stat. 204 (1970), 87 Stat. 139 (1973), 90 Stat. 1320 (1976), 92 Stat. 3467 (1978). — Adv. Council Hist. Pres.
21. Procedures for the Protection of Historic and Cultural Properties (36 CFR 800). — Adv. Council Hist. Pres.
22. E.O. 11593, May 31, 1971, Protection and Enhancement of the Cultural Environment (36 FR 8921, 16 U.S.C. 470). — Adv. Council Hist. Pres.
23. Wild and Scenic Rivers Act of 1968, P.L. 90-542, as amended (16 U.S.C. 1271 et seq.). — Interior
24. Secs. 307(c) and (d) of the Coastal Zone Management Act of 1972, as amended (16 U.S.C. 1451 et seq.). — Commerce

Construction Activities (Grantee Contracts)

25. Archaeological and Historic Preservation Act, May 24, 1974, P.L. 93-291 (16 U.S.C. 469a–469a-2). — Interior

C. Protection and Advancement of Economy
  26. Cargo Preference Act of 1954, 68 Stat. 832. — Commerce
  27. Use of U.S. Flag Air Carriers, International Air Transportation Fair Competitive Practices Act of 1974, P.L. 93-623 (49 U.S.C. 1517). — GSA
  28. Placement of Procurement and Facilities in Labor Surplus Areas, 32 A CFR Part 134. — DOD/GSA

D. Health, Welfare, and Safety
  29. Protection of Human Subjects of Biomedical and Behavioral Research, Sec. 474, National Research Act, P.L. 93-348 (42 U.S.C. 289-3) as implemented by 45 CFR 46. — HEW
  30. Lead-Based Paint Poisoning Prohibition (42 U.S.C. 4831(b)). — HUD
  31. Animal Welfare Act of 1966 (7 U.S.C. 2131-2147). — USDA

E. Minority Participation
  32. Indian Self-Determination and Education Assistance, Sec. 7(g), P.L. 93-638, January 4, 1975, 25 U.S.C. 450e(b). — None assigned

33. E.O. 12138 of May 18, 1979, creating a National Women's Business Enterprise Policy and Prescribing Arrangements for Developing, Coordinating, and Implementing a National Program for Women's Business Enterprise. — ICWB*

F. Labor Standards
   Grantee Contracts only
   34. Davis-Bacon Act, 40 U.S.C. 276a–276a-7 and 27 CFR Pt. 1, 46 Stat. 1494, Appendix A. — Labor
   35. Anti-Kickback (Copeland) Act (18 U.S.C. 874; 40 U.S.C. 276c). — Labor
   36. Contract Work Hours and Safety Standards Act (40 U.S.C. 327–332). — Labor

ADMINISTRATIVE AND FISCAL POLICY REQUIREMENTS

A. Public Employee Standards
   37. Intergovernmental Personnel Act of 1970, as amended by Title VI, Sec. 602, Civil Service Reform Act, P.L. 95-454 (42 U.S.C. 4728–4763). — OPM
   38. The Hatch Act (5 U.S.C. 1501–1508). — OPM

B. Administrative and Procedural Requirements (General)
   39. Federal Grant and Cooperative Agreement Act of 1977, P.L. 95-224 (41 U.S.C. 501–509). — OMB
   40. OMB Circular No. A-40: *Management of Federal Reporting Requirements.* — OMB
   41. OMB Circular No. A-95: *Evaluation, Review, and Coordination of Federal and Federally Assisted Programs and Projects,* Revised January 13, 1976. — OMB
   42. OMB Circular No. A-111: *Jointly Funded Assistance to State and Local Governments and Nonprofit Organizations—Policies and Procedures,* July 6, 1976. — OMB
   43. Executive Order 12044: *Improving Government Regulations,* March 23, 1978. — OMB
   44. *Department of Commerce Directives for the Conduct of Federal Statistical Activities,* May 1978 (Formerly OMB Circular No. A-46). — Commerce

*Interagency Commission on Women's Business

45. FMC 74-8: *Guidelines for Agency Implementation of the Uniform Relocation Assistance and Real Property Acquisition Policies of 1970 Public Law 91-646,* October 4, 1976. GSA
46. Treasury Circular No. 1082: *Notification to States of Grant-in-Aid Information,* August 8, 1973. Treasury
47. Treasury Circular No. 1075 (Fourth Revision): *Regulation Governing the Withdrawal of Cash from Treasury for Advance Payments under Federal Grant and Other Programs,* December 14, 1947. Treasury
48. Claims Collection Act of 1966, P.L. 89-508, 89 Stat. 309 (31 U.S.C. 952). GAO

C. Recipient-Related Administrative and Fiscal Requirements

NONPROFIT ORGANIZATIONS AND INSTITUTIONS

49. OMB Circular No. A-21 (Formerly FMC 73-8, December 19, 1973): *Cost Principles for Educational Institutions,* March 6, 1979. OMB
50. OMB Circular No. A-110: *Grants and Agreements with Institutions of Higher Education, Hospitals and Other Nonprofit Organizations—Uniform Administrative Requirements,* July 30, 1976. OMB
51. FMC 73-3: *Cost Sharing on Federal Research,* December 4, 1973. OMB
52. OMB Circular No. A-88 (Formerly FMC 73-6): *Coordinating Indirect Cost Rates and Audit at Educational Institutions,* December 5, 1979. OMB
53. FMC 73-7: *Administration of College and University Research Grants,* December 19, 1973. OMB

State and/or Local Governments

54. OMB Circular No. A-90: *Cooperating with State and Local Governments to Coordinate and Improve Information Systems,* September 21, 1968. OMB
55. OMB Circular No. A-102: *Uniform Administrative Requirements for Grants-in-Aid to State and Local Governments,* Revised, August 24, 1977. OMB
56. OMB Circular No. A-73 (Formerly FMC 73-2): *Audit of Federal Programs,* March 15, 1978. OMB

57. FMC 74-4: *Cost Principles Applicable to Grants and Contracts with State and Local Governments,* July 18, 1974.   OMB

D. Access to Information
58. Freedom of Information Act (5 U.S.C. 552)   None Assigned
59. Privacy Act of 1974, P.L. 93-579 (5 U.S.C. 522a).   OMB

BIBLIOGRAPHY

Anderson, Martin. *The Federal Bulldozer.* Cambridge, Mass.: MIT Press, 1964.
Arnold, R. Douglas. *Congress and the Bureaucracy: A Theory of Influence.* New Haven: Yale University Press, 1979.
Bardach, Eugene and Robert A. Kagan. *Social Regulation: Strategies for Reform.* San Francisco: Institute for Contemporary Studies, 1982.
Bardach, Eugene and Lucian Pugliaresi. "The Environmental Impact Statement vs. the Real World." *The Public Interest,* XLIX (Fall, 1977), 22–38.
Barringer, Felicity. "Rulebook." Washington *Post,* January 18, 1982, p. A9.
Bauer, Raymond A., Ithiel de Sola Pool, and Lewis Anthony Dexter, *American Business and Public Policy: The Politics of Foreign Trade.* Chicago: Aldine Atherton, 1972.
Beer, Samuel H. "The Adoption of General Revenue Sharing: A Case Study in Public Sector Politics." *Public Policy,* XXIV (1976), 127–95.
Benson, George C. S. *The New Centralization: A Study of Intergovernmental Relations in the United States.* New York: Farrar and Rinehart, 1941.
Bernstein, Marver H. *Regulating Business by Independent Commission.* Princeton: Princeton University Press, 1955.
Berry, Jeffrey M. *Lobbying for the People: The Political Behavior of Public Interest Groups.* Princeton: Princeton University Press, 1977.
Blair, John P. "Spending Rates as Evaluative Tools." *Evaluation Review,* V (1981), 712–19.
Brown, George D. "The Courts and Grant Reforms: A Time for Action." *Intergovernmental Perspective,* VII (Fall, 1981), 6–14.
Brown, Raymond, Ann Coil, and Carol Rose. *A Time for Accounting: The Housing and Community Development Act in the South.* Atlanta: Southern Regional Council, 1976.
Bryner, Gary. "Congress, Courts, and Agencies: Equal Employment and the Limits of Policy Implementation." *Political Science Quarterly,* XCVI (Fall, 1981), 411–30.

Bulkeley, William M. "Cities Fear 'New Federalism' Will Further Pinch Budgets Already Hit by Tighter Government Aid." *Wall Street Journal*, March 2, 1982, p. 50.

Canan, James. *War in Space*. New York: Harper and Row, 1982.

Choate, Pat. *As Time Goes By: The Costs and Consequences of Delay*. Washington, D.C.: Academy for Contemporary Problems, 1980.

Clark, Timothy B. "Access for the Handicapped—A Test of Carter's War on Inflation." *National Journal*, X (October 21, 1978), 1672–75.

Cole, Richard L., and David A. Caputo. "Presidential Control of the Senior Civil Service: Assessing the Strategies of the Nixon Years." *American Political Science Review*, LXXIII (1979), 399–413.

Colgate, Craig, Jr. (ed.). *National Trade and Professional Associations of the United States and Canada and Labor Unions*. Washington, D.C.: Columbia Books, 1981.

Coopers and Lybrand. "Recommendations for Near Term Field Organization and Structure." Photocopied report, 1976.

Cutler, Lloyd N. and David R. Johnson. "Regulation and the Political Process." *Yale Law Journal*, LXXXIV (1975), 1395–1418.

Danaceau, Paul. *Regulation: The View from Janesville, Wisconsin and a Regulator's Perspective*. Washington, D.C.: U.S. Government Printing Office, 1980.

Davis, Kenneth Culp. *Discretionary Justice: A Preliminary Inquiry*. Urbana, Ill.: University of Illinois Press, 1971.

Derthick, Martha. *New Towns In-Town*. Washington, D.C.: Urban Institute, 1972.

DeStefano, Frank, and Clay H. Wellborn. "Aspects of Community Development Activities in Selected Localities." Summary of NAACP findings prepared by the Congressional Research Service of the Library of Congress. Washington, D.C.: photocopied, 1976.

Dodd, Lawrence C., and Richard C. Schott. *Congress and the Administrative State*. New York: John Wiley, 1979.

Dommel, Paul R., et al. *Targeting Community Development*. Washington, D.C.: U.S. Government Printing Office, 1980.

Dornan, Paul B., and Claire L. Felbinger. "Of Time and Money: Spending Rates as a Performance Measure in the Community Development Block Grant Program." Paper prepared for delivery at the 1982 Annual Meeting of the Midwest Political Science Association, Milwaukee, Wisconsin.

Fainsod, Merle. "Some Reflections on the Nature of the Regulatory Process." *Public Policy*, I (1940), 299–323.

Fainsod, Merle, and Lincoln Gordon. *Government and the American Economy*. New York: Norton, 1941.

Fallows, James M. *National Defense*. New York: Random House, 1981.

Farkas, Suzanne. *Urban Lobbying: Mayors in the Federal Arena*. New York: New York University Press, 1971.

Feaver, Douglas B. "Another Great Society Milepost Falls." Washington *Post*, May 27, 1982, p. A25.

Fesler, James W. *Area and Administration.* University, Ala.: University of Alabama Press, 1949.
Fiorina, Morris P. *Congress: Keystone of the Washington Establishment.* New Haven: Yale University Press, 1977.
Fisher, Louis. "A Political Context for Legislative Vetoes." *Political Science Quarterly,* XCIII (1978), 241–54.
Gelfand, Mark I. *A Nation of Cities: The Federal Government and Urban America.* New York: Oxford University Press, 1975.
Ginsberg, Robert L. "Second Year Community Development Block Grant Experience: A Summary of Findings of the NAHRO Community Development Monitoring Project (January, 1977)." *Journal of Housing* XXXIV (February, 1977), 80–83.
Grodzins, Morton. *The American System: A New View of Government in the United States.* Ed. Daniel J. Elazar. Chicago: Rand McNally, 1966.
Haider, Donald H. *When Governments Come to Washington: Governors, Mayors, and Intergovernmental Lobbying.* New York: Free Press, 1974.
Hanus, Jerome J. (ed.). *The Nationalization of State Government.* Lexington, Mass.: Lexington Books, 1981.
Harris, Joseph P. *Congressional Control of Administration.* Washington, D.C.: Brookings Institution, 1964.
Herbers, John. "Block Grant Programs Assumed in Most States." *New York Times,* November 3, 1981, p. A14.
Jacob, Herbert, and Kenneth N. Vines (eds.). *Politics in the American States: A Comparative Analysis.* Boston: Little, Brown, 1976.
Kaufman, Herbert. *The Administrative Behavior of Federal Bureau Chiefs.* Washington, D.C.: Brookings Institution, 1981.
———. "Administrative Decentralization and Political Power." *Public Administration Review,* XXIX (1969), 3–15.
———. *The Forest Ranger: A Study in Administrative Behavior.* Baltimore: Johns Hopkins University Press, 1960.
———. *Red Tape: Its Origins, Uses, and Abuses.* Washington, D.C.: Brookings Institution, 1977.
Kettl, Donald F. *Managing Community Development in the New Federalism.* New York: Praeger, 1980.
Key, V. O. *The Administration of Federal Grants to States.* Chicago: Public Administration Service, 1937.
King, Anthony (ed.). *The New American Political System.* Washington, D.C.: American Enterprise Institute, 1978.
Koch, Edward I. "The Mandate Millstone." *The Public Interest,* LXI (Fall, 1980), 42–57.
Kohlmeier, Louis M., Jr. *The Regulators: Watchdog Agencies and the Public Interest.* New York: Harper and Row, 1969.
Kushner, James A. "Litigation Strategies and Judicial Review under Title I of the Housing and Community Development Act of 1974." *Urban Law Annual,* XI (1976), 37–100.
Lilley III, William, and James C. Miller III. "The New 'Social Regulation.'" *The Public Interest,* XLVII (Spring, 1977), 49–61.

Lovell, Catherine, and Charles Tobin. "The Mandate Issue." *Public Administration Review*, XLI (1981), 318–31.
Lowi, Theodore J. *The End of Liberalism: The Second Republic of the United States*. New York: Norton, 1979.
Macmahon, Arthur W. *Administering Federalism in a Democracy*. New York: Oxford University Press, 1972.
Madden, Thomas J., and Patrick R. Harkins. "New Block Grant Program Faces Period of Adjustment in the Courts." *National Law Journal*, IV (March 8, 1982), 29–31.
Masters, Kim. "OMB Asserts Contacts Need Not Be Logged." *Legal Times of Washington*, June 22, 1981, p. 1.
Mayhew, David R. *Congress: The Electoral Connection*. New Haven: Yale University Press, 1974.
Michigan Advisory Committee to the U.S. Commission on Civil Rights. *Civil Rights and the Housing and Community Development Act of 1974, Vol. 1: Livonia*. Washington, D.C.: U.S. Commission on Civil Rights, 1975.
———. *Civil Rights and the Housing and Community Development Act of 1974, Vol. III: The Chippewa People of Sault Ste. Marie*. Washington, D.C.: U.S. Commission on Civil Rights, 1976.
Milbrath, Lester W. *The Washington Lobbyists*. Westport, Conn.: Greenwood Press, 1976.
Mitnick, Barry M. *The Political Economy of Regulation: Creating, Designing, and Removing Regulatory Forms*. New York: Columbia University Press, 1980.
Mosher, Frederick C. "The Changing Responsibilities and Tactics of the Federal Government." *Public Administration Review*, XL (1980), 541–48.
Muller, Thomas, and Michael Fix. "Federal Solicitude, Local Costs: The Impact of Federal Regulation on Municipal Finances." *Regulation*, IV (July/August, 1980), 29–36.
Nathan, Richard P. *The Plot That Failed: Nixon and the Administrative Presidency*. New York: Wiley, 1975.
Nathan, Richard P., and associates. *Block Grants for Community Development*. Washington, D.C.: U.S. Government Printing Office, 1977.
———. *Public Service Employment: A Field Evaluation*. Washington, D.C.: Brookings Institution, 1981.
Nathan, Richard P., Charles F. Adams, Jr., and associates. *Revenue Sharing: The Second Round*. Washington, D.C.: Brookings Institution, 1977.
National Commission on Urban Problems. *Building the American City*. Washington, D.C.: U.S. Government Printing Office, 1968.
National Urban League. "The New Housing Programs: Who Benefits." New York, mimeographed, 1975.
Ogul, Morris S. *Congress Oversees the Bureaucracy: Studies in Legislative Supervision*. Pittsburgh: University of Pittsburgh Press, 1976.
Okun, Arthur M. *Equality and Efficiency: The Big Tradeoff*. Washington, D.C.: Brookings Institution, 1975.
Orren, Karen. "Standing to Sue: Interest Group Conflict in the Federal Courts." *American Political Science Review*, LXX (1976), 723–41.

Polsby, Nelson W. "Contemporary Transformations of American Politics: Thoughts on the Research Agendas of Political Scientists." *Political Science Quarterly*, XCVI (Winter, 1981–82), 551–70.

Potomac Institute. "The Housing Assistance Plan: A Non-Working Program for Community Improvement?" Washington, D.C.: photocopied, 1975.

Pressman, Jeffrey L., and Aaron Wildavsky. *Implementation*. Berkeley: University of California Press, 1973.

Reagan, Michael D. *The New Federalism*. New York: Oxford University Press, 1972.

Redford, Emmette S. *Administration of National Economic Control*. New York: Macmillan, 1952.

Rosenberg, Morton. "Beyond the Limits of Executive Power: Presidential Control of Agency Rulemaking Under Executive Order 12,291." *Michigan Law Review*, LXXX (December, 1981), 193–247.

Ross, William Warfield. "New Rules for 'Major' Rulemaking: Living with Executive Order 12291." *National Law Journal*, III (April 27, 1981), 19.

Rourke, Francis E. *Bureaucracy, Politics, and Public Policy*. Boston: Little, Brown, 1976.

Scher, Seymour. "Conditions for Legislative Control." *Journal of Politics*, XXV (1963), 526–51.

Seidman, Harold. *Politics, Position, and Power: The Dynamics of Federal Organization*. New York: Oxford University Press, 1980.

Short, Raymond S. "Municipalities and the Federal Government." *Annals of the American Academy of Political and Social Science*, CCVII (January, 1940), 44–53.

Smallwood, Frank (ed.). *The New Federalism*. Hanover, N.H.: Public Affairs Center of Dartmouth College, 1967.

Struyk, Raymond. *Saving the Housing Assistance Plan: Improving Incentives to State and Local Governments*. Washington, D.C.: Urban Institute, 1979.

Sundquist, James L., with David W. Davis. *Making Federalism Work: A Study of Program Coordination at the Community Level*. Washington, D.C.: Brookings Institution, 1969.

Truman, David B. *Administrative Decentralization*. Chicago: University of Chicago Press, 1940.

———. *The Governmental Process: Political Interests and Public Opinion*. New York: Knopf, 1971.

U.S. Advisory Commission on Intergovernmental Relations. *A Catalog of Federal Grant-in-Aid Programs to State and Local Governments: Grants Funded FY 1978*. Washington, D.C.: U.S. Government Printing Office, 1979.

———. *Categorical Grants: Their Role and Design*. Washington, D.C.: U.S. Government Printing Office, 1978.

———. *Citizen Participation in the American Federal System*. Washington, D.C.: U.S. Government Printing Office, 1979.

———. *A Crisis of Confidence and Competence*. Washington, D.C.: U.S. Government Printing Office, 1980.

---. *The Intergovernmental Grant System: Summary and Concluding Observations.* Washington, D.C.: U.S. Government Printing Office, 1978.

---. *Significant Features of Fiscal Federalism, 1980–81 Edition.* Washington, D.C.: U.S. Government Printing Office, 1981.

---. *Urban America in the Federal System.* Washington, D.C.: U.S. Government Printing Office, 1969.

U.S. Commission on Federal Paperwork. *Environmental Impact Statements.* Washington, D.C.: U.S. Government Printing Office, 1977.

---. *Impact of Federal Paperwork on State and Local Governments: An Assessment by the Academy for Contemporary Problems.* Washington, D.C.: U.S. Government Printing Office, 1977.

U.S. Comptroller General. *Agencies When Providing Federal Financial Assistance Should Ensure Compliance with Title VI.* Washington, D.C.: U.S. General Accounting Office, April 15, 1980, Report HRD-80-22.

---. *Analysis of Community Development Block Grant Program Drawdown Rates.* Washington, D.C.: U.S. General Accounting Office, August 20, 1980, Report CED-80-137.

---. *The Community Development Block Grant Program Can Be More Effective in Revitalizing the Nation's Cities.* Washington, D.C.: U.S. General Accounting Office, April 30, 1981, Report CED-81-76.

---. *Environmental Reviews Done by Communities: Are They Needed? Are They Adequate?* Washington, D.C.: U.S. General Accounting Office, September 1, 1977, Report CED-77-123.

---. *The Federal Government Should But Doesn't Know the Cost of Administering Its Assistance Programs.* Washington, D.C.: U.S. General Accounting Office, February 14, 1978, Report GGD-77-87.

---. *Fundamental Changes Are Needed in Federal Assistance to State and Local Governments.* Washington, D.C.: U.S. General Accounting Office, August 19, 1975, Report GGD-75-75.

---. *Management and Evaluation of the Community Development Block Grant Program Need to Be Strengthened.* Washington, D.C.: U.S. General Accounting Office, August 30, 1978, Report CED-78-160.

---. *Meeting Application and Review Requirements for Block Grants under Title I of the Housing and Community Development Act of 1974.* Washington, D.C.: U.S. General Accounting Office, June 23, 1976, Report RED-76-106.

---. *Weak Internal Controls Make the Department of Labor and Selected CETA Grantees Vulnerable to Fraud, Waste, and Abuse.* Washington, D.C.: U.S. General Accounting Office, March 27, 1981, Report AFMD-81-46.

U.S. Council on Environmental Quality. "Community Development Block Grants and NEPA: Delegation of National Environmental Policy Act Reponsibilities to Community Development Block Grant Recipients." Washington, D.C.: photocopied, 1977.

U.S. Department of Housing and Urban Development. *Community Development Block Grant Program: First Annual Report.* Washington, D.C.: U.S. Government Printing Office, 1975.

———. *Community Development Block Grant Program: Second Annual Report.* Washington, D.C.: U.S. Government Printing Office, 1976.
———. *Community Development Block Grant Program: Third Annual Report.* Washington, D.C.: U.S. Government Printing Office, 1978.
———. *Fourth Annual Community Development Block Grant Report.* Washington D.C.: U.S. Government Printing Office, 1979.
———. *Fifth Annual Community Development Block Grant Report.* Washington, D.C.: U.S. Government Printing Office, 1980.
———. *Sixth Annual Community Development Block Grant Report.* Washington, D.C.: U.S. Government Printing Office, 1981.
U.S. House of Representatives, Committee on Appropriations, Subcommittee on HUD—Independent Agencies. *Department of Housing and Urban Development—Independent Agencies, Appropriations for 1976.* Hearing, 94th Cong., 1st sess., 1975.
———. *Department of Housing and Urban Development—Independent Agencies, Appropriations for 1977.* Hearing, 94th Cong., 2nd sess., 1976.
———. *Department of Housing and Urban Development—Independent Agencies, Appropriations for 1981.* Hearing, 96th Cong., 2nd sess., 1980.
U.S. House of Representatives, Committee on Banking, Currency and Housing, Subcommittee on Housing and Community Development. *Oversight Hearing on Community Development Block Grant Program.* Hearing, 94th Cong., 1st sess., 1975.
U.S. House of Representatives, Committee on Banking, Finance and Urban Affairs, Subcommittee on Housing and Community Development. *Community Development Block Grant Program.* Committee print, 95th Cong., 1st sess., 1977.
———. *Community Development Block Grant—Small Cities Regulations.* Hearing, 97th Cong., 1st sess., 1981, pp. 1–2.
———. *Housing and Community Development Act of 1977.* Hearings, 95th Cong., 1st sess., 1977.
———. *Housing and Community Development Amendments of 1981.* Hearings, 97th Cong., 1st sess., 1981.
U.S. House of Representatives, Committee on Rules, Subcommittee on Rules of the House. *Studies on the Legislative Veto.* Committee print, 96th Cong., 2nd sess., 1980.
U.S. Office of Management and Budget. *The Budget of the United States Government, Fiscal Year 1983.* Washington, D.C.: U.S. Government Printing Office, 1982.
———. *Improving Government Regulations: Current Status and Future Directions.* Washington, D.C.: U.S. Government Printing Office, 1980.
———. *Information Collection Budget, Fiscal Year 1982.* Washington, D.C.: U.S. Government Printing Office, 1981.
———. *Managing Federal Assistance in the 1980's.* Washington, D.C.: U.S. Government Printing Office, 1980.
U.S. Senate, Committee on Banking, Housing and Urban Affairs. *Community Development Block Grant Program.* Hearings, 94th Cong., 2nd sess., 1976.

———. *Housing and Community Development Legislation of 1977.* Hearings, 95th Cong., 1st sess., 1977.
VanHorn, Carl E. *Policy Implementation in the Federal System.* Lexington, Mass.: Lexington Books, 1979.
Walker, David B., Albert J. Richter, and Cynthia Cates Colella. "The First Ten Months: Grant-in-Aid, Regulatory, and Other Changes." *Intergovernmental Perspective,* VIII (Winter, 1982), 5–22.
Weissert, Carol. "The Politics-Administration Dichotomy Revisited: An Intergovernmental Perspective." Prepared for the 1981 Annual Meeting of the Midwest Political Science Association, Cincinnati, Ohio.
Wilson, James Q. (ed.). *The Politics of Regulation.* New York: Basic Books, 1980.
———. *Urban Renewal: The Record and the Controversy.* Cambridge, Mass.: MIT Press, 1966.
Working Group for Community Development Reform. "Community Development Block Grants—Implementing National Priorities." Washington, D.C.: mimeographed, 1976.

INDEX

Abuse of programs, 7, 36–37, 102, 117–19, 156
ACIR. *See* Advisory Commission on Intergovernmental Relations
Adams, Betty, 73n
Adams, Charles F., Jr., 55n
Administrative discretion. *See* Discretion
Administrative Procedure Act, 107n, 152
Advisory Commission on Intergovernmental Relations, 4n, 7n, 31n, 157
Affirmative action. *See* Civil rights
AFL-CIO, 107–109
Agenda: and interest groups, 100, 104–15, 122; reactive, 126–27
Akey, Denise S., 108
Alcoholism program, 138
Anderson, Martin, 15n
Applications: as condition for funding, 6–7; urban renewal, 16; in Comprehensive Employment and Training Act, 18; in Community Development Block Grant Program, 18–19, 21, 58; in Great Society, 26–27, 30–33; in New Deal, 29; federal review, 34, 96–97, 103, 133, 169; coordination, 44; and civil rights, 48–49; and environmental protection, 50–53; and benefits for the poor, 59–60; and Housing Assistance Plan, 68–74; and monitoring, 79, 82
Arnold, R. Douglas, 38
Ashley, Thomas, 119

Association of Rehabilitation Facilities, 108
Audits. *See* Financial controls

Baltimore, Md., 52
Bardach, Eugene, 53n, 125n
Barringer, Felicity, 135n
Bauer, Raymond A., 89n
Beals, Alan, 110n, 143n
Beam, David R., 37 n
Beer, Samuel H., 37, 108, 112
Benefit-cost analysis, 134–35
Benson, George C. S., 28 n
Bernstein, Marver H., 2n
Berry, Jeffrey M., 107n, 109
Bilingual Education Act of 1974, p. 9. *See also* Education
Blair, John P., 163n, 164
Block grants: defined, 17; information problems, 78; Reagan proposals, 138–41; threat to congressional power, 148–49; instability, 166
Bloyd, Paul, 143n
Blumenfeld, M. Joseph, 71
Bollinger, Stephen J., 144
Bond, Christopher S., 142n
Brown, Garry, 119–20
Brown, George D., 122, 123n
Brown, Raymond, 62n, 90n
Brooke, Edward W., 66
Brookings Institution, 63, 93–94

/ 195

Bryner, Gary, 54n, 57n
Budget cuts, 131–32, 140–41
Bulkeley, William L., 140n
Buschbaum, Peter, 63n
Bush, George, 134

Canan, James W., 166n
Caputo, David A., 38–39n
Categorical grants: criticism of, 15–16; varieties of, 16–17; in 1960s, 31–33; and lobbying, 106
Carter, Jimmy: administration of, 67, 72, 96, 103–104, 132–35, 137, 166; regulatory reform, 129–30
CD. *See* Community Development Block Grant Program
Center for Community Change, 108
Centralization: and regulation, 75, 85–86; incentives for, 152–53; cycles of, 154–59; and field administration, 166–73
CETA. *See* Comprehensive Employment and Training Act
Choate, Pat, 163n
Citizen participation, 7, 32, 59
Civil rights: in Community Development Block Grant Program, 20, 46–49; in war on poverty, 32; in revenue sharing, 54–56; and federal supervision, 86, 95, 134–35, 161; and Congress, 117
Civil Rights Act of 1964, pp. 6, 9, 54
Clark, Timothy B., 9n
Clean Water Act, 9
Cleveland, Ohio, 80
Coalition for Block Grant Compliance, 70, 107, 108, 115
Code of Federal Regulations, 21, 35–36
Coil, Ann, 62n
Cole, Richard L., 38–39n
Colean, Miles L., 14n
Colgate, Craig, Jr., 86n
Commission on Civil Rights, 70, 90
Commission on Federal Paperwork, 53, 54
Communication: administrative, 84–85; and regulation, 95–98; through congressional committees, 119–22
Community Development Block Grant Program: benefits for the poor, 13–14, 59–68, 91–93, 142–46; features, 18–19, 119–21, 131; increased federal supervision, 21, 36, 133; civil rights regulations, 46–49; environmental regulations, 49–53; interest group complaints, 62–63, 89–93, 106–15; field administration, 78–88; training of Housing and Urban Development officials, 83–84; legislative review (veto), 119–22, 143–46; congressional review of rules, 120–22; role of courts, 122–25; for small cities, 138, 141–46; problems of delay, 163–65. *See also* Applications; Congress; Courts; Housing and Urban Development; Housing Assistance Plan; Neighborhood Strategy Areas; Urban Development Action Grants
Comprehensive Employment and Training Act: beneficiaries, 7; complaints about, 13, 33–34, 102–103; passage, 17–18, 131, 138; growing regulation, 34, 36, 102–103; and interest groups, 89, 106; end of, 119
Comptroller General of the United States. *See* General Accounting Office
Conference of Mayors, 106, 108, 114–15, 136, 150, 157
Congress: and grant formulas, 33, 38, 40; suspicions of New Federalism, 33; party unity, 38; distributive politics, 40; and vague goals, 45–46; committee review of Community Development Block Grant Program, 63–66, 72–73, 85, 91; policy making through regulation, 98; administrative oversight, 115–22, 118–22; interest groups and the agenda, 122; legislative review (veto), 143–46; and grant reform, 143–44, 148–49; conflict with Office of Management and Budget, 149. *See also* Delegation
Consumer Product Safety Commission, 44
Coopers and Lybrand, 84n, 86n
Copeland Act, 6
Corpus Christi, Tex., 90
Council on Environmental Quality, 52
Council on Wage and Price Stability, 129, 134
Courts: and housing rules, 71–72; and regulation, 122–25; interest group influence, 125; regulatory reform, 149–51
Crosscutting regulations. *See* Regulation
Cutler, Lloyd N., 23

Danaceau, Paul, 12, 13
Davis-Bacon Act, 5–6, 9, 56

Day care, 160
Deaton, Philip L., 12
Decentralization: and monitoring, 82–83; and interest groups, 113–15; cycles of, 154–56; and national goals, 159–61; difficulty of, 166–73
Defense, Department of, 162, 166
Delay, costs of, 10–12, 163–64
Delegation, 46, 56–57, 159–61
Depression, 25
Derthick, Martha, 15
DeStefano, Frank, 90n
Dexter, Lewis Anthony, 89n
DiLieto, Biagio, 140
Discretion: in grant programs, 14–21, 24, 159–61; and Congress, 56–58; and Community Development Block Grant Program, 92–93, 118; in Reagan proposals, 130–31, 138–40; and courts, 150
Dodd, Lawrence C., 117n
Dommel, Paul R., 93n
Drug abuse, 138

Eads, George C., 147n
Eckrose, Roy, 11–12
Economic development, 14, 163
Education: and handicapped, 9; bilingual, 9; block grant proposal, 17, 138
Education, Department of, 135
Elazar, Daniel J., 28n
Elementary and Secondary Education Act, 5, 35–36
Eligibility questions, 86
Embry, Robert, 103, 104, 119
Energy program, 138
Environmental protection: federal rules, 6, 10, 43–45, 53–54, 161; in Community Development Block Grant Program, 49–53; and experts, 84; interpretation, 95; and benefit-cost analysis, 134–35
Environmental Protection Agency, 4, 44
Equal opportunity. See Civil rights
Euclid, Ohio, 48
Executive Order 11821, p. 128
Executive Order 12044, p. 129
Executive Order 12291, p. 133–34
Expected to reside, 69–74, 85, 87, 124
Experts, 84–85

Fainsod, Merle, 2, 22n
Fallows, James M., 166n

Farkas, Suzanne, 110
Feaver, Douglas B., 132n
Federal grants. See Grants
Federalist, 104
Federal Register: and regulatory volume, 35–36; as communication, 58, 71, 95–98, 113, 170; mentioned, 19, 120, 134–37, 143–44
Fesler, James W., 168n
Field administration: and civil rights, 47–49; interpretation of regulations, 61–62; performance measurement, 75, 78–88; communication, 84–86, 97; problems for, 168–73
Financial regulations: as grant requirements, 5–6, 43, 159–61; mentioned, 10, 24, 150
Fish and Wildlife Coordination Act, 6
Fisher, Louis, 119n
Fix, Michael, 9–10
Flood insurance, 44
Ford, Gerald: administration of, 63, 67, 72, 96, 100, 103, 126; regulatory reform, 128–29, 132–34, 137; mentioned, 60
Formulas: and regulation, 5, 37–39, 156–59; in categorical grants, 17, 32; in Community Development Block Grant Program, 18–19; in Comprehensive Employment and Training Act, 18; and Congress, 116, 148–49; and centralization, 157–58
Fragmentation, 82–85, 87–88
Fraud, 7, 36–37, 102–103
Freedom of information, 44

GAO. See General Accounting Office
Gelfand, Mark I., 14n, 28
General Accounting Office studies: environmental protection, 51–52; civil rights, 54–56; Housing and Urban Development monitoring, 80–81; sanctions, 165–66
General revenue sharing. See Revenue sharing
Ginsberg, Robert L., 63n
Gonzalez, Henry B., 144
Gordon, Lincoln, 2
Governors, as lobbyists, 37
Grants: number and amount, 4–5; constituency, 5, 109; criticism of, 15–16; land, 24; reform, 130–32, 138–41, 166–73; and budget cuts, 140–41; instability, 166. See also Applications;

198 / INDEX

Block grants; Categorical grants; Formulas; Revenue sharing
Great Society: and administrative control, 16; grant programs, 25–26, 30–33; and bureaucrats, 38–39; and intergovernmental lobbying, 105–106; expansion of federal power, 158
Grodzins, Morton, 28n
Gunther, John J., 110n

Haider, Donald J., 89n, 105, 110
Handicapped: accessibility of federally funded projects, 6, 8–9, 43, 45–46, 134–35; coordination of federal rules, 11; and interest groups, 109; and Congress, 117
HAP. See Housing Assistance Plan
Harkins, Patrick R., 123n, 150n
Harris, Joseph P., 117n
Harris, Patricia Roberts, 64–65, 72, 103
Hartford v. *Hills*, 71, 102, 124, 151
Hatch Act, 6
Health: planning regulations, 4; mental health, 4–5; block grant, 138
Health, Education, and Welfare, Department of, 54
Heclo, Hugh, 118, 157
Herbers, John, 139n
Highways, 30–31, 134, 154, 160, 171
Hills, Carla, 103
Historic preservation, 6, 43–44, 50
Housing Act of 1949, p. 14
Housing Act of 1954, p. 14
Housing and Urban Development, Department of: handbooks, 3; crosscutting regulations, 10–12; supervision of Community Development Block Grant Program, 34, 133; field administration, 19, 78–88, 97, 169–71; and civil rights, 47–49; and enviromental protection, 49–53; and benefits for the poor, 59–68; complaints about administration, 70–74, 80–88; and information, 76–98, 103; fragmentation, 82–85, 87; training of officials, 83–84; reorganization of, 83–85, 169–71; concentration of power, 86–87; congressional relations, 115–22; judicial oversight, 124–25; agenda, 125–27; small cities program, 142–46; performance measurement, 163–66; sanctions, 164–66. See also Agenda; Housing Assistance Plan; Neighborhood Strategy Areas

Housing Assistance Plan: features, 68–74; and experts, 85; and courts, 124
Housing programs: in New Deal, 28; federally subsidized, 68–74, 160–61
Houston, Tex., 165
HUD. See Housing and Urban Development, Department of

Inducements, 2–3
Inequality, 31
Information: difficulty of obtaining, 76–78; and interest groups, 88–95; biases, 94; weaknesses, 103; and congressional oversight, 118–22
Interest groups: and grant support, 5; fear of New Federalism, 33; and formula grants, 37–38; monitoring by, 62–63, 70, 88–95, 111–15; concentration of power, 86, 153; and administrative agenda, 100, 104–15; varieties of, 106–10; cost of access, 109; motivation, 109–10; constituencies of, 112–15; conflict, 113–15; role in congressional oversight, 122; and courts, 123–25; coalitions, 157
Internal regulation, 3
Interstate Commerce Commission, 2
Issue networks, 118, 157, 161

Johnson, David R., 23
Johnson, Lyndon B., and war on poverty, 25, 31–33
Job training. See Comprehensive Employment and Training Act
Justice, Department of, 54

Kaufman, Herbert, 22, 154
Kettl, Donald F., 34n, 53n
Key, V. O., 129
Kickbacks, 6
Knapp, John L., 144
Koch, Edward, 8
Kohlmeier, Louis H., Jr., 2n
Kushner, James A., 122, 125n

Law Enforcement Assistance Act, 17
Law Enforcement Assistance Administration, 102–103
Law enforcement grants in New Deal, 28
Leadership Conference on Civil Rights, 108
League of Women Voters, 108
Legislative review (veto), 143–46

INDEX / 199

Lilley, William III, 2n, 43n
Little Rock, Ark., 91
Livonia, Mich., 47, 70, 102
Loan guarantees, 2–3
Lovell, Catherine, 44n, 46, 161n
Lundine, Stanley N., 145n

Macmahon, Arthur W., 159
Madden, Thomas J., 23n, 150n
Madison, James, 104
Maine v. Thiboutot, 124
Manufactured Housing Institute, 106
Mass transit: federal grants, 4, 11–12, 17, 36; and handicapped, 9, 135
Masters, Kim, 151n
Mayhew, David R., 45, 115–16
Mayors: as lobbyists, 37, 105; goals in Community Development Block Grant Program, 110
McMurray, Gerald R., 144n
Meeker, David, 61, 64, 70, 103
Medicaid, 4
Mental health, 138
Middletown, Conn., 48
Milbrath, Lester W., 89
Milgram, Grace, 121
Miller, James C. III, 2n, 43n
Mine safety, 4
Mitnick, Barry M., 159n
Model Cities, 15, 31, 61
Monitoring: as federal control, 34, 109, 159–73; and crosscutting rules, 53; by interest groups, 63–64, 70, 88–95, 111–15; and field administration, 75, 82–88, 169–73. *See also* Performance; Spending rates
Mortgage Bankers Association of America, 106
Mosher, Frederick C., 3n
Mott, Andrew, 104
Muller, Thomas, 9–10

NAACP, 90, 106–108, 156
NAHRO. *See* National Association of Housing and Redevelopment Officials
Nathan, Richard P., 13n, 38n, 55n, 63
National Association for Retarded Citizens, 108
National Association of Counties, 106, 108
National Association of Home Builders, 106
National Association of Housing and Redevelopment Officials, 63, 91–93, 107–108
National Citizen Participation Council, 108
National Committee Against Discrimination in Housing, 70, 108
National Community Development Association, 107, 108, 110
National Easter Seal Society, 108, 113
National Environmental Policy Act of 1969, pp. 6, 50
National Governors Association, 140, 142, 153
National Highway Traffic Safety Administration, 44
National Housing Law Project, 143
National League of Cities, 106, 108, 142–43, 157
National Urban League, 90, 108
Neighborhood Strategy Areas, 67–68
New Deal: federal control in, 25–30, 39–40, 42; and intergovernmental lobbying, 105; expansion of federal power, 158
New Federalism: debate over local discretion, 110; Reagan version, 130–46
—Nixon version: proposals, 16–18, 33, 58–59; and civil rights, 49; administration of, 75–76, 164; and interest groups, 106; congressional role, 117–18; expansion of federal power, 158
New Haven, Conn., 140
Nixon, Richard M.: New Federalism proposal, 16–18, 33, 58–59; bureaucratic strategies, 38–39; administration of, 60, 67, 83, 131, 141, 164; and federal control, 131; grant reform, 171
NSAs. *See* Neighborhood Strategy Areas

Oakland, Calif., 162
Occupational Safety and Health Administration, 44
Office of Environmental Quality, 86
Office of Management and Budget: circulars, 3; and crosscutting regulations, 6, 43; assessment of grants' burdens, 8, 11; and monitoring, 81; regulatory review by, 133–39, 146–48; small cities program, 142–46; ex parte contacts, 151–52
Ogul, Morris S., 117n
Okun, Arthur M., 90

OMB. *See* Office of Management and Budget
Orlinsky, Walter, 52n, 73n
Orren, Karen, 125n
Oversight, congressional, 115–22

Paperwork: in environmental protection, 52; for compliance, 75, 81–82; reduction, 136–39; Office of Management and Budget review, 146
Partnership for Health Act, 17, 138
Performance: reports, 7; measuring, 78–88, 161–73; and regulation, 96–97, 172–73; congressional review, 116–22. *See also* Sanctions; Spending rates
Petkas, Peter J., 62, 101
Pierce, Samuel R., Jr., 144
Pool, Ithiel de Sola, 89n
Poor, benefits for: in Community Development Block Grant Program, 20–21, 59–69;interest group complaints, 91–93, 103–104; Housing and Urban Development supervision, 142–46; and centralization, 171–72
Potomac Institute, 90, 108
Pressman, Jeffrey L., 15n, 162
Privacy, 44
Private sector regulations, 1–3
Program-based regulations. *See* Regulations
Proxmire, William, 64, 66, 91, 98, 101–102
Pugliaresi, Lucian, 53n, 125n

Reagan, Michael D., 16n
Reagan, Ronald: New Federalism proposal, 21, 130–46, 151, 156–57, 171; budget cuts, 131
Redford, Emmette S., 57, 78
Regulation: varieties of, 1–7; command and control, 2; interpretation of, 11, 54–55, 61–62; as dynamic process, 22–23; case for, 34–35; social, 42–43; as communication, 58, 71, 95–98, 113, 170; and centralization, 75, 85–86, 146–48; and Congress, 117, 120–22; reform, 128–46; benefit-cost analysis, 134–35; minimal, 136–39, 150; growth, 155–57; of performance, 161–63, 172–73
—program-based regulations: defined, 5
—crosscutting regulations: defined, 5–6; growth of, 43; vague goals, 57; congressional role, 116–17; judicial role, 123–25; coordination, 132–33
—problems of: administrative, 10, 102, 156–57; costs, 8–10, 128–29, 135, 156–57; uncertainty and delay, 10–12; adversarial proceedings, 12–13; compliance, 12–14, 34; worst case, 101–102, 122; reactive, 126–27; openness, 151–53. *See also* Performance; Sanctions
Regulatory Analysis Review Group, 129, 134
Regulatory Council, 101
Rehabilitation Act of 1973. *See* Handicapped
Retsinas, Nicholas P., 110n
Revenue sharing: Nixon proposal, 17, 106, 131; regulation of, 36, 102–103; number of recipients, 40; and civil rights, 54–55; complaints, 89; financial record keeping, 160
Risk, 101
Romney, George, 169
Roosevelt, Franklin D., 25–30
Rose, Carol, 62n
Rosenberg, Morton, 151–52
Ross, William Warfield, 151
Rourke, Francis E., 101n, 119
Rural Housing Alliance, 108

Safe streets block grant. *See* Law Enforcement; Assistance Administration
St. Germain, Fernand J., 144
Salem, Ore., 80
Sanctions: withdrawal of funds, 29, 54–55; through congressional hearings, 102, 119–120; conditional grants, 164–66
Sault Ste. Marie, Mich., 47–48
Schechter, Henry B., 109n
Scheiber, Harry N., 28n
Scher, Seymour, 117n
Schott, Richard C., 117n
Section 8 program, 68–74
Section 1983, pp. 123–24
Seidman, Harold, 87, 117n
Sewage treatment, 36, 134
Short, Raymond S., 28
Sierra Club, 107–108, 156
Snail darter, 50
Social services grants, 36, 138
Southern Regional Council, 90–91, 94, 106–107

INDEX / 201

Spending rates, 80, 162–66. *See also* Performance; Sanctions
Stability, 101
Standing, 123, 125
Struyk, Raymond J., 73–74
Suburban Action, 108
Sundquist, James L., 15n

Task Force on Regulatory Relief, 134–35
Tellico Dam, 50
Tobin, Charles, 44n
Transportation. *See* Highways; Mass transit
Treasury, Department of, 55–56
Trucking, 2
Truman, David B., 114n, 173

Uncertainty, 10–12
Unemployment Insurance Compensation Act, 9
United Cerebral Palsy Association, 108, 113
Urban Development Action Grants, 86
Urban Institute, 73–74

Urban Mass Transit Administration, 11–12
Urban renewal: early programs, 14–15; goals, 14–15; complexity, 15–16; in 1950s, 31

Van Horn, Carl E., 102
Vines, Kenneth N., 31n

Wage standards, 9
Walker, David B., 138n
War on poverty, 25, 32–33, 154
Waste, 7, 36–37, 102
Water programs, 4
Weiner, Frances E., 143n
Weissert, Carol, 5n
Welfare, 132
Wellborn, Clay H., 90n
Wildavsky, Aaron, 15n, 162
Wilson, James Q., 15n, 101, 109n
Winter, William F., 142n
Working Group for Community Development Reform, 62–63, 104, 143